TRAINING MISSIONARIES

TRAINING MISSIONARIES

Principles and Possibilities

Evelyn and Richard Hibbert

WILLIAM CAREY
LIBRARY

Training Missionaries: Principles and Possibilities
Copyright © 2016 by Evelyn and Richard Hibbert

Published by William Carey Library
1605 E. Elizabeth St.
Pasadena, CA 91104 | www.missionbooks.org

Melissa Hughes, editor
Joanne Leong, graphic design

William Carey Library is a ministry of
Frontier Ventures | www.frontierventures.org

Printed in the United States of America
20 19 18 17 16   5 4 3 2 1 BP300

Library of Congress Cataloging-in-Publication Data
Names: Hibbert, Evelyn, author.
Title: Training missionaries : principles and possibilities / by Evelyn and
    Richard Hibbert.
Description: Pasadena, CA : William Carey Library, 2016. | Includes
    bibliographical references and index.
Identifiers: LCCN 2016032553 (print) | LCCN 2016033009 (ebook) | ISBN
    9780878085477 (pbk.) | ISBN 0878085475 (pbk.) | ISBN 9780878088850
    (eBook)
Subjects: LCSH: Missionaries--Training of.
Classification: LCC BV2091 .H48 2016 (print) | LCC BV2091 (ebook) | DDC
    266.0071--dc23
LC record available at https://lccn.loc.gov/2016032553

CONTENTS

ACKNOWLEDGMENTS

Although this book revolves around ideas, it could not have come into being if these ideas had not been tested in the crucible of experience. Two testing grounds proved the value of these ideas: the discipling of new believers and training of Millet leaders in Bulgaria, and the training of missionaries in Australia. In each case, there would have been no training without both trainees and trainers. The Millet proved that the same principles apply for the poor and disadvantaged as for those with higher education in more prosperous situations. In Australia, the ideas could not have been put into practice apart from the wholehearted support and commitment of the WEC International Australian Leadership and Journey Training Teams. Not only Australian WEC, but a number of WEC missionaries around the world, Australian missionaries from other mission agencies, and Australian church and theological education leaders willingly gave their time and support to participate in the long process of review and development required for accreditation. In this way, this book has been a corporate endeavor over many years.

PREFACE

Before we became missionaries we were medical doctors. We chose to become missionaries because we saw that while doctors patch up people so they can live a short while longer, missionaries offer healing that lasts for eternity. Our experiences as trainee doctors has undoubtedly influenced our views on missionary training.

Doctors are trained to be reflective practitioners. Although they have a huge body of knowledge to learn, it is critically important that they master a range of skills and learn how to relate well to people. Doctors have to think about what they are doing and continually consider whether there might be ways of doing things better. They also belong to learning communities of peers. They are trained from very early on that they have a responsibility to pass on to more junior colleagues everything that they have learned, and to keep on learning themselves. We long to see this same commitment to ongoing learning and this devotion to discovering good practice and passing it on to others among missionaries.

We set out for the field in 1989, learned language and a little about culture and, after the fall of communism in Eastern Europe, moved to Bulgaria as pioneering missionaries to Turkish-speakers. We had the privilege of planting a church and establishing nationwide leadership training for the thousands of Millet believers who were flooding into the church at that time. A number of missionaries came to join us, and many short-term workers passed through our field. Later we became part of the international leadership group of our mission agency and visited many fields to provide support and training. Richard now works as the director of the School of Cross-Cultural Mission at the Sydney Missionary and Bible College. Evelyn is the academic dean of the School for Christian Studies, The Salvation Army Booth College in Sydney.

WHO THIS BOOK IS FOR

This book is written for people who train missionaries. You might be a faculty member at a Bible college, seminary, or university who teaches in the area of missions. You might be involved in the leadership of a training institution for Christian workers including missionaries, pastors, and other people working in multicultural contexts. Perhaps you are a mission agency leader or trainer, or a missionary who works with local churches or missions networks that are sending people to work in other cultures. We believe that the principles we advocate apply across all these training contexts, but also that the specific ways these principles are applied should vary according to the specific training context.

THE WAY THE BOOK IS ORGANIZED

In order to organize the book we struggled for a long time to find an integrating framework that created a cohesive flow of thought across the whole book. In the end we found that the most helpful way of thinking about missionary training was to apply a framework that combines two basic ways of understanding the process of learning. These two fundamental perspectives are, first, to see learning as the making of connections between theory and practice, and second, to see learning as the transformation of systems of meaning. We have integrated these two fundamental conceptions of learning into the framework that is portrayed visually in Figure 1 and have used it as a way of organizing the whole book.

This basic framework for understanding the process of learning is based on two models of adult learning that are grounded in the issues and challenges of life and ministry. The first component of our framework rests on the work of Ted Ward and Samuel Rowen who portrayed the process of learning using a two-rail fence. A railway track seen from above, with its two rails running horizontally and sleepers that "connect" the two rails, conveys the same idea. The bottom rail represents real-life experience and the top rail represents theory. They proposed that learning requires three elements: cognitive inputs (the top rail), field experience (the bottom rail), and strong connections made between the cognitive input and experience (the sleepers). Connections are made by helping learners reflect on their experience in the light of theory and theology, evaluate their experience in the light of cognitive input, and hypothesize about better ways of approaching life and ministry. An ideal way of teaching is to start with the lived experience of the students, progress to looking at what the Bible says about these issues and at the insights of missiological and other theories, and then move back down to apply insights gained to life and ministry.[1]

The second key component of our framework is based on Jack Mezirow's thinking about learning. He developed the idea of transformative learning that sees learning as the transformation of a person's frame of reference. These frames of reference are the network of assumptions on which we base our points of view, habits of thinking, and beliefs. These frames of reference help people to interpret and make sense of what they encounter.[2] In this book, we refer to these frames of reference as "meaning frameworks" as they are the way people structure what they already know in order to interpret and therefore make meaning of the world around them. When people encounter new information, their ability to relate to, accept, and utilize that information depends on how well it can be fitted into their existing meaning framework. Part of the trainer's role is therefore to scaffold new information so that it can be added to the person's own meaning framework or gently disrupt the existing framework so it can be reconfigured without causing it to completely disintegrate. The idea of a meaning framework is particularly helpful for learning in the field of intercultural communication because it corresponds quite well with the anthropological concept of worldview. Both frame of reference and worldview refer to a systems of meaning-making held by an individual (in the case of a frame of reference) or a group (in the case of a worldview).[3]

Learning to be a missionary is a holistic endeavor that affects all the dimensions of human experience—spiritual, emotional, interpersonal, practical, and intellectual. The framework for seeing the learning process that is portrayed in Figure 1 can be applied to each of these dimensions individually or to all of them at once. The process of learning begins with the trainee's existing meaning framework, as well as the issues and challenges they face in life and ministry.

---

1.   A concise explanation of their idea is summarised in Ted Warren Ward and Samuel F. Rowen, "The Significance of the Extension Seminary," *Evangelical Missions Quarterly* 9, no. 1 (1972).

2.   Jack Mezirow, "Transformative Learning: Theory to Practice," *New Directions for Adult and Continuing Education* 74 (1997).

3.   For a helpful explanation of the concept of the anthropological concept of worldview, see Charles H. Kraft, *Worldview for Christian Witness* (Pasadena, CA: William Carey Library, 2008), 11–31.

It introduces them to insights from the Bible and other cognitive inputs such as missiology. They are helped to analyze and reflect on the issues and challenges in life and ministry (both in their own experience and in that of others). Learners are helped to make connections between experience and cognitive inputs and to find integrative solutions to apply to ministry needs. In the process of exploring the connections between experience and theory, and between the different theories, learners' assumptions about needs, the world, and other related elements are exposed and may even be shaken. In this way, their meaning frameworks are being brought to conscious awareness and then modified and extended. The process of finding practical solutions to life and ministry issues by reflecting on them in the light of the Bible and various theories, and then hypothesizing a solution and applying, testing, and reflecting on it results in a reconfiguration and strengthening our meaning frameworks.

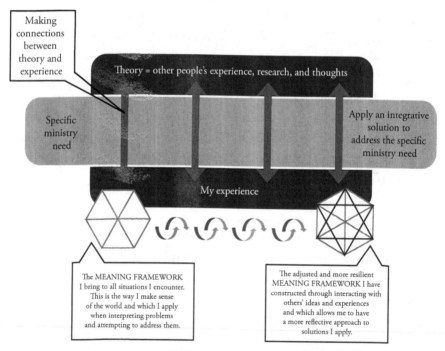

Figure 1 Learning process (developed from Ward, Rowen and Mezirow's ideas)

To be effective in cross-cultural ministry, missionaries need to become outstanding learners. Within one lifetime we can never learn all there is to know about God or the people he has created and the way they organize their lives. Whether in language learning, culture learning, ministry development, or theological exploration, missionaries need to keep on learning. They need to keep testing the assumptions of their existing meaning frameworks and developing their complexity and resilience. Only then will they be able to facilitate the ongoing development of authentic cultural expressions of Christlikeness and growth in all the dimensions of relationship with God.

This book is divided into two main sections. The first discusses the foundations on which we believe missionary training should be designed, while the second focuses on the practical outworkings of these foundations. The first section begins (in Chapter 1) by exploring why specific training for missionaries that is different to the training of pastors, chaplains, and other Christian workers serving in culturally similar contexts is needed. It then outlines four essential elements of this training: experiencing God (Chapter 2), relating to people (Chapter 3), using the Bible (Chapter 4), and engaging with culture (Chapter 5). Lessons from the Bible and from recent history that inform missionary training are discussed in Chapters 6 and 7.

The second half of the book begins (in Chapter 8) by describing a set of steps that can be used to design or shape a missionary training program. These are based on educational insights. Chapter 9 describes how these steps were put into practice in an experimental missionary training situation and reflect on that experience. The final chapter (Chapter 10) considers implications and possibilities for applying these principles in other missionary training contexts.

THE NEED FOR AND PURPOSE OF SPECIALIZED MISSIONARY TRAINING

A missionary is someone who is sent out by a church in one cultural context to serve God among people from another culture by communicating the gospel, discipling believers, planting churches, teaching the Bible, and training leaders. Missionaries need a different kind of training than pastors, evangelists, and other Christian workers serving among people who are culturally similar to themselves. Three aspects of cross-cultural ministry distinguish it from monocultural ministry: its focus on relating to people who are culturally different, its emphasis on contextualizing or adapting ways of communicating and practicing Christianity in order to make sense to the local people, and its unpredictability. The unpredictability arises from lack of familiarity with the context and the lack of control over our lives when we live in different political and social settings. This can range from not knowing when, what, or how to eat, to precarious residence permits, and even war and other kinds of physical danger. Each of these three aspects of cross-cultural ministry requires missionary training to have additional emphases in contrast to training for ministry in one's home culture.

THE NEED FOR SPECIALIZED MISSIONARY TRAINING

Missionaries who lack specific training in cross-cultural ministry tend to replicate methods of evangelism, church life and ministry from their home context that are often unsuited to the new cultural context they work in. Without special training, it is natural for all of us to uncritically export our culturally shaped ways of sharing the gospel, discipling people, meeting as a church, and training leaders. But this approach can have negative consequences. It leads to churches and practices that local people see as alien and ugly, not because of the offense of the cross but because they have been shaped by a foreign culture.[4]

---

4.   Darrell Whiteman, "Contextualization: The Theory, the Gap, the Challenge," *International Bulletin of Missionary Research* 21: 3–4.

The need to provide specialized training for missionaries has been recognized for at least a century. The 1910 World Missionary Conference in Edinburgh highlighted the need for such specialized missionary training. One of the conference's focus groups researched missionary training around the world for two years prior to the conference and wrote a detailed, book-length report.[5] David Harley, who has dedicated decades to the study of missionary training, believes this group's report "is probably the most thorough report on missionary training that has ever been produced."[6]

The Edinburgh Conference's missionary training group discovered that most missionaries were being sent out with no specialist missionary training. They praised the character qualities and spiritual life that they saw in missionary graduates of Bible colleges such as those set up by D.L. Moody and A.B. Simpson whose aim was to prepare missionaries, but they felt that there was too little specialist training for cross-cultural ministry. They also noted that the vast majority of missionaries were educated in theological colleges where they received no missions training.[7]

The widespread lack of dedicated training for missionaries stimulated the Edinburgh group to recommend that specialist missionary training colleges be started. They felt that this training should be oriented around four dimensions: spiritual, moral, intellectual, and practical. Genuine spiritual vitality was in their view the most important of these. Training, they believed, should help prepare missionaries in how to maintain their spiritual life in situations of hardship and little or no Christian fellowship. Secondly, they saw moral or character qualities such as humility, respect for people of other cultures, and an attitude of being a learner about culture as vital. The third "intellectual" area included training in the Bible and Christian doctrine, and missiological subjects such as the science and history of missions and world religions. The final area the group considered important was practical training in things like elementary medicine and hygiene.[8]

---

5.   "Report of Commission V," (Edinburgh & London: World Missionary Conference, 1910).

6.   C. David Harley, "Missionary Training : The History of All Nations Christian College and Its Predecessors (1911–1981)" (doctoral, Rijksuniversiteit Utrecht, 2000), 25.

7.   Ibid., 28.

8.   Ibid., 29–30.

The conference's report singled out one of the very few colleges that was dedicated to providing specialist missionary training at that time—Edinburgh Missionary Training College. The missionary training group felt that this college gave the kind of specialized training they thought was needed. It had been founded just over two decades earlier to train women missionaries. The founding principal, previously a missionary in India, had set up an integrated program of worship, study, and practical training. The course was highly interactive, with nearly all classwork conducted by discussion. Community life was foundational in nurturing students' relationship with God and discovery of their unique identity, and conflicts were treated as a vehicle for growth. An atmosphere of freedom was intentionally fostered, with very few rules, so that trainees could develop in their ability to make good decisions in complex situations as they would have to do on the mission field.[9]

In the mid-1990's and the early 2000's, two multi-agency, wide-ranging international studies of missionary attrition—exploring why missionaries leave the field and how to keep them longer on the field—convincingly reaffirm the need for pre-field training in cross-cultural ministry. These studies were published as *Too Valuable to Lose*[10] and *Worth Keeping*.[11]

The first of these studies showed that pre-field missionary training that addresses being, doing, and knowing is among the top three factors that prevent long-term missionaries leaving the field prematurely.[12] The follow-up study of nearly six hundred mission agencies in twenty-two countries found that agencies that retained missionaries better had much higher pre-field training requirements than low retaining agencies. High retaining agencies expected their missionary candidates to have two to three times as much formal missiological training and 50 percent more practical missionary training than low

---

9. Ibid., 52–54.

10. William David Taylor, ed., *Too Valuable to Lose: Exploring the Causes and Cures of Missionary Attrition*, Globalization of Mission Series (Pasadena, CA: William Carey Library, 1997).

11. Rob Hay, *Worth Keeping: Global Perspectives on Best Practice in Missionary Retention*, Globalization of Mission Series (Pasadena, CA: William Carey Library, 2007).

12. Detlef Blöcher and Jonathan Lewis, "Further Findings in the Research Data," in *Too Valuable to Lose: Exploring the Causes and Cures of Missionary Attrition*, ed. William David Taylor (Pasadena, CA: William Carey Library, 1997), 105–25.

retaining agencies. In addition, high retaining agencies had a considerably higher emphasis on ongoing training than low retaining agencies.[13]

Summarizing the implications of these studies for missionary training, Detlef Blöcher, a member of the team coordinating this study, emphasizes that there is a clear correlation between retention and pre-field missionary training in missiology and practical missionary skills. He writes:

> Best practice mission agencies provide careful candidate se-
> lection and sound pre-field training. They encourage their
> missionaries to engage in continuous training and develop-
> ment of new gifts and to actively work towards the continuous
> improvement of their ministries. . . . This global trend calls for
> increasing training standards of missionaries and a lifestyle of
> lifelong learning.[14]

THE QUALITIES OF EFFECTIVE MISSIONARIES

Missionary trainers and agencies often design their training with a profile of an effective missionary in mind. The profile outlines the qualities that they expect missionaries to have. Profiles help mission agencies select candidates who are best suited for missionary work and help training institutions develop curricula that develop the characteristics outlined in the profile. The Gateway Mission-ary Training Centre in Canada, for example, has produced a particularly well thought through profile, or list of training outcomes, to guide their missionary training.[15] It contains the following qualities, which they expect trainees to grow in as a result of their training:

Spirituality: Demonstrates growth in relationship with God
Character: Reflects Christlikeness in attitude and action
Interpersonal skills: Demonstrates ability in relating to others

---

13. Detlef Blöcher, "Training Builds up Missionaries: Lessons from ReMAP II," *Connections: The Journal of the World Evangelical Alliance Missions Commission* 4 (2005): 23.
14. Ibid., 24–25.
15. Robert Brynjolfson, "Student Assessment in an Outcomes-Based Program," in *Integral Ministry Training: Design and Evaluation*, ed. Robert Brynjolfson and Jonathan Lewis (Pasadena, CA: William Carey Library, 2006).

Physical and emotional health: Evidences a balanced holistic approach to life

Church: Demonstrates a commitment to the universal body of Christ locally and globally

Bible and theology of missions: Has a firm grasp of the Bible and mission theology

Teamwork: Able to function effectively in a team

Cross-cultural adaptation: Understands and values cultural differences and demonstrates adaptability

Contextualization: Understands the culture and adapts the gospel message to communicate it effectively

Language learning: Demonstrates competence in acquiring another language

Communication: Communicates effectively in a variety of settings

Evangelism: Intentionally seeks opportunities to introduce people to Jesus Christ

Discipleship: Is a disciple and makes disciples of Jesus

Practical skills: Willing to learn and to perform activities related to daily living

Family and single life: Understands and demonstrates what family and/or single life involves here and on the mission field

Pre-field ministry: Knows the steps and practices skills/activities that are essential to getting to the field

The focus in this list on character qualities and ministry skills is reflected in most training outcomes profiles developed by other organizations as well as profiles listing the desired characteristics of missionaries beyond their training.[16] This same focus can be seen, for example, in the profile of qualifications for

---

16. These include the profiles produced by Latin American missionary trainers in Robert Ferris, ed. *Establishing Ministry Training: A Manual for Program Developers* (Pasadena, CA: William Carey Library, 1995), 147–52; the profiles produced by Asian missionary trainers for missionaries and for missionary trainers by the Evangelical Fellowship of Asia Missions Commission that can be found in Titus Loong and Steve Hoke, "Working Consultation for Asian Missionary Trainers," *Training for Cross-Cultural Ministries*, no. 2 (1993); and the partial outcomes profile of Redcliffe College described in Colin Bulley, "Non-Formal and Community-Based Learning," in *Integral Ministry Training: Design and Evaluation*, ed. Robert Brynjolfson and Jonathan Lewis (Pasadena, CA: William Carey Library, 2006).

Indian missionaries published by the Indian Missions Association. Their belief was that "understanding and informational requirements should be instrumental to character and ministry ends."[17] The list reads as follows:

CHARACTER AREAS
- Spiritually mature
- Zeal for cross-cultural evangelism
- Disciplined and accountable
- Adaptable
- Rightly related to God
- Rightly related to one's family
- Rightly related to one's community

MINISTRY AREAS
- Exercises spiritual disciplines
- Engages in spiritual warfare
- Communicates effectively (in one's own language)
- Builds relationships and friendships
- Understands and communicates cross-culturally
- Learns a language
- Evangelizes and preaches
- Teaches, trains, and disciples
- Plants the church
- Manages time and resources
- Copes with stress and loneliness

This list of qualifications strikingly illustrates the emphasis that mission agencies put on the character of missionary candidates and their ability to do certain things. It has no knowledge outcomes that stand alone. Missionaries clearly need to know some things in order to be able to be effective in their work in the ministry areas and in order to live out the character qualities. But in no instance does knowledge exist separately from its effects on being and doing.

The missions commission of Latin American evangelicals, COMIBAM, organized a series of missionary training workshops and consultations to address curricular design for missionary training centers in Latin America from

---

17. Indian Missions Association, "Qualifications for Indian Missionaries," in *Establishing Ministry Training: A Manual for Program Developers*, ed. Robert Ferris (Pasadena, CA: William Carey Library, 1995).

2003 to 2005. One of the conclusions of this group was that effective mission-ary training institutions "are deliberately oriented towards the development of the character and abilities necessary for cross-cultural ministry."[18] Missionary trainers and agency personnel agreed that missionary training should nurture the following qualities in trainees:

- Spiritual maturity
- Christian character and ethics
- Healthy family relationships
- Physical and emotional well-being
- Proper relationship with others
- Biblical and theological understanding
- Ministerial skills
- Practical skills

Of the eight areas in this list, seven focus on character qualities and min-istry skills. Only one focuses on knowledge or understanding. It is clear that when missionary trainers think about what characteristics missionaries need to be effective, they consistently generate lists in which character qualities and life and ministry skills predominate, and that in their conceptualization of mis-sionary qualities, knowledge of the Bible and theology, while essential, is only one of many areas that training should address.

FOUR ESSENTIAL ELEMENTS

Working with long lists of desired missionary characteristics can be difficult to work with day-to-day, so it can be helpful to organize the items into meaningful categories. Items from the four different profiles—The Edinburgh Conference, Gateway, Indian Missions Association, and COMIBAM—can be categorized under four major areas of missionary life and work: Experiencing God, Relat-ing to people, Engaging with culture, Using the Bible. These categories are not definitive, but they fit well with our personal meaning frameworks. "Experi-encing God" relates to the missionary's relationship with God. "Relating to people" refers to interpersonal relationships. "Engaging with culture" means interacting with the systems of meaning and practice that groups of people

---

18. Omar Gava, "COMIBAM Training Coordinator's Report: Towards Excellence in Missionary Training," *Connections* 4, no. 2 (2005).

establish together. "Using the Bible" is about looking to the Bible to inform and guide all aspects of missionary life and ministry.

	Experiencing God	Relating to people		Engaging with culture	Using the Bible	Other
	Spiritual	Practical	Moral	Moral	Intellectual	
Edinburgh Group	Maintain spiritual life in situations of hardship and little or no Christian fellowship	Elementary medicine & hygiene	Humility	Respect for people of other cultures	Bible & Christian doctrine	
				Learner about culture	Science & history of missions	
					World religions	
Gateway Missionary Training Centre	Demonstrates growth in relationship with God	Evidences a balanced holistic approach to life	Reflects Christlikeness in attitude and action	Understands and values cultural differences and demonstrates adaptability	Has a firm grasp of the Bible and mission theology	Knows the steps and practices skills/activities that are essential to getting to the field
	Is a disciple	Willing to learn and to perform activities related to daily living	Demonstrates ability in relating to others	Understands the culture	Adapts the Gospel message to communicate it effectively (according to the culture)	
		Understands and demonstrates what family and/or single life involves here and on the mission field	Demonstrates a commitment to the universal body of Christ locally and globally	Demonstrates competence in acquiring another language		
			Able to function effectively in a team			

	Experiencing God		Relating to people	Engaging with culture	Using the Bible	Other
Gateway Missionary Training Centre (cont.)			Communicates effectively in a variety of settings			
			Intentionally seeks opportunities to introduce people to Jesus Christ			
			Makes disciples of Jesus			
Indian Missions Association	Spiritually mature	Manages time and resources	Zeal for cross-cultural evangelism	Understands and communicates cross-culturally	Evangelizes and preaches	
	Disciplined	Copes with stress and loneliness	Accountable	Learns a language	Teaches, trains, disciples	
	Adaptable		Rightly related to one's family		Plants the church	
	Rightly related to God		Rightly related to one's community			
	Exercises spiritual disciplines		Communicates effectively			
	Engages in spiritual warfare		Builds relationships and friendships			
COMIBAM	Spiritual maturity	Physical and emotional well-being	Healthy family relationships		Biblical and theological understanding	
	Christian character and ethics	Practical skills	Proper relationship with others			
			Ministerial skills			

Table 1 Categorizing profile items under four key areas

Categorizing desired missionary qualities under the four essential elements gives trainers a quick checklist of areas that missionaries need to become competent in. The next four chapters are organized according to these four elements. These four categories will, from now on, be referred to as the *essential elements of missionary training*. They constitute four interlocking elements which are each both outcomes and processes. They are summarized in Figure 2.

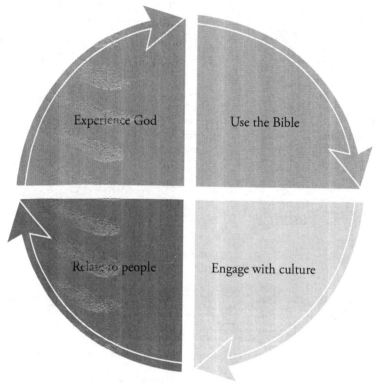

Figure 2 Essential elements of missionary training

DEFINING LEARNING OUTCOMES

After stakeholders[19] have identified a set of desired missionary qualities, the next step in designing a training program is to express these qualities in terms of learning outcomes. Learning outcomes differ from qualities in that they

---

19.   Stakeholders are people who have a vested interest in the outcomes of the training program. They include mission agency leaders, church leaders and mission field leaders.

must state what successful trainees will be able to be, do, or know by the end of their training, in specific terms. The quality "builds relationships and friendships," for example, expressed as a learning outcome would be something like "is able to build relationships and friendships with a broad variety of people."

Training methods needed to achieve each outcome differ according to the nature of the outcome. Learning outcomes are therefore classified according to their implications for training. Character-related learning outcomes are best achieved through exposure to role models who embody the outcomes and through reflection on personal performance. These types of outcomes are referred to as "being" outcomes. If the focus of an outcome is a skill, it is referred to as a "doing" outcome. Skills are best learned by practicing them and receiving specific feedback. Where stakeholders are concerned that graduates need foundational knowledge for ministry, outcomes are designated "knowing" outcomes. The best way of helping adult trainees gain knowledge is through problem-solving and other active tasks which incorporate active research and use of information. Where a single learning outcome appears to fall under more than one category, it is placed under the category that it most strongly corresponds with. The qualities listed in each category should answer the questions:

Being: What kind of person does the missionary need to be?
Doing: What does the missionary need to be able to do?
Knowing: What do missionaries need to know in order to be the person God wants them to be and do the work he has given them to do?

Qualities under each of these three categories are best developed using different means. Character qualities are best developed through interaction with other people and the challenges of life, and reflecting on that interaction. Skills are best developed by doing, by giving people opportunity to see them being performed by someone who is good at them, by giving opportunities to practice them, and by giving feedback on how well trainees did them. Knowledge is best developed by explaining theory and theology in the context of trying to answer questions and problems from real life so that strong connections between theory/theology and practice can be made.

The qualities from the four different profiles (Edinburgh Conference, Gateway, Indian Missions Association, and COMIBAM) have been rearranged according to these three categories in Table 2.

Be	Do	Know
Rightly related to God	Practical skills	Bible & Christian doctrine
Spiritually mature	Willing to learn and to perform activities related to daily living	Biblical and theological understanding
Spiritual maturity	Knows the steps and practices skills/activities that are essential to getting to the field	Science & history of missions
Christian character and ethics	Elementary medicine & hygiene	Has a firm grasp of the Bible and mission theology
Reflects Christlikeness in attitude and action	Learner about culture	Understands the culture
Disciplined	Demonstrates cultural adaptability	Understands and values cultural differences
Exercised spiritual disciplines	Learns a language	World religions
Maintain spiritual life in situations of hardship and little or no Christian fellowship	Demonstrates competence in acquiring another language	
Copes with stress and loneliness	Demonstrates ability in relating to others	
Demonstrates growth in relationship with God	Builds relationships and friendships	
Is a disciple	Communicates effectively in a variety of settings	
Physical and emotional well-being	Communicates effectively	
Evidences a balanced holistic approach to life	Understands and communicates cross-culturally	
Understands and demonstrates what family and/or single life involves here and on the mission field	Able to function effectively in a team	
Healthy family relationships	Manages time and resources	
Rightly related to one's family	Accountable	
Rightly related to one's community	Ministerial skills	
Proper relationship with others	Adapts the Gospel message to communicate it effectively (according to the culture)	
Respect for people of other cultures	Zeal for cross-cultural evangelism	
Humility	Evangelizes and preaches	
Adaptable	Intentionally seeks opportunities to introduce people to Jesus Christ	

Be	Do	Know
	Makes disciples of Jesus	
	Teaches, trains, disciples	
	Plants the church	
	Engages in spiritual warfare	
	Demonstrates a commitment to the universal body of Christ locally and globally	

Table 2 Missionary profile items arranged according to Being, Doing, & Knowing

Categorizing the qualities of effective missionaries in this way reminds us that the development of character and skills is of greater importance than knowledge acquisition. In many institutions, it seems as if knowing, being, and doing are competitors, and preferential treatment is often given to theoretical knowledge.[20] Through highlighting this issue, we are not saying that knowledge is not important, but that a stronger emphasis needs to be placed on developing character and skills.

Since qualities relating to being are developed through time spent with role models such as the trainers, and qualities relating to doing are developed through practice, it also suggests that training programs for missionaries should devote as much time and effort to modeling, mentoring, and coaching as to the transfer of information.

CONTEXTS OF MISSIONARY TRAINING

Authentic Cross-cultural Ministry

Christian ministry is all about people. It requires lots and lots of time with people. It involves going to people where they are, listening to them, spending time with them, eating with them, crying with them, and laughing with them. It also means learning to respect them and looking for things to appreciate even when our prejudices cause us to pre-judge them. If students are to grow in these skills, they need to see good models in real ministry situations and to receive feedback on how well they are doing these things in authentic contexts. They

---

20. This observation about the competition between knowledge, being, and doing came from Philip Crooks in a personal email, 24th February, 2015.

need time to practice and experiment with different approaches. In the process, trainees will learn skills not only of relating to the people they are ministering to, but also of learning to work with others. This is vital preparation for working in ministry teams.

Having authentic ministry exposure is also important because it is usually only as people start working in close contact with others that they start to understand themselves. Very often, we have found, people either do not know themselves well, or they have a conception of themselves based on what they have been trained to think that they should be. It can take a long time for people—especially those who do not fit conservative stereotypes of the ideal Christian—to come to understand and accept who they are in Christ and what they have to offer to others. This issue of self-identity is particularly significant for pioneer missionaries who, as people who are willing to make the sacrifice of going to new and difficult areas for Jesus' sake, are often less conservative types of people. Having a "sober judgment" of oneself, understanding our own strengths and weaknesses and what we bring to a relationship, and learning to accept and forgive ourselves, is an essential foundation for effective ministry, as well as important for long-term resilience (cf. Rom 12:3).

Learning Community

Teachers are the heart of any training program. Every training program stands or falls on the quality of its trainers. Regardless of the curriculum or the content of the teaching sessions, students will look to their teachers as role models and begin to imitate their attitudes and behavior.

The importance of teachers modeling what they want to see in their students is confirmed by biblical patterns of teaching, discipling, and training. The Apostle Paul told the Corinthians to imitate him as he imitated Christ (1 Cor 4:16, 11:1). He told Timothy to be an example not only in the way he taught but also in the way he lived, and specifically in his love, faith, and purity (1 Tim 4:12). He taught that church leaders must be mature people of proven good character (1 Tim 3:2–7; Tit 1:6–9). This emphasis on having leaders as character exemplars is central to the Bible's teaching about expectations of leaders and the way they should be developed or trained.

Jesus devoted three years to being with his disciples so that, above all, they could be "with him" (Mark 3:13–14). Joshua watched what Moses did for over forty years and learned how he responded in the many challenges of leading the Israelites. Elisha patterned his ministry on that of his model and mentor,

Elijah, who he spent several years traveling with. These apprentices not only saw what their mentors did but they saw how they did it and observed their emotional responses to what they encountered. The lives and feelings of their mentors were transparent to the apprentices, and these apprentices were intent on emulating their mentors.

Each of the mentors or teachers described above reproduced themselves in their trainees. It was expected that students would become like their teachers, and this is why Jesus said, "the student who works hard will become like the teacher" (Luke 6:40). This is not only true of teachers in Jesus' time. Students today, whether they realize it or not, pattern their lives, at least to some extent, on the teachers and mentors they respect.

Paulo Freire emphasized that students are not just empty containers waiting to be filled up with knowledge.[21] Instead, they watch their teachers, expecting them to be holistic examples who embody the qualities they hope their students will develop. Whatever students respect or like in those that teach them, they will seek to imitate. In many cases, students will seek out teachers and teaching institutions that have reputations that they admire in order to acquire the things they value.

Healthy learning contexts are characterized by transparency, diversity, an acceptance that some conflict is normal, and an ability to manage that conflict. In missionary training, a healthy learning environment exposes missionary trainees not only to divergent viewpoints but also to living models of conflict management. Trainees experience how a healthy community can be formed among diverse people.

Missionary trainees need the skills to understand the questions people from different cultures are asking and to formulate real answers to down-to-earth problems encountered in cross-cultural life and ministry. Useful answers will be expressed in the lives and actions of those giving answers, not only in their words. Students therefore need to see their teachers engaging with the world. They need to see how their teachers approach searching the Scriptures to find answers that are more than platitudes. Students need to see their teachers engaging in serving people who are struggling and see them helping these people discover the living Savior. They need to see how exemplary lives, even in all their weakness, can speak more powerfully than all the right theological

---

21. Paulo Freire, *Pedagogy of the Oppressed*, new rev. 20th anniversary ed. (New York: Continuum, 1993).

answers delivered correctly but without compassion. They need to see how to live when there are no answers and relationship with God himself is the only solution. In intercultural and multicultural contexts, they need to see teachers who are open and flexible, who build relationships with people from very different backgrounds than themselves, and who nevertheless do not compromise the gospel or lose their faith.

TRAINING IMPLICATIONS

The need for missionary trainees to have good role models and to be able to practice ministry skills influences how and where missionary training should be done. Although trainees can still benefit from interacting with role models in non-ministry contexts and practicing skills in simulated environments, the effect of these is more potent when they occur in authentic cross-cultural ministry. This real-life context makes learning easier to transfer and apply to other contexts elsewhere in the world.

Andrew Wingate, who served as a theological educator missionary in India in the 1970s, described his seminary as "a laboratory of the gospel" that employed an action-reflection approach to learning. Faculty members and students were "deeply engaged with the world outside, as a learning and acting community" (Wingate 2010, 223). Teachers were expected to be involved in practical ministry outside the college. Wingate, for example, was assigned together with a group of students to prison ministry where he recalls experiencing the power of the gospel to change lives and faced the complexity of sharing the gospel with Hindus and discipling life prisoners. Engagement with the practice of ministry outside the classroom enlarged his and his students' appreciation of the gospel and the complexity of human problems, and their ability to minister to people from vastly different religious, cultural, and socioeconomic backgrounds than their own. Students together with individual faculty members formed a learning community as they engaged in and reflected on ministry they did together.[22]

---

22. Andrew Wingate, "Training for Ministry in a Multifaith Context: A Case Study from Britain," in *Handbook of Theological Education in World Christianity: Theological Perspectives, Regional Surveys, Ecumenical Trends*, ed. Dietrich Werner, et al. (Oxford, England: Regnum Books International, 2010).

In this chapter we have outlined four essential elements of missionary training and pointed to two key contexts in which training ideally occurs. These are shown in Figure 3. Each element is interwoven with the others, and the learning community cannot be separated from the cross-cultural ministry in which it corporately engages. The next four chapters will examine each essential element in more detail.

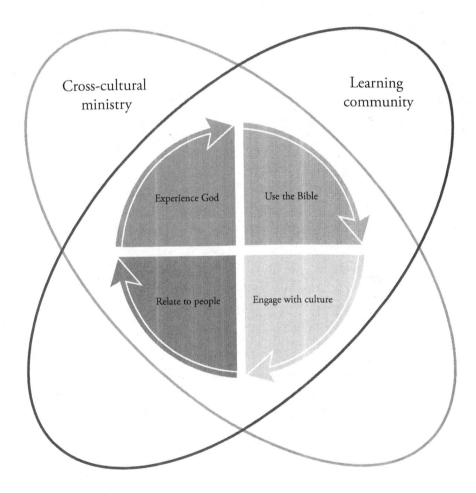

Figure 3 Essential elements and contexts of missionary training

2

EXPERIENCING GOD

This chapter focuses on the essential element around which all other aspects of being an effective missionary revolve: an ongoing experience of God that results in a continuing transformation so that the missionary becomes more like Jesus year by year. A missionary who maintains a vital fellowship with God bears fruit especially by growing in key qualities of character such as obedience to God and being willing to suffer for Christ (John 15: 1–17; Gal 5:22). Missiologist Edgar Elliston, an expert in leadership training, and J. Timothy Kauffman write: "Effective ministry emerges out of the quality of character—not out of technical competence."[23]

Spiritual health is a missionary's lifeblood. Missionaries are God's ambassadors to those who have not met him. Their task—to invite people into relationship with Jesus and to keep growing in him—is spiritual, and missionaries can only joyfully endure the isolation and sometimes impossible challenges of missionary life by spiritual means. Missionaries must develop a resilient faith that can cope with the physical, emotional, and spiritual challenges of leaving home, living in an unfamiliar climate and culture, and grappling with other religious systems.[24]

A recent international survey of theological education asked more than 1,500 Christian leaders what the most important elements in preparation for Christian ministry are. One of the four key areas they felt needed strengthening was spiritual formation.[25] In our own experience of participating in

23. Edgar J. Elliston and J. Timothy Kauffman, *Developing Leaders for Urban Ministries*, American University Studies Series VII, Theology and Religion, (New York: P. Lang, 1993), 165.

24. Ron Brown, "Resilience in Ministry Despite Trauma," in *Worth Keeping: Global Perspectives on Best Practice in Missionary Retention*, ed. Rob Hay (Pasadena, CA: William Carey Library, 2007), 315–18.

25. David Esterline et al., "Global Survey on Theological Education 2011–2013: Summary of Main Findings," (Busan: Global Digital Library on Theology and Ecumenism (GlobeTheoLib), 2013), 5.

evaluation teams of several missionary training colleges, spiritual formation was consistently noted as an area of weakness.

Many books have been written about spiritual formation, but few focus specifically on how to help missionaries grow spiritually.[26] This chapter describes the key qualities of character and spiritual life that missionaries need.

QUALITIES OF CHARACTER AND SPIRITUALITY NEEDED BY MISSIONARIES

A Transforming Experience of God

Missionaries need to have experienced and continue to be experiencing a relationship with God through which they are being transformed to become more like Jesus. This involves being filled with, directed by, and keeping in step with the Holy Spirit so that the fruit of the Spirit—love, joy, peace, forbearance, kindness, goodness, faithfulness, gentleness, self-control—is displayed in their lives (Eph 5:18; Gal 5:16–26).

Missionaries' experience of God should lead to a holistic, all-encompassing, lifelong response to him, " . . . a Christ-centred orientation to every component of life."[27] Central to this response to God is loving him with heart, soul, mind, and strength (Deut 6:1–9; Matt 22: 37–38). The central need in training for missionary work is to know God experientially and to enjoy him. "In fact, this great need is so central to all life, and so definitive for all ministries, and so relevant to all cultures, and so ultimate compared to all other values, that is should be the all-absorbing passion of every Christian scholar and teacher."[28] Like the exemplary missionary of the New Testament, the Apostle Paul, missionaries need more than anything else to know Christ and to get to the point where

---

26.   Two books we found especially helpful in preparing this chapter were: Thomas Hale and Gene Daniels, *On Being a Missionary*, rev. ed. (Pasadena, CA: William Carey Library, 2012) and J. Oswald Sanders, *Spiritual Leadership: Principles of Excellence for Every Believer* (Chicago, IL: Moody Publishers, 2007).

27.   Kenneth Boa, *Conformed to His Image: Biblical and Practical Approaches to Spiritual Formation* (Grand Rapids, MI: Zondervan, 2001), 19.

28.   John Piper, "Training the Next Generation of Evangelical Pastors and Missionaries," in *Teaching Them Obedience in All Things: Equipping for the 21st Century*, ed. Edgar J. Elliston (Pasadena, CA: William Carey Library, 1999), 16.

they can say "everything else is worthless when compared to the priceless gain of knowing Christ Jesus my Lord" (Phil 3:8, cf. Eph 1:17; Eph 3:16–18; Phil 1:9; Phil 3:8–10; Col 1:9–10).

Ability to Discern God's Voice

A vital part of growing in our personal relationship with God is learning to discern God's voice and work out what he wants in the situations we face. The issues that they have to deal with are usually complex and unpredictable. They do not fit into neat theological patterns and rarely replicate scenarios that are discussed in theological education that focuses on preparing pastors and teachers for the church in their home cultures. Quite commonly, missionaries will search in vain through the textbooks they used in their Bible college or seminary for answers to the questions they face in cross-cultural ministry.

Missionary trainees need to know their Bibles well but also how to search the Scriptures for answers to questions they do not have prepared answers for. They need to know how to hear the "gentle whisper" of God's voice (1 Kgs 19:12) that indicates which way to turn (Isa 30:21), and that directs the missionary to people God has prepared (Acts 16:9–10). They also need to be able to discern whether it is the Holy Spirit, or something else, speaking through a dream, vision, or other medium to local people. For example, when a person in the same form as the actor portraying Jesus in the Jesus film started appearing in the dreams of a young woman in the church and giving her messages for the church we had started in Bulgaria, we needed to help the church work out whether this was Jesus or an evil spirit.

Obedience to God

Missionaries are God's servants, and must focus on serving God's agenda rather than their own or other people's.[29] In doing this, they are following in the footsteps of all God's servants who have lived before them. Israel's model king, David, is called God's servant more than seventy times in the Bible. The prophets are also frequently called God's servants, and the characteristic word used for the work of priests is "serving." The apostles similarly call themselves servants of Christ (Ex 30:30; 2 Ki 9:7; Dan 9:6, 10–11, 17; Rom 1:1; 2 Pet 1:1). Servants are characterized by obedience to their masters.

---

29. Elliston and Kauffman, *Developing Leaders for Urban Ministries*, 8.

Jesus commanded his disciples to do over forty specific things, which missionaries in turn have been commanded to do and to teach others to do (Matt 28:19). These things have helpfully been grouped under seven basic commands by George Patterson:[30]

- Repent, believe, and receive the Holy Spirit (Mark 1:15; John 6:29; John 20:22)
- Be baptized (Matt 28:28–20)
- Love God, neighbor, fellow disciples, the needy, and enemies (Matt 22:36–40; John 13:34–35; Luke 10:25–37; Matt 5:43–48)
- Break bread (Matt 26:26–28)
- Pray (John 16:24)
- Give (Luke 6:38)
- Make disciples (Matt 28:18–19)

It is crucial that missionaries exemplify these things in their lives, so that those they disciple can see what they should be doing by observing the missionaries' lifestyle as they, in turn, follow the example of Christ (cf. 1 Cor 11:1).

Holiness

Nothing mars the fragrance of Jesus so much in our lives or disrupts our ability to delight in him than persisting in sin. God has set apart his people for himself and wants them to live holy lives that reflect the special relationship they have with him. We are commanded to be holy as God is holy and to confess our sins to ensure fellowship with God and with each other (1 Pet 1:15–16; 1 John 1:5–2:11). We are also warned that Satan is prowling around looking for prey and that sin opens a connection to the devil (1 Pet 5:8–9; 1 John 3:8). Sin is a poison that harms individuals and destroys relationships when it is not dealt with.

When the Turkish-speaking Roma in Bulgaria first streamed into the kingdom of God in the late 1980s, their most common question was to ask whether specific things they had done were sinful. They were constantly on alert so that they would not offend God by what they did. New believers were unrestrained in their gossiping of the gospel but also afraid of distorting it. They had a deep awe of an all-seeing God who loved them and who required holiness.

One key area of temptation that must be addressed in missionary training is sexual temptation. Phil Parshall, in his survey of 390 missionaries, found

---

30. George Patterson and Richard Scoggins, *Church Multiplication Guide: The Miracle of Church Reproduction*, rev. ed. (Pasadena, CA: William Carey Library, 2002), 22.

that "sexual temptation is an ongoing battle for a large number of respondents" and noted that sex was rarely dealt with in pre-field orientation.[31] Moral failure in sexuality continues to be an issue today and opportunities for secret sin have increased with the advent of the internet.

A Clear Sense of Calling

The call to be a missionary is a crucial part of a missionary's spiritual formation and journey with God but the idea of the missionary call is easily misunderstood. Some people are locked into the idea that a call has to come in the form of a single dramatic and mystical experience through which God's will for them is revealed. Although the Bible describes some highly dramatic, one-time calls to God's service such as that of Moses, Samuel, Isaiah, and Saul (Ex 3; 1 Sam 3; Isa 6:1–9; Acts 9), it also points to less dramatic ways of being called or sent out by God, such as the cases of Silas and Timothy. Their guidance seemed to consist of being recommended by their home churches, being confirmed by others for missionary work, and by receiving gifts for this ministry through prophecy and the laying on of hands (Acts 15:36–41; Acts 16:1–3; 1 Tim 4:14; 2 Tim 1:6).

The missionary call is a special kind of guidance from God that a person experiences as a growing conviction leading to a decision point to serve God as a missionary.[32] This conviction should be confirmed by others (Acts 22:12–21; Rom 1:5; Acts 9:5; Acts 13:1–3). The process of receiving this kind of guidance relies on being obedient, stepping out, and trusting God to keep directing the prospective missionary's path.

Defining the missionary call as God's guidance that leads someone to become convinced that they should serve as a missionary allows for multiple ways this guidance and resulting conviction can be experienced. It also suggests that the experience of being guided into missionary service is often comprised of a sequence of events and that the exact sequence and combination of events may

---

31. Phil Parshall, "How Spiritual Are Missionaries?," in *Helping Missionaries Grow: Readings in Mental Health and Missions*, ed. Michele Lewis O'Donnell and Kelly S. O'Donnell (Pasadena, CA: William Carey Library, 1988).

32. e.g., Tom A. Steffen and Lois McKinney Douglas, *Encountering Missionary Life and Work: Preparing for Intercultural Ministry* (Grand Rapids, MI: Baker Academic, 2008), 48–61.

be different for each person.[33] If God gives visions or other dramatic ways of guiding someone, it is at his prerogative and in his timing.

Missionaries need a specific call or sense of conviction from God that missionary work is what he wants them to do. This is in contrast to the wider call shared by all Christians to keep trusting and obeying Jesus, make disciples, and offer their bodies to God as living sacrifices. Knowing they have been called to this task enables missionaries to persevere when things seem overwhelmingly difficult. Recent research has suggested that a clear sense of being called is very important in keeping missionaries on the field.[34] Thomas Hale explains that the missionary call is "a much more profound and life-changing event than ordinary guidance is." He argues that the additional duties that missionaries have as spiritual leaders on the forefront of the spiritual battle requires them to have a special calling. "It is my experience that those who arrive on the mission field without this sense of call are much more vulnerable to doubt and discouragement when the going gets tough."[35]

A Healthy Sense of Self

Missionaries need to understand and accept who God has made them to be. Paul puts it this way: "Don't think you are better than you really are. Be honest in your evaluation of yourselves" (Rom 12:3). This requires a balance between being aware of personal inadequacy or weakness and knowing that God has made you, is able to use you, and loves you as you are (Ex 4:10–11; Ps 139:13–16; Rom 12:3–8; 2 Cor 4; 12:9).

People need help from others to see who they are in terms of personality and gifting, and the best way of accessing this help is to work together with other people. The unique and valuable contributions that each person has to offer become clear in this process of serving God together. The conflict and difficulties involved in working together help potential missionaries to come face-to-face with their own inadequacies and to learn how to find God's help to grow.

---

33. Michael David Sills, *The Missionary Call: Find Your Place in God's Plan for the World* (Chicago, IL: Moody Publishers, 2008), 113.

34. Peter Brierley, "Missionary Attrition: The ReMAP Research Report," in *Too Valuable to Lose: Exploring the Causes and Cures of Missionary Attrition*, ed. William David Taylor (Pasadena, CA: William Carey Library, 1997); Detlef Blöcher and Jonathan Lewis, "Further Findings in the Research Data," ibid., 114; Hay, *Worth Keeping: Global Perspectives on Best Practice in Missionary Retention*, 16–19, 75–87, 101–12.

35. Hale and Daniels, *On Being a Missionary*, 20.

Accepting who we are means also accepting our own style of spirituality. Part of authentic spirituality is freedom to nurture spirituality in different ways. In an effort to help Christians grow in their faith, churches, colleges, and Christian organizations, including mission agencies, can tend to prescribe what people should do to develop their relationship with God. This may include specific expectations about personal devotional times, attendance at corporate worship and prayer meetings, and particular patterns of prayer or worship. While these are all good things, God's ways of enabling people to experience his presence are not as restrictive as these, and he delights in difference.[36] One large-scale survey of missionary spirituality revealed that there is a wide variety in how missionaries maintain their spirituality.[37] A particularly helpful book that explores the different ways in which people can draw closer to God is Gary Thomas's *Sacred Pathways*.[38] It moves us beyond a one-size-fits-all prescription for developing spirituality to describe a wide variety of ways that different people connect with God.

Missionaries need to be allowed the freedom to explore their spirituality in ways that are most meaningful and helpful for their spiritual growth. This is especially true since they go to cultures where people may have different ways of encountering God. If the training community recognizes and accepts differences in the ways Christians grow spiritually, it will help trainee missionaries to develop an openness to other ways of worshipping and growing in Christ. This openness will help them to be able to contextualize the gospel, and develop ways of doing discipleship and church, that are appropriate for people from different cultures.

Patience, Perseverance, and Faith

Missionaries have to do a lot of waiting. They wait to be accepted into a mission agency. They wait for financial support to be sufficient for them to leave for the field. They wait for visas. They have to be patient while they travel, meet new people, do mundane but challenging life-maintenance tasks, negotiate bureaucracy, wrestle with major life decisions, and interact with co-workers. They wait

---

36. We explore this in more depth in Evelyn Hibbert and Richard Hibbert, *Leading Multicultural Teams* (Pasadena, CA: William Carey Library, 2014), 47–68.

37. Parshall, "How Spiritual Are Missionaries?."

38. Gary Thomas, *Sacred Pathways: Discover Your Soul's Path to God* (Grand Rapids, MI: Zondervan, 2000).

for people to come to faith and wait for illness, depression, and discouragement to pass. Patience is needed to accept things as they are and not try to force things that we do not have control over to happen.

Missionaries must also be able to persevere and even thrive when there is little support and even active opposition. They often encounter situations where answers from home do not address the questions they face. Missionaries therefore need to have faith that God's purposes will prevail. They have to be confident that God will complete his work in the world, in and through them, and in others they are working with (Ps 33:10–11; 145:13; Phil 1:6; 2 Tim 2:13) even when they cannot see any evidence of change occurring.

Being convinced that the work of changing others' lives is God's work and not the missionary's is central to being a servant of God (cf. Matt 16:17; 2 Cor 4:3–5). Getting caught up in false guilt about apparent lack of success or, alternatively, becoming proud when things go well, cripples missionary effectiveness (Isa 26:12). Missionaries should strive like athletes, keep focused, disciplined, and obedient like soldiers, but leave the results to God. This is because they are in a spiritual battle in which the ultimate outcome is not dependent on human effort (Zech 4:61; Cor 9:24–27; 2 Tim 2:3–5). Observing living examples, discussing the issues with experienced missionaries, reflecting on personal experience, and having committed intercessors praying for them, all help the missionary to find a balanced perspective.

Faith is independent of guaranteed outcomes. The timing and mode in which God's promises are fulfilled are his prerogative. We often cannot predict how things in the short term, or even in our lifetimes, will turn out. True faith has to be content with this, just as Shadrach, Meshach, and Abednego demonstrated in being comfortable with ambiguous outcomes in their confrontation with Nebuchadnezzar (Dan 3).

Faith requires action regardless of our feelings and what we can see. Faith is like a soldier's courage. It is not necessarily something that is felt inside (although it may be). It is more often a stepping out in obedience regardless of what might happen. This mirrors the balance between expecting God to act and needing to take action ourselves. Missionaries need to be able to find this balance, and it is very helpful for new missionaries to spend time learning and working alongside more experienced workers who demonstrate it.

Faith is developed through experiencing God's faithfulness in difficulties and suffering. It needs to be tested and developed by experience. It is also developed through participation in a community of people that together can testify to God's faithfulness, give concrete examples, and actively encourage each other to trust.

Faith enables missionaries to keep focusing on the harvest fields where there are still no workers, to keep casting a vision for those who have not heard, locally and further afield, and to keep believing that God will bring a harvest there too (cf. Mark 1:38; Luke 10:2). It enables them to keep working for the evangelization of the whole city, region, and people group they are working among, and believing that Jesus will build his church there (Matt 16:18).

Resilience

Cross-cultural mission is characterized by unpredictability and relative isolation from the supports that are available at home. Missionaries' lives are marked by more uncertainty than if they were living in their home countries. They are faced with completely new and unfamiliar ministry situations and problems. They face constant ambiguity because the people they work among usually have very different values and a completely different way of seeing the world. They may work among people who have a solid system of belief that they are confident in and who do not seem at all open to considering Christianity. They may even meet local people who appear to have more genuine faith than they feel themselves have. Missionaries are also caught up in spiritual warfare and can face fierce opposition as they attempt to break new ground with the gospel.

To face all these challenges, missionaries must develop spiritual resilience. This has three key facets: 1) perseverance in the face of opposition, lack of support, and other difficulties (discussed above); 2) confidence in the foundation they stand on while being able to adjust their understanding and expression of faith in response to the unfamiliar challenges of cross-cultural ministry; and 3) the ability to build and draw on relationships.

Resilience enables missionaries to hold many things loosely while being sure of the unshakeable foundations of their faith. Resilient missionaries are able to discern what is important yet be flexible regarding things that are of secondary importance. Inflexible missionaries, in contrast, tightly hold on to their own ways of thinking and doing things. Hale and Daniels observe:

> The person who is predominantly determined and single-minded will be an asset on the field, as long as he is also willing to listen to others' ideas and to adapt and compromise when appropriate. The predominantly rigid and inflexible

person, on the other hand, is threatened by new ideas and unable to adapt, and thus would be a liability of the field.[39]

Rigidity in faith and personality, as well as in how things must be done, will inhibit the missionary from relating to people from other cultures and being able to effectively communicate the gospel and make disciples among them. It will also cause problems when working in teams with diverse membership.

The kingdom of God will only advance if people are willing to venture into the unknown and try things that may not work. Resilience enables missionaries to embrace the risks needed to take the gospel into new areas and plant new churches where there are none. They need to be secure enough in who they are and their relationship with God and with others that they are willing to take risks and even to fail.

Another aspect of spiritual resilience is being able to cope with discouragement and failure. Trials and discouragement are inevitable. These provide opportunities to find God's strength, wisdom, and sufficiency. Discouragement and depression are normal human responses to setbacks, disappointments and frustrations, and bad news. Friends are the best therapy as they help us to keep things in perspective. Friends only have to listen, not counsel. They can accept/validate the emotion while maintaining normal life and coaxing gradual recovery. When the emotion is disproportionate or there is no recovery within a reasonable time frame, friends can urge or arrange for intervention from outside.

Being able to praise God regardless of what is happening lifts our gaze from ourselves and onto God, and brings relief. This is what the African American slaves did in the face of their oppression, what the Turkish Gypsy Christians do in the face of their many challenges of being stigmatized and marginalized in Bulgarian society, and what the Korean Christians do in their early morning prayer meetings as they cry out to God all together. Prayer and songs are just two examples of ways in which human beings can abandon themselves in the experience of God, find emotional release and healing, and return refreshed to ministry. This ability to find refreshment despite sometimes overwhelming challenges and discouragement is a key factor in resilience.

Resilience is promoted by living a healthy lifestyle and by having a healthy outlook on life. Personal discipline in rest, healthy eating and exercise,

---

39. Hale and Daniels, *On Being a Missionary*, 55.

continuing to learn, maintaining healthy relationships (especially marriage and family), good sleeping habits, a healthy devotional life, and taking time to "smell the roses" all help the missionary to maintain a healthy perspective. But more than in any other way, resilience is developed through experiencing God in the face of difficulties. Missionaries need to have experienced the power of God in their personal life and in ministry. Without this, they may have difficulty being able to access the Holy Spirit's help during the confusion and challenges of cross-cultural experiences.[40]

Ability to Cope with Stress

Missionaries face huge stresses when moving to another country and learning a new language and culture, as well as the repeated stress of re-entering the culture they left behind and engaging with people at home who find it difficult to understand the demands of the missionary's life and ministry.

Missionaries also work in situations that are very poorly resourced. There simply are not the personnel or other resources that would be expected in a similar ministry situation in the home country. The missionary must be able to manage their stress and set reasonable boundaries. Feeling trapped, frustrated, angry, discouraged, exhausted, depressed, irritable, are all absolutely normal human emotions in missionary life. They are not in themselves sinful but are symptoms of being pushed beyond the normal human capacity for endurance. The challenge is that under stress it is easier to give in to sin (Eph 4:26).

Missionaries need to understand the ways they typically react to stress and be able to take measures to keep stress at manageable levels. They need to understand how stress can affect their personal feelings and also their perception of their own spirituality. For example, if a person becomes tired they are more likely to feel depressed and discouraged. This may cause them to feel as if God is far away and to lose hope in God's promises. Recognizing the connection between physical and mental well-being and spiritual feelings or perceptions can help missionaries keep a balanced and healthy perspective, as well as take time for rest and refreshment. Missionaries need to learn how to find peace, how to endure the impossible with God's help (within reasonable boundaries) and how to recover through resting. They need to develop a healthy recognition of their own and others' humanity.

---

40. Ibid., 67.

Willingness to Suffer

Suffering is unavoidable in missionary life. Just as God's perfect servant, Jesus, endured the ultimate suffering, so missionaries must expect suffering and willingly endure it when it comes (1 Pet 2:21). Jesus impressed on his disciples that they would suffer, and that they would need to be single-minded in enduring it for his sake (Mark 8:34–38; Luke 9:57–62; John 15:18). While every Christian should expect to suffer for Christ and be willing to do this, missionaries are particularly likely to suffer, as the apostles did, partly because of the self-sacrifice involved in living among a culturally different people in an unfamiliar environment, and partly because many people will oppose the message they bring and them as the messengers (Acts 14: 22; 1 Pet 4:12–19; Matt 10:24–25; 2 Tim 1:8–12; 2:3). It does not help to downplay the sacrifices that missionaries make. They are real and unavoidable, and their cost should be calculated and accepted before embarking on a missionary career.

Once sacrifice has been accepted as integral to the missionary calling, it requires discipline to continue on this path. Many missionaries revert to comfortable, middle-class lifestyles once on the field. In some cases, where missionaries come from less affluent backgrounds, missionary lifestyles can actually be materially better than what they left behind. While there is nothing intrinsically wrong with comfort, the missionary call is to sacrifice. Even on the mission field, the insidious creep of possessions, comfort, and status can gradually erode the willingness to continue moving out to the edges, and taking the risks that are necessary to make disciples of all nations.

Missionaries are not called to sacrifice for sacrifice's sake. They are called, though, to obedience and to give up their comfort and security and go to places that are unfamiliar and may be highly uncomfortable. They are often asked by God to give up their professions and homes and to accept lower income and jobs with less status. More than most Christians in their home churches, missionaries will face hardship.

Jesus asks missionaries to do nothing more than he already did for us. He instructed his disciples not to worry about the things they needed (Matt 6:25; Luke 12:22) or to store up treasures on earth (Matt 6:19–21; Luke 12:17–21). Paul gave an outstanding living example of a person willing to endure whatever was necessary to take the gospel to the ends of the earth (2 Cor 11:23–27). At the same time missionaries need to be able to relate to affluent Christians and enjoy the good things God has given. Again, Paul provides a living testimony of learning to be content in all circumstances (Phil 4:12).

Another issue that has to be dealt with is the subtle expectation of reward for service or sacrifice. Many Christians still expect that if they do what is right and especially if they sacrifice for God, they should receive blessing in return. When they instead encounter suffering and misfortune they find it difficult to accept and even more difficult to comprehend. There is an implicit expectation, for example, that if you sacrifice your children's opportunities (compared to their home-based peers) for the sake of the gospel, they will only benefit, not be disadvantaged or harmed through the experience. However, there are no such guarantees. Missionaries are not promised more blessings because they have given up more. In fact, in many cases, they will suffer more trouble, discouragement, and misfortune.

Loneliness is a sacrifice that is rarely talked about except in the context of single missionaries, but whether single or married, missionaries need to be able to cope with loneliness. Being dislocated from family, friends, and familiar supports can take a severe emotional toll. It can take a long time to establish friendships in the new culture, and these friendships may be associated with demands that the missionary is unable to fulfill. This may mean that it is not possible to relax in a relationship in the same way that it is possible to do with a friend at home. Even in their home countries missionaries can experience loneliness. They have often changed so much that they feel they no longer fit in and find it difficult to relate to people who seem to have remained the same despite the passage of many years.

DEVELOPING HABITS THAT PROMOTE TRANSFORMATION INTO CHRISTLIKENESS

The essence of spiritual formation is growth in our relationship with and obedience to Jesus and becoming like him. Our part in this process is to develop habits or disciplines that promote this kind of growth and which become a part of our way of life.

The relationship of discipline to spiritual development has long been recognized and was clearly demonstrated by the monastic orders. A generation ago this recognition of the importance of spiritual disciplines was expressed in sayings like "No Bible, no breakfast." The importance of discipline for spiritual development is discussed in books like Richard Foster's *Celebration of Discipline* and Dallas Willard's *The Spirit of the Disciplines*.[41]

Another word used to describe discipline is habitus. Habitus is a way of being that is continually developing and which embodies, internally and physically, the beliefs, assumptions, and practices of a group of people.[42] In this case, the group is missionaries. The word "discipline" usually refers to a fixed practice. One example of this would be soldiers performing a physical drill on the parade ground. The discipline that going over and over the same drill instills in soldiers is not just the physical actions of the drill itself but the attitude of unhesitating obedience to superior officers and the automating of essential skills for battle. In other words, habitual practices result in the embodiment of specific, unhesitating attitudes and automated skills. In the same way that an army is intentional in developing habits of obedience in its soldiers, Dallas Willard stresses that Christians should be intentional in engaging in spiritual transformation.[43]

A habit is reinforced by repeated practice until it becomes an integral part of life and is applied continually without having to consciously think about it. Whatever practices we choose to engage in repetitively, it is essential that they achieve the purpose that we want them to. Missionaries are not soldiers, but they are meant to be like soldiers in their discipline (2 Tim 2:3–4). While an army focuses on developing uniformity and suppressing individuality, God is developing diversity in harmony (1 Cor 12:12–30). In contrast to military formation, spiritual formation should result in the affirmation of individuality, encouraging each person to develop into all that God has created her or him to be (Rom 9:19–21; 2 Tim 2:20).

A habitus or way of being that promotes ongoing spiritual formation needs to be nurtured by engaging in disciplines related to our thought life, our feelings, and our wills. Saba Mahmood found that engaging in physical acts of

---

41.   Richard Foster, *Celebration of Discipline* (Hachette UK, 2012), 6; Dallas Willard, *The Spirit of the Disciplines* (Hodder & Stoughton, 1996).

42.   We are extending the idea of habitus here originally described by Pierre Bourdieu and applied to Islamic women's movements by Saba Mahmood, *Politics of Piety: The Islamic Revival and the Feminist Subject* (Princeton University Press, 2005), and education by Megan Watkins and Greg Noble, *Disposed to Learn: Schooling, Ethnicity and the Scholarly Habitus* (Bloomsbury Academic, 2013).

43.   Dallas Willard, *Renovation of the Heart* (Hovel Audio, 2005), 59–65.

worship helped Muslim women develop pious attitudes and behaviors.[44] Her descriptions resonate with Paul's admonition to the Philippians to discipline themselves to think well of others (Phil 4:8–9) and Jesus' command to forgive and keep forgiving (Matt 18:21–22). In both these activities, the believer has to act first and trust that the appropriate feelings will follow.

This development of good habits is dependent on a supportive context, clear expectations, proactive encouragement, and consistent role models. This has been demonstrated in the case of academic achievement. Megan Watkins and Greg Noble investigated how certain ethnic groups appeared to achieve better academic results than others. They discovered that academic achievement was associated with parents instilling a scholarly habitus in their children. This scholarly habitus was promoted by providing a context that promoted study, by proactive parental support of study practices and by clear parental expectations about their children's study.[45] Additionally, a great deal of recent educational research has been exploring how schools can develop good habits of behavior in their students. These patterns of behavior relate to academic study, social skill development, as well as the attitudes and behavior characteristic of good citizens.[46]

Missionary spiritual formation is facilitated by the same set of factors. The support of others, clear expectations, encouragement, and modeling should all be included as key ingredients in missionary spiritual formation. Missionary trainers should provide a context that supports the development of relevant spiritual attitudes and behaviors, explicitly describe what these spiritual attitudes and behaviors look like, focus on encouragement rather than penalties, and model missionary attitudes and ministry skills to trainees.

THE NEED FOR TRAINERS TO BE LIVING MODELS

The overarching goal of missionary training is to motivate and help trainees to keep getting to know, love, and obey Jesus more and so to become more like

---

44. Saba Mahmood, *Politics of Piety: The Islamic Revival and the Feminist Subject*, (Princeton, NJ: Princeton University Press, 2005).

45. Megan Watkins and Greg Noble, *Disposed to Learn: Schooling, Ethnicity and the Scholarly Habitus* (New York: Bloomsbury Academic, 2013).

46. Research in this field usually refers to Positive Behavioral Interventions and Support (PBIS) or Positive Behaviour for Learning (PBL).

him, not only through the designated period of training, but through their whole lives.[47] God has always wanted people to become like him. Though sin marred his image or likeness in people, he still calls his people to become like him. He wants his people to be holy as he is holy (Lev 11:44; Lev 19:2; 20:26; 1 Pet 1:15–16). God wants his people to "to walk in all his ways," which means imitating him.[48] One of God's purposes in sending Jesus to earth to become a man was to show us what he is like so that we could imitate (John 1:1, 14, 18; 14:7; 17:26). When Jesus called his disciples to follow him, it meant not only following him around from place to place, but patterning their lives on his, just as rabbis of his time expected their students to do.[49] Jesus expected his disciples to imitate him and, by doing this, to become like their master, just as the society of that time expected disciples of any rabbi would become like their teacher (Luke 6:40).

Every believer is meant to imitate Jesus and to grow to be more like him (1 John 2:6; Rom 8:29). Since Jesus is no longer physically with us, knowing what imitating Christ looks like is immeasurably helped by following the example of Christians whose lives have been shaped by God. This is why Paul told the Corinthians to imitate him (1 Cor 11:1) and reminded Timothy of his own lifestyle (2 Tim 3:10–11).

Living models of the Christian life become reference points from which we extrapolate appropriate responses for new situations. Missionary trainers should model, among other things, disciplines of thinking, feeling, and behavior that they expect their trainees to imitate. One way of doing this is for trainers to share with trainees honest testimonies about what they think God is doing in their lives and how they are growing in and applying the disciplines. It is also important that trainers pro-actively encourage trainees about what they are doing well in putting the disciplines into practice.

Paul Hiebert was one of these living examples for me (Richard). As a student in several of his doctoral seminars, I not only learned some valuable missiological theory but was influenced by what I saw of his character and

---

47.   Jonathan Lewis, "Philosophy of Integral Ministry Training," in *Integral Ministry Training: Design and Evaluation*, ed. Robert Brynjolfson and Jonathan Lewis (Pasadena, CA: William Carey Library, 2006), 22.

48.   Christopher J. H. Wright, *Deuteronomy*, New International Biblical Commentary Old Testament Series (Peabody, MA: Hendrickson Publishers, 1996), 145.

49.   Günter Krallmann, *Mentoring for Mission: A Handbook on Leadership Principles Exemplified by Jesus Christ*, 2nd ed. (Waynesboro, GA: Gabriel Publishing, 2002), 61.

convictions, and especially the way he made himself and his home available to his students. It was often difficult for doctoral students to find affordable accommodation and so he opened his home for several students to stay with him. This was invaluable for them to be able to complete their studies. He also hosted a meal for a wider group of missions students every few weeks where we talked about all kinds of things including missions dilemmas being faced by students in their work. Finally, his ongoing practical commitment to mission was evident in his giving, even in his seventies, nearly half of each year to serving in India.

Training programs should combine the role modeling of trainers with explicit verbal explanation of what appropriate behavior and attitudes entail. When the specific behaviors associated with a character quality are clearly defined, trainees know much more clearly what to aim for and to work on. Having clearly articulated criteria not only helps students to know what to aspire to, but also acts as a health check for teachers' own behavior and attitudes. It helps trainees who come from different backgrounds and who may not be familiar with the sociocultural bases on which assessments are made in the training program to have explicit guidance that helps them to understand what they need to work on and demonstrate in order to develop in the more subjective areas of character and spirituality. This can be particularly important when trainees come from different cultures or socioeconomic classes than the trainers. For example, if the training is occurring in a high context culture[50] where older people must be addressed with honorifics and their statements are not questioned in public, respect might be articulated as addressing older people using honorifics and being quiet in group situations even when you disagree with what the older person says. In a low context culture, respect might instead be defined as waiting for the older person to finish what they are saying before offering an opinion.

Spirituality is more caught than taught. The most helpful thing that missionary trainers can do to help people grow in qualities of missionary spirituality

---

50. The different orientations of people from high and low context cultures was first described by Edward Hall in *Beyond Culture* (New York: Anchor Press, 1976). People from high context cultures are more aware of the many non-verbal cues in the context including other things going on in the room. They place as much or more value on these non-verbal elements as they do on the words themselves. People from low context cultures, in contrast, pay attention almost exclusively to the words of the communication and ignore many of the elements in the wider context.

is to model these in their own lives. Missionary trainees need to see how these qualities are expressed in their teachers and this means they need to spend time with them outside a classroom. Ideally, trainers and trainees will eat together, spend time in each other's homes, and serve alongside each other in practical ministry tasks. In this way trainers can be holistic examples of Christian life and ministry. Some aspects of this role modeling can be provided through testimonies, including in biographies, but the most powerful models are those that new missionaries can see and touch (cf. 1 John 1:1).

Role modeling becomes even more powerful in affecting trainees' lives when they see multiple role models among both trainers and trainees in the learning community. They observe not only individual responses but also how the group is able to flex and grow as each member participates. Every community develops a set of symbols, rituals, and stories that is unique to it. These symbols, rituals, and stories then become a resource that can be used to inform new relationship and community-building in the missionaries' new contexts. These communal experiences develop a bank of intuitive knowledge. In this way, both planned and unplanned experiences in the training program help the trainees develop "in a relational-experiential manner."[51]

The character qualities that are needed by missionaries are expressed in complexes of behavior that are different in different cultures. Patience among Americans looks very different to patience among Pacific Islanders, for example. For this reason, trainees need holistic role models who can contextualize the display of Christian maturity in various contexts.

The type of learning that is achieved through observing and interacting with role models is not a bank of decontextualized knowledge that can be written down. It is more holistic and intuitive. Donald Schön describes this type of learning as being about tacit knowledge. It is something that accomplished professionals such as concert pianists have developed. It is expert and intuitive and that cannot be broken down into components. Students learn this tacit knowledge through receiving feedback based on the intuitive understanding of the expert. When music reviewers compare one performer's performance with that of another, they are also making judgments according to this same kind of knowledge. Although some specific elements might be able to be articulated,

---

51. Elizabeth Conde-Frazier, S. Steve Kang, and Gary A. Parrett, *A Many Colored Kingdom: Multicultural Dynamics for Spiritual Formation* (Grand Rapids, MI: Baker Academic, 2004), 87.

it is more about a holistic impression of many elements that combine into a unique way of doing things that is singular to each specific expert. This allows for individual personality to express itself even though the musical score may be exactly the same.[52] In the same way, each experienced missionary will interact in an individual way yet still demonstrate an expert approach that others can learn from. They will also benefit from seeing the way different experts handle similar situations and, by reflecting on and integrating their observations and experiences, be able to develop their own approach.

THE NEED FOR TRAINING TO OCCUR IN AN AUTHENTIC CONTEXT

There is no substitute for cross-cultural experience in missionary training. Exposure to the new and unfamiliar challenges of cross-cultural ministry, combined with mentoring by experienced workers can help the new missionary to develop resilience, learn to manage stress, and develop intercultural competence. Being placed in ministry situations that the trainees cannot control, such as when they do not understand the language being spoken, cannot dictate when to leave, where they sit, or who they interact with, or where they are powerless to effect change, is an important step in developing self-awareness and the fruit of the Spirit.

Trainees who are constantly seeing a group of trainers modeling character qualities, spirituality, and ways of responding to people can then experiment with "trying on" these ways of acting, reacting, and nurturing spiritual health that different trainers display. Through experiments in imitating various trainers and modifying how they do things, trainees can develop their own approach that uniquely suits them and the ministry context they are working in. When they go into new contexts, they have living models they can refer to and imagine how those living models might have approached what they encounter.[53]

---

52. Donald A. Schön, *The Reflective Practitioner: How Professionals Think in Action* (Aldershot, England: Arena, 1991).

53. This is the approach popularized through Charles Sheldon's book *In His Steps* (New York: Grosset & Dunlap, 1935). In this book Sheldon is, in effect, actively contextualizing—by providing fictional living models—the imitation of Jesus for the American audience of his time.

Training in a cross-cultural context is further enhanced by working in a multicultural ministry team as trainees are helped to develop in character and fruits of the Spirit as they learn to work together with people with significantly different backgrounds and expectations than themselves. Training that occurs in multicultural contexts with diverse trainers also helps missionary candidates to become more flexible and interculturally competent. Learning in multicultural communities can help to overcome the tendency each participant has to be limited by their own cultural blind spots and limited experience. Cultural blind spots can result in "trained incapacity" to perceive or relate to things outside a homogeneous group's way of seeing things and skill set.[54]

In order to learn how to manage stress, missionary trainees have to practice implementing strategies in stressful situations. Providing a training context that is as close as possible to the situation that missionaries experience on the field helps trainees to experience authentic stressors in a safe environment. Trainers can help trainees to identify what they are experiencing before things escalate, and trainees can trial various strategies for responding to stress. If the training experience is more authentic, this alerts trainees to realistic triggers and responses which makes them more able to recognize them when they arise on the mission field.

Conducting training in the context of cross-cultural ministry with more experienced missionaries helps trainees to see that sacrifice and self-discipline are an ongoing daily choice rather than a once-for-all moment of commitment. Hearing the honest testimonies of missionary trainers and seeing how they live their lives can help both with realistically understanding as well as counting the cost of missionary work (Luke 14:28–33), and with providing guidelines on how to approach the kind of cost-counting Jesus talked about. As a result, trainees are able to be more realistic in their decisions and more confident to move forward despite the prospect of difficulties and suffering. It is not helpful to downplay the sacrifices missionaries have to make, but honest testimonies from missionaries, along with trainees being able to see the quality of these missionaries' faith, character, family, and life, can help them to decide whether they are willing to accept the costs and whether they want to be like their mentors.

---

54. Birgit Herppich, "Cultural Bias in Missionary Education: The Unintentional Dynamic of Trained Incapacity," in *Association of Professors of Mission* (University of Northwestern, St Paul, MN: First Fruits Press, 2014).

3

USING THE BIBLE

Despite going through Bible college or seminary training many of us who have served as missionaries felt unprepared for what we faced on the field. Two recent studies of ministry and missionary training highlight that missionaries particularly feel unable to relate the issues they face in cross-cultural ministry to their studies of Bible and theology.[55]

PUTTING THE BIBLE INTO PRACTICE

As missionaries, we are meant to pass on our understanding of the Bible. We therefore need to know the Bible well. Jesus modeled the importance of knowing Scripture in many ways, including his response to Satan's temptations in which he quoted from the Old Testament, and his quoting of the Bible on the many occasions when he said "It is written . . ." (Matt 4:1–11; Luke 4:1–13). Jesus also expected religious leaders to know and understand the Bible well (e.g., Matt 12:3–8).

Reading or hearing the Scriptures is just the first step towards understanding them. Reflecting and meditating on them is a crucial second part of the process (Ps 119: 15, 23, 27, 48, 78, 97, 99, 148). This involves continually filling one's mind with the Scriptures in order to internalize them and "hide them in the heart" (e.g., v. 11, 20, 44). The goal is not knowledge for its own sake but for the sake of being able to live in a way that pleases and honors God (Col 1:9–10). Knowledge of the Scriptures is a means to an end—never an end in itself.[56] It

---

55. Herbert Brasher, *Important Factors in Pre-Field and Field-Based Preparation of Missionaries Serving with Cross and Crescent International*, Evangelical Missiological Society Dissertation Series (Pasadena, CA: WCIU Press, 2007), 67–76; Les Ball, *Transforming Theology: Student Experience and Transformative Learning in Undergraduate Theological Education* (Preston, Victoria: Mosaic Press, 2012).

56. Perry G. Downs, *Teaching for Spiritual Growth: An Introduction to Christian Education* (Grand Rapids, MI: Zondervan, 1994), 41.

is sadly possible to know the Scriptures well but to miss their purpose. This was true of many of the Jewish religious leaders who interacted with Jesus. He said to them: "You search the Scriptures because you believe they give you eternal life. But these Scriptures point to me! Yet you refuse to come to me so that I can give you this eternal life" (John 5:39–10).

God's intention and expectation is that study of, meditation on, and obedience to his Word would be a lifelong habit for his people and especially for those in leadership roles. Scripture teaches us what is true and right and "is God's way of preparing us in every way, fully equipped for every good thing God wants us to do" (2 Tim 3:16–17).

Meditating on and actively obeying the Bible should be part of who missionaries are. God has given us his Word so that we can put it into practice. This is illustrated in the lives of Israel's leaders. God wanted Joshua, for example, to study and meditate on the Book of the Law continually so that he could do what it said (Josh 1:8). He wanted every Israelite king to write for himself a copy of the law and read from it every day so that "he may learn to revere the Lord his God and follow carefully all the words of this law and these decrees and not consider himself better than his brothers and turn from the law to the right or to the left." (Deut 17:18–20). God's intention was to keep the king on track with God's ways by continually reminding him of God's desires and commands so that the king could put them into practice in his own life and ensure they were followed by his people.

PASSING ON THE MESSAGE OF THE BIBLE TO OTHERS

Missionaries are meant to pass on their understanding of the Bible to others. But this isn't only a matter of cognitive knowledge. Jesus commanded his disciples not simply to teach others what he had taught them, but to teach others to *obey* everything he had commanded them. This required the apostles, and requires missionaries today, to pass on the teaching not only through words but also through the way they live. The missionary's lifestyle should agree with what they teach so that local believers see and hear the same coherent message being expressed through word and deed (cf. 1 Cor 4:17; 1 Tim 4:12–16).

Missionaries have been entrusted with a message from God that is expressed in the Scriptures. It is vital that missionaries have a clear understanding of this message and hold firmly to it so that they can pass it on to others (cf. 1 Tim 6:20; 2 Tim 2:2). They need to be able to teach or pass on the knowledge of God and his ways as they are revealed in the Bible (Matt 28:18–19; 2 Tim 2:2; 1 Tim 3:2). In addition, they must be able to facilitate and empower those who come to faith through their ministry to teach others, just as Jesus enabled his disciples to make new disciples.

The missionary role is a transient one. "The cross-cultural agent is vital, but catalytic and temporary, and must be ready to move on."[57] For this reason, missionaries must be able to teach and pass on the message of the Scriptures in a way that is reproducible. This contrasts with the relative stability of ministry positions in churches and theological colleges at home. The missionary's way of teaching should be reproducible by local believers who should be trained to pass on what they have received (cf. 2 Tim 2:2). The focus is not on reproducing institutions but on reproducing devoted servants of Jesus by selecting and training the right people—people like Priscilla and Aquila, Timothy and Titus—and then encouraging and supporting them, and modeling effective ministry. The teaching skills of missionaries should be honed towards teaching themselves out of a job as quickly as possible.

CONTEXTUALIZING THE MESSAGE OF THE BIBLE

The challenge of missionary work is to determine how to communicate the message of the Bible in meaningful and reproducible ways across sometimes overwhelming cultural barriers. An incarnational approach to missionary life that focuses on identifying with the local people has helped missionaries to represent Jesus as his ambassadors. Although missionaries are able to build relationships with local people, they have long recognized their inability to ever fully become members of the host culture. They are only ever a temporary presence partly due to factors outside their control, such as illness, war, and political upheaval. But they are also only meant to be a temporary presence because once churches have been established and nurtured, those churches become responsible for reaching their own communities, and the missionaries must move on to the remaining unreached. Missionaries therefore need to

---

57. Andrew F. Walls, *The Missionary Movement in Christian History: Studies in the Transmission of Faith* (Maryknoll, NY: Orbis Books, 1996), 258.

provide the local people with access to God's word in their own language and train them to read and interpret it for themselves, in the belief that God's word is sufficient (cf. 2 Tim 3:16–17) for locals to grow in their faith even in the absence of missionaries.

In order to provide the Scriptures in local languages, missionaries must have the commitment to learn the local language and culture in sufficient depth to adequately communicate the riches of the Bible. They have to grapple with how to effectively translate and communicate biblical truths in culturally authentic ways. Engaging effectively in the process of contextualization is an ongoing challenge in all missionary work. In practice, effective contextualization means the difference between establishing a church that local people feel belongs in their culture rather than a foreign institution that is rejected by the majority.

The way that missionaries view the Scriptures strongly affects how they approach contextualization. Missionaries who have not had missiological training are often oblivious to the need to contextualize their ways of living, sharing the gospel, and discipling local people. They often do not realize how much of their own experience of Christianity has been affected by culture and mistakenly assume that their way is the only right way of being Christian. Missionaries without missiological training can tend to have a more rigid, or black and white, understanding of biblical interpretation, translation, and literacy, as well as the Christian practices associated with specific ways of interpreting the Bible. They can also be less inclined to perceive God's word as a seed to be planted in different soils, free to grow into its own form and expression.[58] Wanting to be true to what they understand of the word of God, they may insist on word-for-word translations of Scripture that often result in their meaning being misunderstood. In order for local people to get an understanding of Scripture that is as faithful as possible to its original intent, it is important that missionaries invest the time and effort to find the best possible ways of expressing things in the local language and, where necessary, infuse new meaning into existing words which have different nuances.[59]

---

58. Lamin O. Sanneh, *Translating the Message: The Missionary Impact on Culture*, American Society of Missiology Series. (Maryknoll, NY: Orbis Books, 1989).

59. A convincing illustration of this can be found in Harriet Hill, *The Bible at Cultural Crossroads: From Translation to Communication* (Kinderhook, NY: St. Jerome Publishing, 2006).

Missionaries need different skills in handling the Bible than Christian leaders in working in their own culture. In monocultural settings, when Christian workers are trained in the interpretation and application of the Bible, analysis of the surrounding culture and formulation of a Christian response is assumed to have been done by the teachers and leaders of the established church. The wisdom and experience of previous leaders and theologians is passed on to new leaders as the accepted and right way of thinking and doing things. In cross-cultural missionary work however, especially in pioneer situations, this cultural analysis has not yet been done, and it takes a tremendous amount of commitment, learning, and interaction with local people in order for an authentic expression of Christianity to emerge and become established. Missionaries need to be able to search the Scriptures to find answers to questions and issues in the cultures they are working in and to formulate new theologies and ways of communicating these that are relevant to the local culture. Missionaries whose way of handling the Bible is dependent on pre-formulated responses will struggle to help local people develop a relevant faith and may even find their own faith challenged by things they encounter for which their Bible training did not prepare them.

Missionaries also have to help the local people learn the Bible and to use it to find answers to their own questions and guidance for their own lives. As the Bible is a written text, missionaries have been strongly committed to training people to read and comprehend written texts. This has often been associated with introducing Western-style schooling.[60] If missionaries have not had missiological training, they can find it difficult to critically evaluate their views of literacy, knowledge, teaching, and learning, and be willing to allow indigenous modes of learning the Bible to develop. One major area in which debate has arisen in recent decades is with respect to orality. There has been an increasing interest in missionary circles in the use of storytelling and other oral modes of

---

60. We are not here intending to define "Western culture." It is a term that is frequently used to refer to a cluster of cultures including people from the USA, England, Germany and the Netherlands and other related countries. It is an indiscriminate term that is often used in reference to people from countries with high levels of education and economic development. In the context of this discussion of the dominance of knowledge in education, we use it to refer to low context cultures that emphasize words over the context in which words are spoken and to contexts where this approach to knowledge has been imported and adopted as the predominant form of education. Readers should discern whether or to what degree this analysis applies to their own situations.

communication and considerable discussion of the adequacy of orality in comparison to literacy to transmit and preserve biblical truth.[61]

DEVELOPING OPENNESS TO DIFFERENT PERSPECTIVES

The process of learning to communicate the message of the Scriptures to people from other cultures requires the missionary to be open to different ways of thinking, perceiving the world, and interpreting the Bible. Missionary training should help trainees develop this openness along with the skills to research culture and relate the Bible to different worldviews. This type of training can help to expose rigid views about what is right and wrong that might cause problems in cross-cultural settings and provides a supportive environment where those with a more rigid faith can be helped to develop more flexible meaning frameworks.[62]

The best means of increasing missionary trainees' openness to different perspectives is to expose them to people from other cultures and their values and ways of thinking about the world in a supportive training environment. This can be done in various ways. The most effective is face-to-face interaction with people from other cultures. This should be combined with discussion and supportive debriefing of the different behaviors, values, and worldview assumptions trainees have encountered. Another way to provide exposure to and interaction with other cultures is through case studies that explore unfamiliar cultural issues. Through these, trainees analyze the beliefs, values, and felt needs that seem to underpin the behaviors described in the case studies, and explore what aspects of the Bible might address them. Through this repeated exposure to different views of the world, different ways of approaching the Bible, and seeing the readiness of teacher-models to engage with new ideas and ways of doing things, trainees gain an appreciation and awareness of different cultural perspectives. They also learn that multiple ways of doing things can equally be "right" and learn not to be quick to assume they already know all the answers in any situation.

---

61. If you would like to learn more about this area we recommend Harry Box, *Don't Throw the Book at Them: Communicating the Christian Message to People Who Don't Read* (Pasadena, CA: William Carey Library, 2014).

62. See the Preface for an explanation of meaning frameworks.

Preparing culturally appropriate biblical responses to unfamiliar questions requires missionaries to be comfortable with more inductive approaches to biblical interpretation, rather than relying on pre-prepared formulations. This also requires openness to different ways of doing Bible study and theologizing. If trainees have not been exposed to inductive methods and unfamiliar questions, they will have a tendency to try and force pre-prepared formulas to fit what they encounter rather than creating more appropriate solutions. For example, while it may seem simple to condemn all sacrifices as anti-biblical (cf. Heb 10:18), this may be an inappropriate stance when considering gifts or feasts of thanksgiving celebrated with the church as recognition of God's healing in a person's life, even though the thanksgiving gift is also termed a sacrifice in the local culture. As developing contextual answers to local problems should also involve negotiating with local Christians, training processes which involve collective discussion and debate of issues, preferably some conflict and discussion of apparently irreconcilable viewpoints, as well as different cultural methods of decision-making, will better prepare missionaries for engaging in effective contextualization in their place of ministry.

TRUTH IS MORE THAN WORDS

One vital aspect of using the Bible is in helping God's people know how to live. As we are to be holy, how we interpret the Bible, especially in terms of understanding sin and right living, is very important. In addition, as evangelists, missionaries work alongside the Holy Spirit to help people understand what sin is in order to encourage them to repent and turn to God. The Bible provides the foundation for this message. The concept of sin is inseparable from truth and righteousness as God's truth defines what is right and how people should behave. We judge people as doing what is right, or being truthful, according to what we believe the Bible teaches us about these things. For this reason, the way we perceive truth and how we interpret the Bible as communicating it is a critical starting point for cross-cultural ministry. At the same time, it is one of the most profound and complex aspects of culture and not as straightforward as our ethnocentric selves would have us believe.

The dominant Western approach to biblical and theological training tends to focus on words as the primary vehicle of truth rather than the context in which those words are communicated and the nonverbal language of the people doing the communicating.[63] Western evangelicals tend to privilege words and the verbal message about Jesus rather than the person of Jesus as embodying truth (cf. John 14:6). Prioritizing words in theological education can result in what is written down being thought of as the only expression of truth. Verbally telling and explaining the message is often promoted as the only way that truth can be communicated. But this overlooks other crucial dimensions of truth found in embodying and practicing the truth through relationship with God, obedience to Jesus, and serving people (cf. John 7:17).[64] Berhard Ott relates this viewpoint to the scientific worldview that assumes that all knowledge can be objectively known and therefore summarized in words or pictures. He states that,

> Reading the Bible with a positivist mind set leads to the formulation of a theology which presumes to give a copy of God's word, a photographic view of the biblical reality. In theological education this leads to the transmission of truth in the form of propositional theological statements.[65]

---

63. Edward Hall explained that people from high context cultures are aware of the many non-verbal cues in the context such as the room the communication is happening in, the ways the people they are with are dressed, how people are sitting or standing, their tone of voice and gestures, and other things going on in the room. They place as much or more value on these non-verbal elements in the communication than they do on the words themselves. People from low context cultures, in contrast, pay attention almost exclusively to the words of the communication and ignore many of the elements in the wider context such as non-verbal cues. If something has been said or written down, low context people expect that it will be adhered to. High context people are much more sensitive to the non-verbal messages around the words, such as the low context person's impatience, and care much less about what was written down. For low context people, words are binding. For high context people, relationships are binding and words are largely irrelevant." Hall, *Beyond Culture*; Hibbert and Hibbert, *Leading Multicultural Teams*, 32–33.

64. An excellent book that shows how these three dimensions of truth are interwoven throughout the Scriptures is Dean E. Flemming, *Recovering the Full Mission of God: A Biblical Perspective on Being, Doing, and Telling* (Downers Grove, IL: IVP Academic, 2013).

65. Bernhard Ott, "Mission Oriented Theological Education: Moving Beyond Traditional Models of Theological Education," in *Christianity and Education: Shaping Christian Thinking in Context*, ed. David Emmanuel Singh and Bernard C. Farr (Eugene, OR: Wipf & Stock, 2011), 57.

The message that many students receive in Western theological education is that text-based, cognitive knowledge is the most important kind of truth. Students' constant exposure to decontextualized knowledge can further strengthen their propensity to define truth almost exclusively in terms of text-based propositions. In contrast, those from more people-oriented cultures quickly relate to Jesus, the person who said "I am the truth." They are more inclined to make judgments about truth and righteousness according to an intuitive sense of what they consider Jesus the man would have done in a similar situation.

A missionary's view of truth strongly influences how they see sin. The question for missionaries and missionary trainers is how they make their judgments about what is sinful. If we define sin simply as something that is "wrong," with what is "right" being determined by what "everyone" knows to be "true," we can easily fall into the trap of judging everything according to the norms of our culture rather than those of the Bible. When missionaries without adequate cross-cultural understanding do refer to the Bible to work out whether something is sinful, though, they are often unaware of their cultural bias in the way they interpret the Bible to define what is true, right, and just.

Different cultural understandings of what is right and good result in different views of what constitutes sin.[66] Commonly, missionaries from low context cultures define truth as black and white, word-defined statements such as, "Let your 'yes' be yes, and your 'no,' no." (Matt 5:37; Jas 5:12). Using the Bible to justify their judgment, they can be quick to judge people as having sinned when they say, "Yes" but then do the opposite. We found this in Bulgaria when we asked Millet people if they were coming to the church meeting that day. They would often say, "Yes," but then not come. At first we were offended and judged them as having lied. We were confused about what was happening. Later we began to realize that the Millet, who are highly people-oriented and concerned above all to maintain relationships, meant "No" when they said "Yes." They interpreted our question relationally. Duane Elmer calls this the "relational yes."[67]

By saying, "Yes" the Millet meant "I affirm you as a person and respect you. Whether or not I go to the meeting will not affect our relationship. I cannot go

---

66. For a more detailed exploration of different cultural perspectives on sin refer to the following article: Richard Yates Hibbert and Evelyn Catherine Hibbert, "Contextualising Sin for Cross-Cultural Evangelism," *Missiology: An International Review* 42, no. 3 (2014).

67. Duane Elmer, *Cross-Cultural Conflict: Building Relationships for Effective Ministry* (Downers Grove, IL: InterVarsity Press, 1993), 118–20.

to the meeting, but I don't want this to affect our relationship." All this extra meaning is conveyed through nonverbal communication that is picked up by other members of the high context culture. When the low context missionary subsequently gets angry and takes them to task over not telling the truth, the high context Millet see this behavior as sinful in that it does not fulfill the biblical commands to bear with one another and love one another. It is easy to see how these different perspectives on truth and sin can significantly affect what is taught as truth, judged as sin, and consequently addressed in Christian teaching. Sometimes the misunderstanding can escalate so much that each side questions whether the other is truly a Christian.

That our understanding of truth is partly shaped by our culture is an issue that should be carefully explored in missionary training. Without an awareness of this reality, missionaries may focus on correcting local believers' sense of what is true according to their own culture rather than by examining the Scriptures together. Missionaries' cross-cultural discipling and training of leaders is then likely to be compromised in its effectiveness and may even damage the growth of local believers.

APPLYING THE BIBLE AS A PRACTICAL TEXTBOOK FOR LIFE

Effective training for cross-cultural ministry requires far more than the transmission of cognitive knowledge about the Bible. Missionaries need to perceive the Bible as a practical textbook for life that can be studied and applied to every situation they encounter. It must be a book that is being continually put into practice rather than only being talked about. When faced with fears, discouragements, overwhelming challenges and anxieties, we need to know through experience that the word of God acts as balm for the soul and spirit (cf. Prov 16:24; Matt 11:28–30) and a light that specifically shows them the way (cf. Ps 119:105). We need to have an affective element in our relationship with God's word (cf. Ps 119:111) and be able to spiritually discern how it speaks to specific situations (cf. Isa 30:21).

The best way for missionaries to learn how to apply the Bible as a practical textbook for life, as well as experience God through it, is to be part of a community that is actively modeling its application to all of life in the context of cross-cultural ministry. This provides an authentic training environment in which trainee missionaries can see how the Bible is a balm that comforts, a sword that convicts, and a lamp that guides the way in life and ministry dilemmas (cf. Ps 119:105; Heb 4:12), in both the lives of their trainers as well as their own lives. They can also practically observe how trainers search the Bible for answers and comfort and, if the training community is diverse, learn to appreciate the different ways that different Christians approach and gain help through its pages. Belonging to a community that actively applies the Bible to all aspects of life develops confidence in the trainees in the vitality of Christian faith, strengthens their sense of belonging to Christ, and provides a model they can emulate on the field.

Effective missionaries know the content of the Bible well (2 Tim 1:13; 2:2, 15; 3:16–17). Knowledge of God and his ways is an essential underpinning to the cross-cultural worker's ministry. Spiritual wisdom and understanding that comes from God's word and the Holy Spirit's application of it to our lives enables missionaries to know God's will and direct their energies to things that please and honor God (Phil 1:9–10; Col 1:9–10).

Missionaries also need to be confident that the Bible has answers to questions and issues that people from other cultures are raising and which they have never previously encountered (cf. Rom 1:17; 2 Tim 3:15–17). Without knowledge of God's word a missionary can be led into attitudes and actions that do not contribute to God's mission. "Enthusiasm without knowledge is not good" (Prov 19:2; cf. Rom 10:1–3).

Learning the Bible is best seen as a process rather than as a product. Where knowing the Bible is conceived of as a product, the focus is on a bounded, complete, definable concrete outcome that students need to acquire. In contrast, seeing learning the Bible as a process releases teachers and their students from the false assumption that the Bible can ever be completely mastered. It reinforces that teachers, as well as students, are continuing to learn about the Bible and how to apply it in real life, and concentrates on providing resources and skills for ongoing learning beyond the end of the course. If assessments are needed for Bible content, tests can be repeated until every student achieves high marks. This is more likely to motivate them to keep learning more. This approach to assessment of content may also encourage trainees to seek to achieve better familiarity with biblical content in other areas, as it gives them a better understanding of what good familiarity with content looks like.

HELPING MISSIONARIES TO USE THE BIBLE IN A CONTEXTUALLY APPROPRIATE WAY

In cross-cultural ministry, an ethnocentric approach to the Bible that assumes one's own way of interpreting the Bible is the only or best way can prevent hearers from understanding God's message to them. It can also inhibit missionaries from learning more of the riches of God that can only be appreciated through diverse perspectives.

The way any of us sees the Bible is shaped by our home culture, and Bible training done from a single cultural perspective tends to rigidify students' views of what is right. Training for monocultural ministry also tends to focus on clarifying theological boundaries and developing skills in ways of doing ministry that have proved successful in one cultural context. If the same kind of training is used in the training of cross-cultural workers, the result can be that graduates develop a "trained incapacity" to adjust their thinking and practices. They become unable to think outside the interpretive categories reinforced by their training and are restricted in their ability to respond to the needs of the new cultural contexts that they encounter.[68]

In contrast to training for monocultural ministry where the focus is on strengthening the trainee's understanding of a single culture's perspective of the Bible, missionary training needs to expose trainees to different cultural perspectives of biblical truth. It should give them tools for developing contextually appropriate and relevant expressions of faith that are still faithful to Scripture. Culturally bound structures of interpretation need to be challenged and evaluated so that trainees can begin to appreciate the positive aspects of the ways that people from other cultures and denominational backgrounds interpret and interact with God's word. Trainees should be helped to see the ways that their home culture has influenced their theology and way of practicing their faith.

The kind of openness that missionary training seeks to develop is a tolerance for ambiguity and for keeping opposites in tension. These qualities enable trainees to engage in dialogue with people from other cultures who think very

---

68. Herppich, "Cultural Bias in Missionary Education: The Unintentional Dynamic of Trained Incapacity."

differently than they do and who see different things in the Scriptures.[69] It also enables them to think critically about their own faith traditions and practices.

As adults are motivated to learn when they have specific problems they need answers for, providing missionary trainees with cross-cultural ministry dilemmas can motivate them to want to learn by searching the Scriptures to find answers. As trainees apply what they are learning from the Bible to the unfamiliar dilemmas faced in other cultures, they start to integrate this new learning into their own meaning frameworks. Their own meaning frameworks are strengthened and are more likely to weather the storms that they will encounter in cross-cultural ministry.

This means that missionary trainees should be exposed to questions about the Bible and Christianity that make them uncomfortable because they challenge the monocultural perspective of faith they are familiar with. They also need to be provided with the practical tools necessary to guide the development of an authentic cultural expression of Christianity in new cultural contexts. These include various kinds of inductive methods of biblical inquiry, Bible storytelling, different culturally shaped methods of biblical interpretation, and ways of helping local people think biblically about the issues and challenges of living in their cultural context.

---

69. Conde-Frazier, Kang, and Parrett, *A Many Colored Kingdom: Multicultural Dynamics for Spiritual Formation*, 177.

4

ENGAGING WITH CULTURE

THE NEED FOR CROSS-CULTURAL UNDERSTANDING

To be effective in cross-cultural ministry, we need specialized training that helps them understand the different ways people from other cultures engage with the world. When missionaries go to the field without this kind of specialized training, "the consequences can be disastrous on themselves, their families and their ministry."[70] They need to develop skills for communicating effectively with people who have a different language, culture, and way of seeing the world.

Cultural differences affect not only the ministry of missionaries to local people but also their relationships with their co-workers who are often from different countries. Missionaries usually expect to struggle with the local culture but are often unprepared for cross-cultural conflict with their co-workers.[71]

Missionaries need to understand the concept of culture and how it affects the whole way of life and thought of a people. They also need to understand that they are cultural beings themselves and that their own understanding of Christianity has been shaped by their culture. This understanding is a vital foundation for contextualizing the message of the Bible and communicating it effectively in a new cultural context.

When a missionary's pre-field training has focused almost entirely on their own cultural (often Western) traditions, things such as folk religion, belief in the spirit world, ancestor veneration, and conversion from other religious identities will almost certainly be considered by that missionary as less important than the traditions they have been trained in. The result is that he or she is

---

70. C. David Harley, *Preparing to Serve: Training for Cross-Cultural Mission* (Pasadena, CA: William Carey Library, 1995), 7.

71. For more detailed information about working in multicultural teams please refer to our book, Hibbert and Hibbert, *Leading Multicultural Teams*.

unlikely to appreciate the need to contextualize Christianity and will not have the tools to undertake this vital task.[72]

One example of the need for training in understanding one's own and others' cultures is helping missionaries engage with the reality of spiritual warfare. This is particularly an issue for Western missionaries as the predominant worldview in the West has tended to minimize or overlook the reality of unseen spirits that are at work in this world. Herbert Brasher, in his research on the effectiveness of pre-field training, found that a lack of training in spiritual warfare often resulted in missionaries responding to new experiences of spiritual warfare in unhelpful ways such as denying its existence or engaging in biblically unsupportable teachings and practices.[73]

Another example of the need for specific cross-cultural training is the tendency for cross-cultural workers to stereotype folk religious beliefs and practices as superstitious or magical. Folk religion practices are often dismissed by missionaries as corrupt and failing to represent the "true" or formal religion of the people. This can result in the religion of the bulk of the population, with all its attendant meaning and significance for their day-to-day lives, being dismissed.

Missionaries instead need to be able to identify, analyze, and reflect on the specific practices they are encountering in the light of Scripture and missiological insights. This will enable them to help local Christians work out answers for the day-to-day challenges of life and help those Christians overcome the common tendency to resort to traditional remedies for things they perceive Christianity as being powerless to address. It is vital that missionaries are trained to help new churches avoid the dangers of a "split-level Christianity" that trusts God for the ultimate issues of forgiveness and eternal life but resorts to traditional religious practices to try to solve day-to-day problems like sickness, curses, and uncertainty about the future.[74]

If missionaries are not aware of their own cultural bias in the way they express their faith, they can unnecessarily condemn practices that are either

---

72. Kang San Tan, "What Is So Theological About Contextual Mission Training?" in *Contextualisation and Mission Training: Engaging Asia's Religious Worlds*, ed. Jonathan Ingleby, Kang San Tan, and Loun Ling Tan (Oxford: Regnum, 2013), 9.

73. Brasher, *Important Factors in Pre-Field and Field-Based Preparation of Missionaries Serving with Cross and Crescent International*, 123–25.

74. The term "split-level Christianity" was coined by Paul Hiebert, who along with his co-authors give very helpful tools for analyzing folk religions in Paul G. Hiebert, R. Daniel Shaw, and Tite Tienou, *Understanding Folk Religion: A Christian Response to Popular Beliefs and Practices* (Grand Rapids, MI: Baker Books, 1999).

neutral or that could be redeemed by the gospel.[75] Culturally unaware missionaries can mistakenly equate the gospel with their own culturally shaped practice of Christianity. This sometimes leads them to unhelpfully reject all forms of indigenous art, dance, and music and prevent the development of a contextualized theology and forms of worship.[76]

BIBLICAL EXAMPLES OF ENGAGING WITH OTHER CULTURES

Paul exemplified a deep understanding of both the Bible and culture in his remarkable ability to adjust his evangelistic message and approach for very different audiences (e.g., Athenians at the Areopagus—Acts 17:16–34; Zeus worshippers at Lystra—Acts 14:8–18; King Agrippa—Acts 26:1–29). Paul was equipped for his task with cross-cultural understanding that God had arranged through this upbringing as a Jew among Gentiles, his education in Greek, Hebrew, and Aramaic languages, and in Greek, Roman, and Jewish cultures. Paul also used his understanding of culture to develop theological principles to meet the specific challenges new communities of believers were facing such as the complex question of whether and in what circumstances believers could eat meat offered to idols (1 Cor 8:4–13; 10:14–31).[77]

The incarnation serves as the ultimate model for mission.[78] Christ was sent by God as the ultimate missionary, and this involved being prepared by God to have the deepest possible understanding of the culture of his own people. By becoming a human being, growing up in a Jewish home, working as a carpenter, becoming hungry, tired, thirsty, experiencing loneliness and sorrow, and being

---

75. This issue is helpfully explored in the context of Africa in Laurenti Magesa, *What Is Not Sacred?: African Spirituality* (Maryknoll, NY: Orbis Books, 2013).

76. Paul Hiebert describes this approach as noncontextualization and explains that many missionaries begin with this approach, and some continue in it all their lives. Paul G. Hiebert, *The Gospel in Human Contexts: Anthropological Explorations for Contemporary Missions* (Grand Rapids, MI: Baker Academic, 2009), 19–21.

77. A particularly helpful book that traces the various ways Paul and others contextualized the gospel for different audiences is Dean E. Flemming, *Contextualization in the New Testament: Patterns for Theology and Mission* (Downers Grove, IL: InterVarsity Press, 2005).

78. Matthias Zahniser, "The Trinity: Paradigm for Mission in the Spirit," *Missiology: An International Review* 17 (1989): 69.

constantly opposed and ultimately rejected, Jesus identified with the people he came to serve and personally appreciated their deepest longings and needs.

Several of the cross-cultural witnesses described in the Old Testament were similarly prepared by God to gain a deep understanding of the people he sent them to. Joseph, Moses, Jonah, and Daniel were all used by God to communicate to Gentile empires. Joseph and Moses were witnesses to the Egyptians, Jonah to the Assyrians at Nineveh, Daniel to the Babylonians and Persians. All except Jonah can be considered long-term cross-cultural witnesses in that they lived or went to live among people of very different cultures than that of their parents. Each had a profound effect on the people they engaged with, leading them to acknowledge Yahweh's power and majesty. What is striking about each of them is the amount of time God caused them to invest in their learning the languages and cultures of the people who did not know God. Moses, Joseph, and Daniel all had extensive enculturation in the language and culture of the Gentiles they were sent to. They demonstrated deep cultural understanding and an ability to communicate effectively in ways that the local people and their leaders could readily understand.

LEARNING FROM MISSIONARY EXPERIENCE

For centuries, missionaries have been grappling with what it means to communicate the gospel across cultures and to establish healthy churches in contexts very different to their home countries. Their experiences and what they have learned have been recorded in missionary biographies, ethnographic case studies, anthropological analyses, and missiological reflections. These insights have been published to help new missionaries in their quest to understand how to introduce Jesus to people who have not encountered him. Many new missionaries, though, venture out to their fields of service with little or no exposure to this treasure trove of missiological wisdom. Many will repeat the mistakes of their forbears over and over again and fail to benefit from the lessons that have been learned.

Effective missionary training should introduce trainees to the wisdom that generations of missionaries and missions researchers have acquired in the crucible of missionary practice. These insights are found in the discipline of missiology—the multidisciplinary study of missionary practice.[79] Missiologists

---

79. Dwight P. Baker, "Missiology as an Interested Discipline—and Where Is It Happening?," *International Bulletin of Missionary Research* 38, no. 1 (2014): 18.

read widely from other disciplines such as anthropology, linguistics, and organizational studies and reflect on these disciplines in the light of Scripture to bring insights into the wide variety of complex issues encountered in making disciples across cultures.

Missiology is a practical discipline. More than simply recording missionary practice or theorizing about it, its purpose is to help missionaries become more effective in their ministry. It seeks to "reform or reshape missionary practice, missionary theory, even missionary strategy, and to refine missionary self-understanding in ways that will enhance missionary effectiveness."[80] Introducing prospective missionaries to missiological insights should therefore be a key component of missionary training. They should be helped to make connections between their own experience of cross-cultural life and ministry and the theoretical and theological insights of missiology.

Missiology gives cross-cultural workers tools for analyzing and understanding what is going on in other cultures so that missionaries can do their task better. People who grow in their ability to analyze and understand other cultures are better able to make sense of their cross-cultural experiences and to successfully communicate with people from different cultures.[81] For this reason, missiological insights should be foundational in all missionary preparation.

THE IMPORTANCE OF CULTURE AND LEARNING ABOUT DIFFERENT CULTURES

All people are cultural beings. Culture is the way that groups of human beings interpret and organize their world and it determines how people interact with each other. Just as the physical world has been created with infinite variety, and each individual is unique, so cultures demonstrate a similar propensity for creativity and variety.[82] While this diversity is wonderful in its richness, it

---

80. Ibid., 17.

81. Angela K.-Y. Leung, Sau-Lai Lee, and Chi-Yue Chiu, "Meta-Knowledge of Culture Promotes Cultural Competence," *Journal of Cross-Cultural Psychology* 44, no. 6 (2013); Winston R. Sieck, Jennifer L. Smith, and Louise J. Rasmussen, "Metacognitive Strategies for Making Sense of Cross-Cultural Encounters," ibid.

82. To learn more about cultures and cultural differences, we recommend the following books: Sarah A. Lanier, *Foreign to Familiar: A Guide to Understanding Hot- and Cold-Climate Cultures* (Hagerstown, MD: McDougal Publishing, 2000); D. Elmer, *Cross-Cultural Connections* (Downer's Grove, IL: InterVarsity Press, 2002).

leads to significant challenges when people from different cultures attempt to relate to one another. These challenges are compounded by each group's inclination to assume their own way of doing things is the right way and to have limited tolerance for accepting people who do things differently. In missionary situations, this is further complicated by the missionary's tendency to assume that his or her culture's way of doing Christianity is supra-cultural, as if it had descended directly from heaven. This has caused many missionaries, at least initially, to want to impose their own way of doing Christianity on people from other cultures and subsequently to inhibit or even obstruct what God is doing in that context. Unfortunately this also means that the missionary misses out on learning from the insights that people from another culture and perspective bring to the understanding of God and his Word.

Culture affects every dimension of human relationships and communication. When people from one culture communicate something to people from another culture, they usually try to use ways of communication that they are familiar with. But the recipients interpret that communication according to their own culture's values and assumptions. The two ways of communicating are usually not congruent and significant misinterpretation often occurs. For a missionary seeking to communicate the good news about Jesus across cultures, the onus is on them to embody and communicate the good news in ways which are as close to the recipients' culture as possible, in order to try and minimize miscommunication. This requires the missionary to adapt in multiple ways including how they greet people, relate to people of the same and opposite gender, relate to people of different statuses in the social hierarchy, use body language, leave space between them and other people, how long they wait for people to arrive, how they practice hospitality, gift-giving, mediation, and how they manage conflict.

RELATING TO PEOPLE IS DONE DIFFERENTLY IN DIFFERENT CULTURES

Missionary work is all about people. Missionaries must therefore be able to build relationships with people in their home culture, in missionary teams, and with the people they are sent to work with. This requires them to be able to communicate well both in their own culture and across cultures and to be able to make friends. The two fundamental tools for building relationships are a fluency in the local language and an understanding of the local culture.

Building relationships across cultures can be particularly challenging because of the different ways different cultures structure their societies and the rules they have for the ways that different people can interact. One area that can be particularly challenging is knowing how to relate between men and women and across extended family groupings and other social groups. This can be further complicated if the missionary does not have a job that corresponds with an understandable role in the culture. For example, while the role of missionary might be understood in North American culture, to local people in a city where men leave the home early to commute and work long hours in an office, shop, or factory, a foreign man who stays at home all day and does not appear to do any office or business work appears lazy or even suspicious to his neighbors and community.

Different cultures have different expectations of friends as well as rules about who can be friends. Because of this, the more missionaries are adept at meeting people and making friends with a broad range of people in the local context, the better sense they will be able to get of appropriate ways of behaving and the best avenues for introducing and gaining acceptance for the gospel.

It is important for missionaries to have some tools to help them research the way people gather in the local culture and the ways people are grouped. Different groups will have particular forms of leadership, decision-making, and ways of relating to other groups. It is important to understand these not only to work out the best way in which to introduce the good news, but also to begin to work out ideas about how the indigenous church should be established and structured.

Missionaries with a good appreciation of local ways of leading, making decisions, and relating to other people can help new churches express who Jesus is in ways that have the greatest potential to be understood by people in the local culture. Far too often missionaries simply reproduce their own culture's church forms with little thought about how alien it might feel to locals and whether it is something that feels like it belongs to the local society. Missionaries who research and learn to respect and accept local forms of leadership are also more likely to empower and support local leaders from the early stages of their work.

Missionaries, as Christ's ambassadors, represent him not just to the individuals they talk to, but to everyone in the local context. For this reason, missionaries' reputations and behavior towards others will be observed and counted for and against them and will influence the local people's receptivity to Christ. In order to act well before the group and individuals within it, the missionary needs to understand local values and ways of enacting honor, respect, and moral purity. For missionaries from Western cultures where these values have been minimized, recognizing how they are put into practice in another culture can be difficult. Pre-exposure to these concepts in missionary training and some practice in behaving appropriately among people from cultures where these are vital alerts trainee missionaries to their importance and starts them on a journey of learning how to put them into practice in different contexts.

SPIRITUALITY IS EXPRESSED DIFFERENTLY IN DIFFERENT CULTURES

Most missionaries are aware of denominational differences in the ways that people experience God and worship him. Despite this awareness, they can still find it difficult to work in teams with people from different denominational backgrounds. The differences in ways that fellow missionaries from different cultures express their spirituality are far greater than denominational differences, and yet missionaries often go the field quite unaware of them. As a result they can unwittingly judge their colleagues for their "un-Christian" ways of expressing their faith, sometimes leading to serious conflict. Even differences in something as basic as different ways of praying has the potential to cause major conflict between missionaries from different backgrounds.

Far more significant for evangelism and church planting than difference between missionaries and the ways they express spirituality, is the difference between missionaries and the local people in the way they see the spiritual realm. Over the last several hundred years, Westerners have largely come to reject the existence of a spiritual realm or to minimize its significance. As a result, when they arrive on the field, Western missionaries do not usually attach much importance to spirits, curses, amulets, or witchcraft. Paul Hiebert called this vacuum in Westerners' perception of the world the "flaw of the excluded middle."[83] This vacuum is represented in Figure 4.

For most of the people of the world, the spiritual realm is central to their lives and they see it as affecting everything that happens. This realm of beings

---

83. Paul G. Hiebert, "The Flaw of the Excluded Middle," *Missiology: An International Review* 10 (1982).

and forces that are unseen but active in this world bridges the material world and God. It is populated with myriad beings, forces, objects, and practices which are very real in the everyday experience of people in those cultures. In contrast, in the Western worldview, there is nothing between the material world and God. It is a vacuum. Even if Christians in the West acknowledge evil spirits and angels, it is usually only to a token extent and their belief in and experience of these spirits' influence on everyday life is usually very limited.

This gap in Western missionaries' view of the world makes it difficult for them to relate to the spiritual reality of many of the people among whom they live. Western theological textbooks do not provide theological answers for the spiritual dimension except in brief sections announcing Jesus' victory over Satan at the cross. Western pastoral training rarely gives instructions on how to deal with demonized parishioners. Few Western Bible colleges effectively prepare their students for engaging with spiritual entities. Consequently, current long-term missionaries repeatedly ask that pre-field training gives more attention to spiritual warfare.

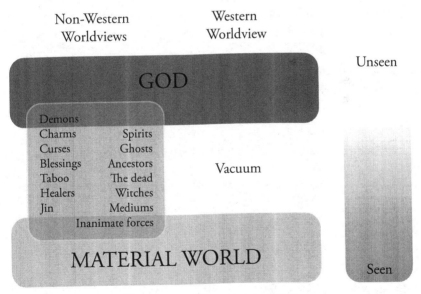

Figure 4 Flaw of the excluded middle[84]

Although many Western missionaries may believe in the existence of evil spirits, most do not practically acknowledge them, and few have experience

---

84. Based on ibid., 40,43.

in dealing with them before going to the field. Folk religious objects such as charms, activities like curses, and practitioners such as shamans are often characterized by Westerners as quaint, superstitious, or fraudulent. While this view can be relatively easily maintained in the West where spiritual practices are hidden away and illness, psychosis, and death are often concealed from public view, it is difficult to maintain in another culture where homage to spirits is found in every home and evil forces animate some of the people missionaries encounter.

Missionaries cannot engage with the unseen forces at work in this world until they acknowledge their existence. They need to come to a balanced understanding of them as part of lived human reality and be shaped by the Scriptures in that understanding. Everyone, from whatever culture they belong to, interprets difficulties and misfortune according to their system of meaning and responds to the spiritual realm according to their meaning framework. Westerners who (often unwittingly) deny the existence of this realm tend to focus on using medicine, science, and the tools of community development to address spiritual needs. Other cultures create different meaning systems and have spirit practitioners who mediate their interaction with this realm.

The way missionaries interact with these meaning systems and spirit practitioners, and whether they condemn or engage with them, will profoundly affect local people's attitudes towards the missionaries' message. Missionaries need to be confident of where they stand in Christ, know through experience the extent of Christ's power, rest in their identity and Jesus' power in the face of things they do not understand or which threaten or cause fear, and have a healthy respect for evil powers.

Missionaries must be also able to deal with unfamiliar spiritual realities. Missionaries are at least familiar with evil spirits in the Bible, but they often encounter other spiritual realities that do not figure in their home culture's worldview or prominently in the Scriptures, such as ancestors, impersonal forces like fate, objects such as amulets and charms, and sorcery or witchcraft. In the case of Western missionaries, this gap in experience is compounded by an inadequate theology.

Because most missionaries will face the powers of the unseen world in new ways in cross-cultural ministry, missionary trainers must teach them about this area and model methods of engagement with it. In his research into the preparation of missionaries, Herbert Brasher found that most missionaries had never had any input on spiritual warfare or deliverance from evil spirits before, or on the field. Less than a third of his missionary interviewees remembered Bible college teaching or ministry experience in spiritual warfare prior to going to the field. Even though almost half of the missionaries he interviewed had engaged in ministry to deal with evil spirits, none of his interviewees could point to any on-field training that had helped them do this.[85]

PEOPLE FROM DIFFERENT CULTURES VALUE THE WRITTEN WORD DIFFERENTLY

The majority of missionaries sent out over the last two centuries have come from highly literate societies that give written documents primacy over oral communication. While this has had major benefits for literacy and the recording of non-literate languages, a bias towards literacy can result in missionaries failing to acknowledge and appreciate other forms of recording and passing on important information that are used in other cultures.[86]

It is very important that missionaries are able to research the place of written texts in the cultures they work in and the different ways in which the local people use and interpret texts. They should also be able to analyze, with an open mind, the way in which any sacred texts are used as these will affect the way that new Christians approach the Bible.

People from different cultures approach written texts in different ways. It can be difficult for Westerners, who tend to be highly text-focused and dispassionate in the way they approach the Bible, to accept these ways. In particular, they can react negatively to more devotional, intuitive, and holistic approaches to God's word. This often occurs when the Bible is referred to as an emotional or spiritual source of strength, illustrated by the impact of verses or stories, even though these may have been taken out of their textual context, or may have been misinterpreted according to linear textual rules of comprehension. Westerners may also be reluctant to accept ritual practices involving the whole book, for example, when Muslim-background believers refuse to place the Bible on the floor. Missionaries need to be able to help local believers position the Bible

---

85. Brasher, *Important Factors in Pre-Field and Field-Based Preparation of Missionaries Serving with Cross and Crescent International*, 116–17.

86. Shirley Brice Heath conducted a major study that clearly demonstrated the different ways in which different communities in an American town introduced their children to language, reading, and books. Shirley Brice Heath, *Ways with Words: Language, Life, and Work in Communities and Classrooms* (New York: Cambridge University Press, 1983).

and the way it is used and interpreted in a meaningful framework in terms of the people's worldview. Otherwise there is a risk of the Bible being rejected as a foreign, irrelevant book.

Written text is a way of storing and transmitting information but information can also be stored, controlled, and passed on in other ways in different cultures. As the Bible is a book, or concrete object, through which the vitally important information about how people can build relationship with God is passed on, it is important that its significance is conveyed in ways which are meaningful in the culture. This makes it imperative for missionaries to research how information is passed on to others in the host culture, and also the ways books relate to this process. This includes who deems the information important and who has the right to interpret it and teach or pass it on. Cross-cultural workers from low context cultures (that give primacy to words rather than nonverbal ways of communicating) rarely perceive the effect of other contextual factors on the acceptance, or otherwise, of text, as they quickly narrow their focus to the written words alone. However, many other factors influence how information, including written texts, is engaged with, including its appearance, who presents it, how it is presented, how it is treated, how others react to it, and its perceived power to influence or change events or people. All these things influence how information is received. In a similar way, low context people's tendency to exclusively focus on the words, can blind them to other ways in which biblical content can be meaningfully communicated, with or without replication of the exact words from the text.

In Islamic cultures, their holy book, the Qur'an, is believed to be the actual word of God handed down to men in the same physical form as it exists in heaven. As such, the written text is treated with great respect and is believed to have implicit power regardless of what the words actually mean. The power of the text can have a beneficial effect on others through its recitation and through making physical copies of the words. In the same way, many Christians are expressing a similar approach when they feel the effect of reading or listening to Scripture is like balm for the soul. Missionaries working among Muslims need to show as much respect to the physical book, the Bible, if they want local people to consider it a book worthy of paying attention to. For example, Muslims do not put the Qur'an on the floor, so Bibles also should not be placed on the floor. Missionaries may also be surprised when local people do not appear to expect to understand what they read, or treat it as an object with magical powers. Missionaries in this situation cannot simply expect people to read the words and try to make practical meaning out of them. They need to actively build bridges between the local understanding of and approaches to holy books and how Christians should engage with their Bibles.

CRITICAL CONTEXTUALIZATION

A distinctive aspect of cross-cultural ministry is the need to contextualize or adapt every aspect of ministry in the light of the local culture and context. Although ministry in one's home culture also involves contextualization, it is usually done unconsciously as Christian workers intuitively exegete their own culture and use ways of communicating that are already familiar to them and to those they minister among. Contextualizing our communication for people from a different culture than our own, however, is a much more demanding process. It requires us to consciously adapt our communication to give the people we are relating to the best chance of understanding us and our message. The goal is to share the gospel, disciple people, and plant churches in ways that make sense to the local people, "in such a way that it meets people's deepest needs and penetrates their worldview, thus allowing them to follow Christ and remain in their own culture."[87]

One of the most helpful and widely used ways of approaching the work of contextualization is that of critical contextualization developed by Paul Hiebert. It involves three main steps, the first of these being observing and listening to local people and especially Christians (where there are some) about the issues they are facing and the ways their culture has traditionally dealt with them. When we applied this process in Bulgaria to the traditional practices revolving around the birth of a child, for example, we discovered a complex of rituals that the local people engaged in around the birth of a new baby. Each part of the complex needed to be identified and examined together in the light of the Bible.

In the second step, local believers and missionaries examine the Bible together to gather insights on the issues they are considering. In addition, other resources that provide insights about how Christians in other cultures have approached or resolved the issues may give additional help at this stage. In the final step the insights from Scripture and analogous situations in other contexts are applied to the issue to provide guidelines for missionaries and the local

---

87. Whiteman, "Contextualization: The Theory, the Gap, the Challenge," 2.

church about how to approach the traditional practice—whether to reject it completely and substitute a practice that better reflects Christian belief, or to accept it as is, or to modify it in some way.[88]

In our case, in the complex of rituals surrounding the birth of a child, one issue related to a special sacrifice that local people made to God when they experienced a blessing. Together with the local people, we examined the reasons why the sacrifice was made and what local non-believers understood it to mean. It would have been easy to simply forbid all sacrifices on the basis of Jesus being the final sacrifice (cf. Hebrews 10:1–18) however this would not have satisfied the needs of the local people nor addressed the reasons why they wanted to kill an animal. Together we examined biblical passages on sacrifice and discussed the similarities and differences with their situation. We also discussed what Christians in other parts of Bulgaria, and Christians from similar backgrounds in other countries were doing. We then allowed the local believers to come to their own conclusions about what would be acceptable practice in the context. They decided that it was acceptable for new believers who wanted to express their gratitude to God for their new child together with their community, the church, to prepare a thanksgiving meal which the whole church joined in. However they stipulated that the believers were taught that such a meal could not be perceived as fulfilling a bargain with God (which was part of the concept of the traditional, pre-Christian sacrifice).

Discussions about contextualization often focus simply on the transfer of the content of biblical text or a pre-prepared gospel message. While this is good as far as it goes, it fails to engage with the broader contextual issues involved in making new disciples of Jesus. Words cannot be separated from their speakers and the contexts in which the speakers speak. Messages have to be lived out in real-life situations in order to have meaning that affects what people do in the comprehensive way in which God intends to bring his kingdom on earth into being. The life of the human messenger of the gospel is a vital part of the message that people perceive. The life of the local church expresses the message about Jesus as much as their words do. For this reason, Lesslie Newbigin referred to the church as the "hermeneutic of the gospel."[89] People in any

---

88. Hiebert, *The Gospel in Human Contexts: Anthropological Explorations for Contemporary Missions*, 26–29, 47–51.

89. Lesslie Newbigin, *The Gospel in a Pluralist Society* (Grand Rapids, MI: W.B. Eerdmans, 1989), 227.

community make sense of the gospel as they look at and interact with God's people. As Christians live out the gospel in community, the people in their neighborhood can see and experience what the gospel means.

In missionary work, every aspect of biblical teaching needs to be effectively contextualized in order for the church to grow as an authentic expression of Christian faith in that culture. The process of arriving at this authentic expression can be arduous and prolonged, involving major negotiation of meaning between the Bible, local cultural practices and understandings, and the missionary's or established church's understandings and practices. Quite often, this process is hampered by missionary, and sometimes local, insistence that foreign forms of Christian practice be established, as if these are the only genuine expression of Christianity. Sometimes the missionary may ban local forms of experiencing God or engaging with the spiritual realm, simply because they are unfamiliar or make the missionary feel uncomfortable. Missionaries who have been trained to engage with culture are likely to be much better at helping the local church to engage in this vital process of contextualization than those who have not had this training.

CONVERSION AND THE NEGOTIATION OF IDENTITY

Conversion is not simply an individual's intellectual assent to the gospel. It involves changing and joining a community of others who also believe in Jesus. But the changes that are central to conversion do not mean that the convert must indiscriminately discard everything from their old way of life. Not only does this result in a vacuum in the convert's life but it also usually results in the rejection of the individual by the home community with the result that the gospel is viewed negatively and is unlikely to be welcome. In addition, this uncritical approach fails to appreciate the good things that exist in the person's culture and the ways in which God is already working in it.

It takes time for new believers to understand the values and practices of the local Christian community and to see how these relate to their family and their culture. It also takes time for them to work out how to relate to their friends and family as a Christian in a way that is faithful to God and helpful for their people. One of the basic challenges that new converts face is to work out their identity. Converts must develop a robust sense of who they are that is based on both their connection with Jesus and his people and on their sense of belonging to their family and society. The process of identity negotiation and its place in the whole journey of conversion to Christ and also the time it can take is shown in Figure 5.

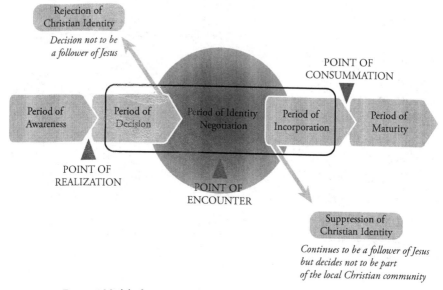

Figure 5 Model of conversion including identity negotiation and a second decision point based on Alan Tippett's model of conversion[90]

The missionary's role is to support the new believer through this process of identity negotiation, recognizing the time it takes and the various dilemmas and conflicts that will be encountered, until the believer arrives at a new formulation of who they are in Christ as well as in relation to their ongoing relationships with others. In order to do this, missionaries must have a sensitivity to the difficulties of this process of identity negotiation, an understanding of the culture and the various issues that are likely to arise during the identity negotiation phase, as well as an appreciation for the cultures and communities the new believer belongs to. The gospel is most likely to spread when it is firmly embedded in local soil and feels like it belongs in the culture. The missionary fosters this by encouraging local ownership of the gospel, expressed collectively through a culturally authentic church and communicated through locally

---

90.   Based on ibid. and Alan Tippett, "The Cultural Anthropology of Conversion," in *Handbook of Religious Conversion*, ed. Newton Maloney and Samuel Southard (Birmingham, AL: Religious Education Press, 1992).

meaningful forms. A missionary's ability to do this is developed through a deep appreciation for the culture acquired through respect for it and ongoing, advanced language and culture study.[91]

HELPING MISSIONARIES ENGAGE WITH CULTURE

In order to get to know people from another culture well, cross-cultural workers need to learn the language and culture of those people. These initial tasks require a long-term commitment of several years and are the platform on which all subsequent ministry is built. International travel and short-term exposure and ministry trips can lull people into thinking that they have understood people from other cultures and are able to communicate well with them. But short-term intercultural interaction rarely extends beyond superficial levels, especially when the intercultural experience is specifically prepared to appeal to the visitor. For this reason, missionary training must prepare trainees to learn at least one other language well and give them tools for researching and understanding another culture to a deep level.

There are many resources available for second language learning and different fields and agencies have different requirements for their missionaries. The Summer Institute of Linguistics (SIL) and similar institutions offer excellent short courses around the world that give pre-field training in how to learn a new language. Most larger mission agencies provide some kind of on-field support for language learning in the first 1–2 years of a missionary's time on the field.

Cross-cultural educators agree that the best way of learning about other cultures is through personal experience living in other cultures. This helps people to overcome their ethnocentric tendencies. Without concrete experience of other cultures it is not possible to imagine the impact that cultural difference has.[92] There is no substitute for person-to-person contact and living in different

---

91. Richard Yates Hibbert, "Negotiating Identity: Extending and Applying Alan Tippett's Model of Conversion," *Missiology: An International Review* [pre-print online version, published 15 July, 2014]. Accessed 11 December, 2014; available from http://mis .sagepub.com/content/early/2014/01/10/0091829614541094

92. Paula J. Pedersen, "Assessing Intercultural Effectiveness Outcomes in a Year-Long Study Abroad Program," *International Journal of Intercultural Relations* 34, no. 1 (2010);

cultures for significant periods of time. Just being exposed to different cultures is not sufficient. People still need to reflect critically on their experience in the light of anthropological and missiological insights into other cultures. Trainees should be exposed to various dimensions of cultural difference and the different ways different cultures do things.

In order to prepare to study the culture of the people they will eventually minister among, trainees need to be given guided experience in using basic methods of anthropological research, and particularly in observing and interviewing (asking questions of) local people. They need to learn how to observe, reserve judgments and test their assumptions, recognize their own presuppositions, and reflect on their experience. They need to be able to sensitively ask open-ended questions and be able to be good listeners. They need to learn how to formulate questions and develop a habit of asking questions. While some of these skills can be learned through role plays and simulations, the best training ground is an authentic cross-cultural situation in which the trainee experiences the unpredictability of life and ministry across cultures. Reflection and learning will be further aided by having the opportunity to discuss discoveries, methods, experiences, and other resources with other trainees and trainers who can add further perspective and provide feedback on what the trainee has been doing.

One area of culture that must be engaged with in training is the spiritual realm. Trainees need opportunities to work alongside experienced missionary trainers who can guide their growth in understanding and engaging in spiritual warfare. This allows them to engage together in cross-cultural ministry and its expressions of the spiritual battle, and debrief those same experiences. In addition, trainers need to be able to help trainees understand spiritual realities they are unfamiliar with and help them develop biblically faithful responses.

Missionaries will inevitably face challenges from the spiritual realm and must be ready to discern, correctly identify, and overcome them. When they are faced with major fear or demonic possession, spiritual platitudes are inadequate. When everything seems impossible and the spiritual oppression is overwhelming, the missionary must know how to break through to victory. The best way to learn this is by being with experienced missionaries as they engage

---

D.C. Hambrick et al., "When Groups Consist of Multiple Nationalities: Towards a New Understanding of the Implications," *Organization Studies* 19, no. 2 (1998); Anne Bartel-Radic, "Intercultural Learning in Global Teams," *Management International Review* 46, no. 6 (2006).

with spiritual forces, and by observing and joining them in what they do. In multicultural training contexts, trainers may be able to organize opportunities for trainees to join in with church groups from other cultures who have more experience in these areas.

Missionaries need to be confident of the power of God. This confidence is gained through experiencing his power personally, seeing God's power at work, and hearing firsthand testimonies of what God has done in people's lives. For this reason, in-ministry training is important both to expose trainees to the various challenges a missionary might face and also to develop in the trainee a sense of confidence that they can handle whatever they will face because they have previously seen similar situations brought to resolution.

A major challenge for today's missions is the tendency for missionaries to stop learning once they have achieved a moderate level of language and cultural understanding that enables them to survive. New missionaries often stop learning language when they complete their formal language course. Similarly, missionaries often seem to arrest in their learning once they have overcome culture shock and learned to function at basic level in their new context. It is vital that missionaries push beyond these basic levels of competency, though, if they are to become effective in their ministry to local people. This requires a commitment to ongoing learning and a continuing effort to keep reading, researching, asking questions, and learning more about other cultures.

One way to encourage ongoing learning is to facilitate the development of missionary learning communities. Having a group of people who are continuing to learn not only means that each can learn from the others, but also that they can hold each other accountable for and stimulate each other to further learning. This happens as members of the learning group share what they are learning about language and culture, and as they research issues and discuss the implications of what they are learning for their lives and ministry. Such learning communities also have the advantage of being able to nurture the development of new missionaries and establish a DNA of continuing to learn which will affect not only the missionary community but also the church it works with.[93]

---

93. For more ideas about establishing missionary learning communities refer to our paper: Richard Yates Hibbert and Evelyn Catherine Hibbert, "Nurturing Missionary Learning Communities," in *Association of Professors of Mission 2014* (University of Northwestern, Saint Paul, MN: First Fruits Press, 2014).

5

RELATING TO PEOPLE

MISSIONARY WORK IS ALL ABOUT PEOPLE

Christian ministry, including cross-cultural ministry, is all about people. Churches are communities of people. Evangelism, discipleship, and gathering people into communities of believers, developing leaders and missionary work are all based on relationships. Being able to talk to people, relate to them, listen to them, care, forgive, resolve conflict, and work with others effectively all require interpersonal skills. If missionary candidates are unable to converse with others beyond initial greetings, they will not be effective missionaries. If they cannot build relationships, they are at risk of social isolation in their adopted country and unlikely to be able to learn the language well.

Missionaries need to know how to make friends with others. They need to know what to do when relationships break down. Broken relationships with fellow missionaries remain a very common reason for leaving the field.[94] Missionary teams too often fail to become effective in their work because their members cannot get on with each other, and a few missionaries' marriages fall apart. Their ministries can be severely compromised as a result. Faith to move mountains means little if the local people consider the missionary unfriendly and unapproachable or see their relationships with their spouses or co-workers in disarray. If missionaries deliver a perfect sermon or an educationally outstanding lesson but fail to respectfully address a local leader in front of others, the worth of their ministry will have been cancelled in the eyes of local people. Likewise, if the ministry seems to be growing well but the missionary's marriage is disintegrating, that will speak more loudly than words.

Many people today, especially in the West, have grown up without learning how to relate to a wide variety of people and how to get to know strangers.

---

94. Brierley, "Missionary Attrition: The ReMAP Research Report," 92–95.

Some are more familiar with interacting with screens than people.[95] For many missionary candidates from Western countries, engaging in meaningful conversation with unfamiliar people in their own culture is a difficult challenge. Yet getting to know strangers and progressing from general conversation to sensitive and respectful communication of the gospel requires significant communication skills. This can be a challenging process even when the responses of the person being interacted with are familiar and predictable as they are when both participants are from the same culture. Missionaries, however, must go the extra mile in learning how to relate to people who speak, behave, and think in ways that are vastly different to themselves and that may make the missionary feel very uncomfortable.

The ability to relate well to people from other cultures is often referred to as having intercultural competence. Guo-Ming Chen describes intercultural competence as the ability to appropriately use both verbal and nonverbal behaviors and feel comfortable in different contexts in order to establish relationships that satisfy the needs of both parties in the relationship.[96] Intercultural competence involves being able to take the initiative in social interaction and be open-minded, flexible, respectful, and curious. Interculturally competent people have a generally positive emotional response to intercultural differences, a desire and commitment to learn, and are able to reserve judgment about cultural differences even when they challenge their core values and beliefs. In essence, being interculturally competent means having a proactive, positive attitude towards people from other cultures and their ways of viewing and interacting with the world.[97] Interculturally competent people also have the tenacity and perseverance to overcome the obstacles and misunderstandings that are inevitable in intercultural interaction. They believe in their ability to build relationships with people who are culturally different despite these obstacles.

Effective cross-cultural ministry is dependent on being able to respect, trust, and empower people. A basic principle of reproducible ministry is encouraging all believers to pass on what they know as soon as they know it.

---

95.   cf. Sherry Turkle, *Alone Together: Why We Expect More from Technology and Less from Each Other* (New York: Basic Books, 2011).

96.   Guo-Ming Chen, "Intercultural Effectiveness," in *Intercultural Communication: A Reader*, ed. Larry A. Samovar, Richard E. Porter, and Edwin R. McDaniel (Boston, MA: Wadsworth Cengage Learning, 2009), 395–98.

97.   Chi-Yue Chiu et al., "Cross-Cultural Competence: Theory, Research, and Application," *Journal of Cross-Cultural Psychology* 44, no. 6 (2013).

We saw this happening extremely effectively in the Millet people movement in Bulgaria. People, and especially the women who were the first to believe, encountered Jesus and gossiped to others what they knew with great passion and determination. They were keen to keep learning more about their wonderful Jesus and would pass on anything they had learned to others as well. Even non-Christians gossiped the wonderful news about Jesus to others and pointed them towards Christians to learn more. Not only did this embed a DNA of evangelism into the movement, it also caused a passionate desire to continue to learn so that they could keep sharing more of their Lord. What was particularly striking was the Millet people's concern for others and their ability to relate to others. Their strong relational networks enabled the gospel to spread rapidly throughout the country.

We saw the same quality of effective evangelism in some new believers in Australia. Several new Muslim-background believers were so passionate about Jesus that they actively took every opportunity to tell others about Him and with only a little encouragement were soon gathering groups of seekers to learn about their new faith.[98]

Many people are concerned that encouraging new believers to tell others about Jesus will result in the spread of heresy. This may be a risk where there is no ongoing discipleship strategy that ensures that believers continue to grow in their faith. However, where such a strategy is in place, not only can the passion for evangelism be encouraged and a movement of multiplying believers and churches grow, but those who evangelize can also be trained as reproducing disciple-makers.

At its most foundational level, Christianity is about relationships—relationship with God and relationship with others. The gospel spreads through relationships and, in churches, relationships help people to grow and protect them from sinning. Missionaries who fail to appreciate this dimension of their faith will struggle to establish vibrant churches and may sever relational bonds that could bear much fruit for the kingdom.[99]

---

98. This recount has been altered slightly to protect the identity of the people involved.

99. Roland Allen addressed this fear as far back as 1927 in a chapter entitled "Fear For the Doctrine" that can be found in Roland Allen, *The Spontaneous Expansion of the Church and the Causes Which Hinder It*, 2nd ed. (London: The World Dominion Press, 1949).

MISSIONARIES MUST BE ABLE TO BUILD CROSS-CULTURAL RELATIONSHIPS

Missionaries must have a strong commitment to communicate effectively with people. Missionary work involves constant relationship-building with strangers who are culturally different than the missionary. As God's ambassadors sent to reconcile the world to himself, missionaries have to know God well enough to be able to represent him with integrity and authenticity as well as get to know the people in their host culture well enough to communicate the gospel in ways that will be relevant to them (2 Cor 5:18–20).

Missionaries also need to be able to manage conflict in cross-cultural relationships since some degree of conflict is inevitable. Their lives are expected to be a sweet fragrance that attracts people to Jesus (2 Cor 2:15). Yet ideas of what is good and appropriate behavior can differ so much between cultures that although missionaries act in a way that is "fragrant" or attractive in their own culture, their behavior can be perceived as a stench in the host culture. It is almost inevitable, then, that at some point in a missionary's ministry their behavior will cause offense to their hosts. Missionaries therefore need to have the interpersonal and intercultural skills to be able to manage the conflict that arises from their cultural mistakes. Even more importantly, they need to have a maturity of character, the resilience to persevere when things are difficult, and a quality of life and faith in which the presence of Jesus is clearly evident.

Missionaries have to be able to manage their emotions. This includes being able to control emotions that rise up unexpectedly in reaction to unpredictable events. It is not sufficient just to control the outward expression of emotion; the emotions themselves also need to be dealt with. The biblical injunction not to let the sun go down on your anger is a good guideline for all negative emotions as it gives a reasonable time frame to attempt to address the feelings and issues. Although how we feel may not necessarily be under our control, how we respond to our feelings is. Along with controlling emotions, missionaries must be able to manage their verbal and nonverbal reactions and responses. All this requires the help of the Holy Spirit. With that empowering, missionaries can dispassionately identify and deal with issues without lashing out at people.

Just to make things more complicated, different cultures have different ways of expressing emotions and missionaries have to learn how to express their emotions in culturally appropriate ways. In multicultural teams, missionaries may also have to learn to identify, respond, and relate to their colleagues' expressions of emotion that are communicated in ways that are often unfamiliar. The ideal is that missionaries are able to respond in a way that promotes the further development of the relationship rather than inhibiting or stifling it.

It is important that missionary trainees learn to identify their emotions, understand what caused them, and be aware of what they can do to manage them. The goal is to learn how to nurture emotional responses that please God, such as the emotional aspects of love, joy, and peace. This is not an intellectual exercise but one involving a holistic personal response of mind, soul, and spirit.

MISSIONARIES ARE ON DISPLAY AS CHRIST'S AMBASSADORS

Missionaries are on display to the watching world in a more intense way than most other Christians. Paul described this as being "on display, like prisoners of war at the end of a victor's parade, condemned to die. We have become a spectacle to the entire world—to people and angels alike" (1 Cor 4:9). Like Paul, missionaries are being observed on the field by both believers and non-believers. They are also on display to churches at home and to other people in their agency and other agencies on the field. As they are on the front line of the kingdom of God they are also on display to the spiritual principalities and powers.

Missionaries are models of what it means to follow Jesus to the people they serve. They should have a quality of spirituality that enables them say to local people, like Paul did, "Follow my example as I follow the example of Christ" (1 Cor 11:1). People will make decisions about whether to follow Christ on the basis of the missionary's quality of life and spirituality.

Missionaries, as Christ's ambassadors and disciple-makers, essentially reproduce themselves—their character, attitudes, skills, and knowledge—in others. As Christ's representatives, they provide a living example of Christlikeness for others to follow. This is even more the case in pioneer missionary situations where there has not previously been a Christian witness and examples of Christian living do not exist. This means that missionary training must ensure that missionary candidates are imitators of Jesus in character and action, and are able to reflect the character of Christ in a way that is meaningful and attractive in different cultural contexts.

Since they are on display, missionaries need to be continually mindful of their context and their own reactions. Our initial reactions to situations are automatic and often dependent on learned ways of behaving. But what we do in response to those first reactions are in our hands. Missionaries need to develop the ability to dispassionately observe themselves and discipline themselves to make the necessary changes in their attitudes and behaviors in response to those observations. In this way, missionaries become habitual reflective practitioners who observe themselves, reflect on what they see, implement changes and continue to observe in an ongoing cycle.

MISSIONARIES ARE LEADERS

Missionaries are ambassadors for Christ and often are in positions of power with more access to resources and influence than the people they serve. They have a key influence on others, and since leading is fundamentally having an influence on others, whether or not they have a formal leadership role, missionaries act as leaders. For this reason, missionaries must meet the biblical criteria for leadership.[100] As such, they are role models for Christian living and service. They also exert influence over others, whether or not they are conscious of it. This can make them vulnerable to misusing their power for personal gain. Missionaries can abuse their positions of power or influence in subtle ways, such as in exaggerated prayer letters, or in more overt forms such as moral failure. Another way that missionaries can misuse power is to hold on to leadership for too long, refusing to hand it over to local people. The exacting biblical standards for leadership, with in-built accountability to a local community, protect both the missionary and those they serve.

What is striking about each of the lists found in the Bible of foundational qualities for God's people that leaders are expected to demonstrate especially clearly is that they are focused on character qualities rather than skills.[101] None of these character qualities stand alone as isolated entities; they are interwoven

---

100. They should, for example, have the qualities required of church elders that are listed in 1 Tim 3:1–7 and Titus 1:6–9. Cf. James E. Plueddemann, "Culture, Learning, and Missionary Training," in *Internationalizing Missionary Training: A Global Perspective*, ed. William David Taylor (Grand Rapids, MI: Baker Book House, 1991), 218.

101. Examples of qualities God wants in his people and especially in Christian leaders can be found in Gal 5:22; Col 3:12–14; 1 Tim 3:1–13; Tit 1:5–9; and 2 Pet 1:5–9.

in the character of the person into an integrated whole. God's plan is that his servants grow in these qualities in a holistic way as they surrender to and are transformed by him (Rom 12:1–2).

Attaining these qualities is not a static, one-time achievement. Missionaries, along with all Christians, need to keep growing in them. That is why Peter writes: "The more you grow like this, the more you will become productive and useful in your knowledge of Jesus Christ" (2 Pet 1:8). Determining the degree to which these qualities must be expressed before trainees begin their missionary service is something that missionary trainers, churches, and sending agencies need to discern.

Examining the biblical expectations of leaders gives us insight into what missionaries should be like and what they should be able to do. Three different leadership roles are particularly prominent in the Old Testament: priests, prophets, and kings and their officials. Priests were Israel's primary teachers, and therefore needed to be able to teach and model to the people what living for God looked like (Lev 10:11; Hos 4:6–7; Mal 2:1–9). The key danger of priests not being faithful to their task was that the people would not walk with God and would turn to idols (Hos 4:7–10; Mal 2:7–8). The prophets' key role was to faithfully proclaim to the people exactly what God had said or shown (Deut 18:20–22), and so they had to be able to listen to God carefully and clearly hear what he was saying or see what he was showing them (Jer 23:18–22). When they failed in this, they led people astray by false visions and prophecies (Ezek 13; Ezek 22:28; Mic 3:1–11). Kings and their officials had to rule God's people with justice (Deut 16:18–2; Jer 21:12 cf. Jer 22:3). The key danger for them was to abuse their power by oppressing their people and acting unjustly (Ezek 11:1–13; 34:1–10; Jer 23:1–4). In the same way, missionaries teach and model God's ways, listen to and proclaim God's word, and lead with justice, fairness, and sensitivity.

Leadership is never a one-person activity but involves followers who are part of a community that recognizes that leadership. This means that leaders have to be acknowledged by those who follow them. God told Moses to appoint leaders who had a good reputation in the community (Deut 1:12). Leaders in the early church were appointed on the basis of having qualities that the church could see. Barnabas, for example, was sent from the church in Jerusalem to Antioch to discern what had happened there and to forge a relationship with them because he was recognized by the church as being "a good man, full of the Holy Spirit and strong in faith" (Acts 11:24). The leaders that Paul wanted Titus to appoint were to be people who were "well thought of for [their] good life" (Tit 1:6).

Each elder was someone "whose life cannot be spoken against" and who had a good reputation both in the church and outside it (1 Tim 3:2, 7; cf. Deut 1:13). There has been a tendency for missionaries (especially from the West) to be self-selected and sent out in relative independence of their churches. It is not surprising therefore that they would tend to repeat this pattern by selecting and training local leaders with little consultation with local church members.[102]

GETTING ON WELL WITH PEOPLE IS A KEY CHARACTER QUALITY FOR MISSIONARIES

Missionaries are servants of others for Jesus' sake, focused on doing what is in the best interests of other people (2 Cor 4:5; 6:4; 1 Pet 5:2). They must love and serve both God's people and people who have yet to come to know Christ. In order to do this, they must become other-oriented, which means to humble themselves and battle pride, just as the first disciples needed to (Matt 23:1–12; John 13). Jesus exemplified a life of loving and serving other people, and he expects his disciples to follow his example by serving one another and the world (John 13:1–17; Matt 10:42–45; Phil 2:6–8; Eph 5:1–2).

A key facet of Christian spirituality is getting on with other people. The Apostle Paul writes to the Ephesians to lead a life worthy of their calling as followers of Jesus. Immediately after this he focuses in on the need for Christians to get on with each other. He writes "Be completely humble and gentle; be patient, bearing with one another in love. Make every effort to keep the unity of the Spirit through the bond of peace" (Eph 4:2–3).

It is easy to feel spiritual—for example, to feel humble—in a room on your own, doing your own thing. Living and working with other people, however, can quickly make our pride and selfishness become apparent. As Christians, our lives are "inextricably bound together" and therefore "incomplete unless committed to and shared with a faith community."[103] It is the community of God's people,

---

102. Most Western books on leadership are very individualistic and task oriented. Recently, women writers have begun to challenge this bias in thinking about leadership. A good book for those who would like to read more about this is by Amanda Sinclair, *Leadership for the Disillusioned: Moving Beyond Myths and Heroes to Leading That Liberates* (Crows Nest, NSW: Allen & Unwin, 2007).

103. Conde-Frazier, Kang, and Parrett, *A Many Colored Kingdom: Multicultural Dynamics for Spiritual Formation*, 81.

the church, living out Jesus' commands in relationship with him and each other that expresses most clearly what the gospel is. Lesslie Newbigin explained that each local church is the most important "hermeneutic of the gospel" or way that the gospel is expressed to its community.[104] Individualistic Westerners can find comprehending this communal dimension of spirituality very difficult.

Just as God is community in himself as Father, Son, and Holy Spirit, so human beings are created for relationships. It is in relationships that the most challenging tests of faith are found. Holiness—being like Jesus in all his purity and passionate love for others—is tested especially powerfully when sin intervenes in relationships and causes conflict and prevents reconciliation. Yet God's word allows us no excuses for broken relationships. Jesus consistently emphasized that his disciples must love one another, serve one another, and forgive one another (e.g., Mark 10:42–45; John 13:34–35). The New Testament repeatedly calls Christians to relinquish their arguments, quarrels, and underlying self-interest and envy and to forgive each other and be reconciled (e.g., 1 Cor 3, Phil 2:1–5; 4:2; Col 3:12–14; Jas 4:1–12).

One major specific way missionaries serve others is by showing hospitality to them. This is such a fundamental quality that it is expected of all church elders (1 Tim 3:2; Tit 1:8). Hospitality is more than just having an open home and inviting people into it. It means having an open life and inviting people to share your life with you. It is welcoming others into your life so that you can get to know them and they, you (1 Thess 2:8). Being hospitable is costly. It involves risk and means being vulnerable.[105] But hospitality or openness to other people is the basis for all relationships, and as the missionary's ministry is all about relationships, it is vital that they demonstrate this quality.

In order to be hospitable and share their lives with others, missionaries must give up the familiar for the uncomfortable (1 Cor 9: 19–22; 1 Thess 1:5; 2:8–9). Missionaries demonstrate Jesus' love by living among a people very different to themselves. They adapt to others' ways of living and communicating so that they can identify with them, share their lives with them, and strive to share the gospel with them in understandable ways. Doing this across cultural boundaries can be costly. It means going into places and doing things that make other people comfortable, regardless of how it makes the missionary feel.

---

104. Newbigin, *The Gospel in a Pluralist Society*, 227.

105. Robert W. Pazmiño, *Foundational Issues in Christian Education: An Introduction in Evangelical Perspective*, 3rd ed. (Grand Rapids, MI: Baker Academic, 2008), 44.

Relationships are a key arena in which faith is demonstrated. A vital part of missionary spirituality is being able to relate well to others and build healthy community. For these reasons, missionary spiritual formation must focus on the quality of relationships that the trainee is able to nurture and draw on, both in their own marriages and families and also with their co-workers. The quality of a missionary's relationships on the field strongly affects their ability to persevere. The largest international study of why missionaries leave the field to date (ReMAP I) found that good relationships with missionary colleagues and supportive family are two of the four most important factors that help keep missionaries on the field.[106] Developing interpersonal skills can help missionaries build healthy relationships, but far more fundamental and essential for healthy relationships is the development of spiritual disciplines like loving, forgiving, bearing with one another, and focusing on what is good in the other person (Col 3:12–14) These qualities also demonstrate the gospel to people outside the missionary team (cf. 1 Pet 2:9–12).

The communal aspect of missionary spirituality is also expressed and challenged in their multiple church relationships. Missionaries often end up belonging to several local church communities and having obligations to the broader church in each country they live and serve in. They receive from churches, but they also have a responsibility to churches to keep lifting their eyes beyond their local context to the world outside the borders of the church, including the unreached regions of the earth. Missionaries must therefore learn how to develop and nurture a wide variety of relationships with different communities of believers.

WHAT A HEALTHY TRAINING COMMUNITY LOOKS LIKE

A healthy missionary training community, like any healthy community, is characterized by hospitality, transparency, acceptance, and balanced accountability. Members of the community spend time in each other's homes and are encouraged to be honest, ask questions, evaluate things that are done, and hold each other accountable. There needs to be a good balance between accepting

---

106. Detlef Blöcher, "What ReMAP I Said, Did, and Achieved," in *Worth Keeping: Global Perspectives on Best Practice in Missionary Retention*, ed. Rob Hay, et al. (Pasadena, CA: William Carey Library, 2007), 15.

one another and holding each other accountable. Paul urged believers both to judge and accept one another, to carry one another's burdens, and to speak the truth in love (1 Cor 5:12; Rom 15:7; Eph 4:15; Gal 6:1–2).

Conflict is a normal part of life and an expected feature of working in a multicultural team. Many conflicts are the result of misinterpretation, poor communication, and wrong assumptions. Effective conflict management focuses on working through misunderstandings and promoting healthy communication. Missionaries will be greatly helped to effectively participate in multicultural teams if they first have the opportunity to be a member of a healthy training community in which conflict is managed in God-honoring ways. A healthy multicultural training team can be a powerful model and training ground for new missionaries. It can provide practical wisdom and support as trainees develop their skills in managing intercultural conflict.

In a healthy community, sin is swiftly but sensitively dealt with, and individuals are quick to identify their own sins, repent, and ask for forgiveness and/ or make restitution, where necessary. Sin affects the health of any community because it damages relationships between people as well as between people and God. It is important for members of a training community to be quick to identify sin, to repent, and to restore relationships . This should be done as transparently as possible, in order to avoid unhelpful speculation and in order to provide a model for relational reconciliation which can be reproduced in other contexts.

Missionaries have to be able to forgive those who hurt them, not just for the sake of interpersonal well-being, but also for intrapersonal healing. Effective missionaries have accepted who they are and are able to engage with others in ways that nurture relationships. They are able to discern and accept when it is best to take separate paths, preferably preserving relationships in the process, as Abraham did with Lot (Gen 13:5–12).

Allowing people to express their own spirituality with integrity is a feature of healthy community. Many leaders make the mistake of assuming that unity means conformity and, because of their own discomfort with difference, suppress expressions of faith that make them feel uncomfortable. When a training community is open to learning about the diverse ways in which God works in individuals, groups, and cultures, each member will be enriched. Not only will the community benefit, but trainees and trainers are likely to encounter God in a deeper way. This will help them develop maturity, resilience, and the strength to persevere on the field.

One example of the way in which differences can be approached in a healthy way that promotes the growth of the training community is by allowing missionary trainees from different heritages to express different ideas about how God speaks today. When trainees who have been brought up to think that God speaks only through the Bible encounter others who can give testimony to God speaking to them personally in other ways, they either have to adjust their theology or simply accept these other trainees whose experience of God is different than theirs. If they cannot adjust to this difference there is a risk that their theology may impede the missionary team they eventually join from seeking God's guidance in ways that are meaningful to some of its members. In addition, there is a risk that their influence may suppress the spiritual development of new churches they are involved in starting.

TRAINING MISSIONARIES IN COMMUNITY

For missionaries to be able to plant healthy churches and build healthy mission teams, they need to have experienced a healthy Christian community. Experiencing a healthy community provides the trainee with a living model to refer back to for comparison when faced with difficult experiences on the field. The more closely their training community resembles their later on-field missionary experience, the more helpful that community will be in the long run.

The cross-cultural dimension of missionary work means trainers need to demonstrate how to keep a vital fellowship with God in the context of the ever-changing demands of cross-cultural ministry. This helps to ensure that the training does not focus only on information or theory, but instead that it includes active demonstration of what spirituality means in practice. For example, when trainers are exhausted and a local visitor knocks on the door, the trainer not only models how to manage the situation but is able to explain to trainees how they find strength from God to be gracious and hospitable as well as modeling how to set aside time to rest.

Ministry does not occur in a vacuum. Exposure to the demands of teamwork and of relating both to team members and those they minister to helps trainees to understand what missionary service involves and enables them to experience and learn from the reactions they have to the things they encounter. In this context of real ministry, trainees experience authentic emotional reactions and can be helped to develop healthy patterns of response. A training community provides a supportive environment in which trainees can learn to practice self-control and emotional self-regulation, and receive reassurance and encouragement when they make mistakes.

Training in the context of community requires trainers to make their way of thinking and making decisions explicit. They need to explain to trainees why they do what they do. Trainees cannot be expected to interpret, understand, or reproduce what they see unless trainers explain their thoughts and actions.

Observing trainers in action is very important, but is not sufficient on its own. It must be accompanied by trainees actively making connections between what they are experiencing and God's word together with missiological insights. Trainees need to develop the habit of continually observing themselves and what is happening around them, monitoring their own responses, and reflecting on their decisions and actions with a view to continually growing and improving. This reflective process is helped by debriefing with mentors or peers and by journaling their reflections. Written or oral reflections ideally will involve trainees describing what they have encountered, identifying their assumptions, evaluating the effectiveness of previous strategies, and suggesting steps for change and plans for application. This habit of reflective learning that is central to the process by which adults learn is shown in Figure 6, which is based on two foundational conceptualizations of how adults learn—David Kolb's learning cycle and Kemmis and McTaggart's action research spiral.[107]

Ideally, missionary trainees should be exposed to authentic cross-cultural ministry problems through participation in authentic cross-cultural ministry. They should be confronted with questions for which they have no pre-prepared answers, and experiences that do not easily fit their inherited Christian frameworks. It is even better if they are interacting with a multicultural missionary team that exposes them to diverse Christian expressions of faith at the same time. In this context of dilemmas thrown up by the practice of cross-cultural ministry, trainees can be helped to grow by being in a supportive learning community that helps them learn to discern God's voice, develop methods of searching the Scriptures to find the answers they need, and experiment with implementing their proposed solutions.

---

107. David A. Kolb, *Experiential Learning: Experience as the Source of Learning and Development* (Englewood Cliffs, NJ: Prentice-Hall, 1984).

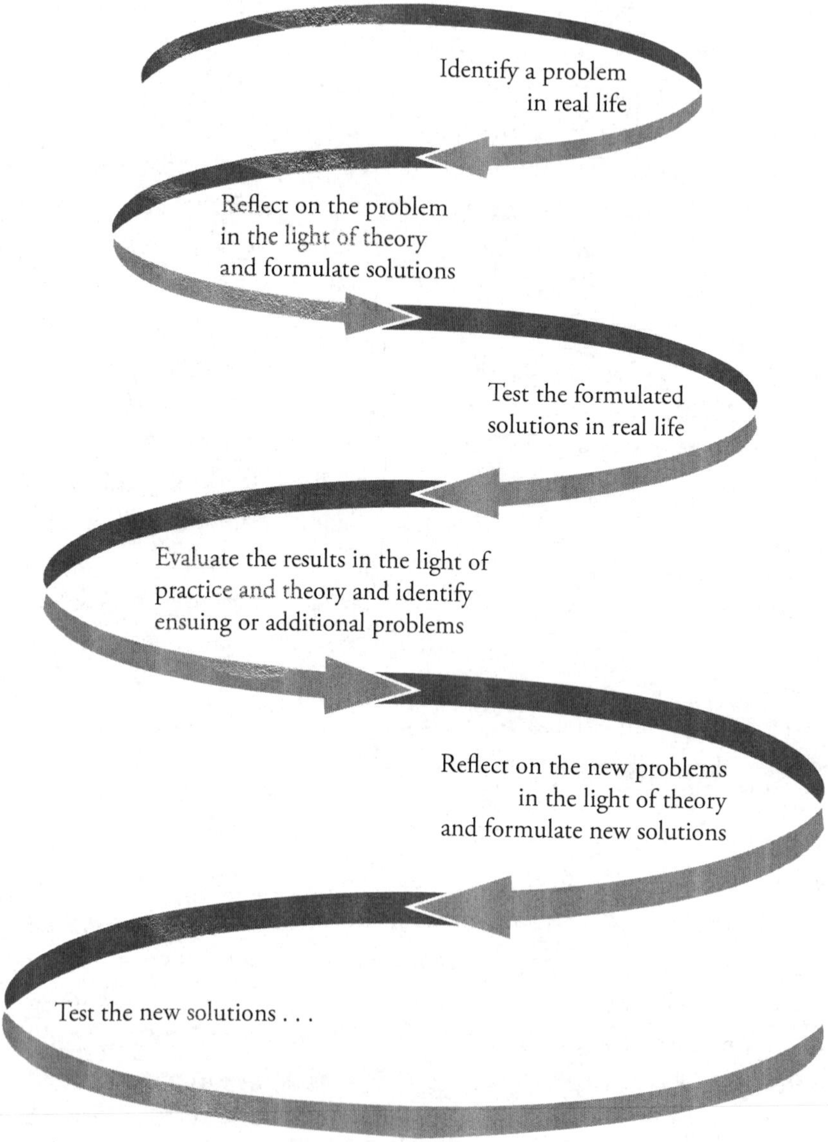

Identify a problem
in real life

Reflect on the problem
in the light of theory
and formulate solutions

Test the formulated
solutions in real life

Evaluate the results in the light of
practice and theory and identify
ensuing or additional problems

Reflect on the new problems
in the light of theory
and formulate new solutions

Test the new solutions . . .

Figure 6 Reflective learning spiral[108]

---

108. Evelyn Catherine Hibbert, "Designing Training for Adults," in *Integral Ministry Training: Design and Evaluation*, ed. Robert Brynjolfson and Jonathan Lewis (Pasadena, CA: William Carey Library, 2006), 60.

6

BUILDING ON PAST EXPERIENCE IN MISSIONARY TRAINING

For several hundred years missionary training has reflected a tension between the enthusiasm to send people out to the field as soon as possible and the realization that poor selection and lack of specific pre-field training for cross-cultural ministry can result in major problems on the field. These problems include trauma to new missionaries, overload for those who care for them, damage to the reputation of the gospel, and weak churches.

The early Bible college movement aimed to train everyone who felt that God was leading them into Christian service, and this meant being open to people of all educational backgrounds and ages. They maximized the accessibility of training by providing evening classes, extension programs, and correspondence schools. Many began in churches with evening Bible classes. Another feature of accessibility was the Bible colleges' concern to keep the training relatively short, in contrast to the minimum of 7 years of higher education required of those going to seminaries. This avoided the problem of missionary fervor being dissipated by many years of preparation and helped ensure missionaries saw themselves as learners rather than leaders when they reached the field.[109]

CURRENT FORMS OF MISSIONARY TRAINING

Bible colleges and seminaries continue to be highly influential in the formation and preparation of missionaries. Since the majority of missionaries train at either a Bible college or seminary, one writer has called these institutions "the linchpins that hold the missionary enterprise together—or weaken it

---

109. Kenneth Mulholland, "Missiological Education in the Bible College Tradition," in *Missiological Education for the Twenty-First Century: The Book, the Circle, and the Sandals: Essays in Honor of Paul E. Pierson*, ed. Paul Everett Pierson, et al. (Maryknoll, NY: Orbis Books, 1996), 45–46.

irreparably."[110] Many missionaries receive little missiological preparation beyond their Bible college and/or seminary training, so this becomes the only formal pre-field training they receive. It is therefore particularly influential.

Preparation for missionary service at Bible colleges and seminaries, though, is by no means the only type of pre-field training available to missionaries today. The relative lack of missiological training offered at many Bible colleges and seminaries has led to mission agencies and mission training colleges developing a range of cross-cultural orientation programs aimed at preparing potential missionaries for the challenges they will face as they enter new cultures. These basic orientation programs are usually designed for people who have already completed a Bible college or seminary course, and usually last between one and 12 weeks. Several agencies including Wycliffe Bible Translators with its sister organization SIL International, as well as New Tribes Mission, have developed more extensive pre-field training programs for their missionaries that last one or two years and are based on the specific types of ministry—Bible translation, linguistics, anthropology, and literacy in Wycliffe's case, and pioneer church planting in New Tribes Mission's case—that their missionaries will be engaged in.[111]

Many larger mission agencies also provide some kind of ongoing training for their missionaries on the field, although this is often limited because of the lack of personnel and the geographical spread of workers. They also usually have established systems for helping new missionaries adjust to their field, as well as some system for language learning. Training institutions such as missionary training institutes and some Bible and theological colleges also offer in-ministry training courses for missionaries, ranging from non-formal training to masters and doctoral programs in missiology or intercultural studies that can be taken for credit or simply audited by missionaries wanting missiological input as part of their lifelong learning. Some of these classes are available as intensive modules of one or two weeks per subject, and a few are available by distance or online. All these features make them fairly accessible to missionaries who can study alongside their ministry on the field or while on home assignment.

---

110. Larry Poston, "The Role of Higher Education in the Christian World Mission: Past, Present, and Future," in *Teaching Them Obedience in All Things: Equipping for the 21st Century*, ed. Edgar J. Elliston and Evangelical Missiological Society. (Pasadena, CA: William Carey Library, 1999), 146.

111. More details about these programs can be found at http://www.sil.org/training/training-programs-language-development and http://usa.ntm.org/mtc-overview

EMPHASES OF TRAINING AT BIBLE AND MISSIONARY TRAINING COLLEGES

The primary purpose of many of the Bible colleges that emerged from the evangelical awakenings of the 1800s was the training of missionaries. This influence is illustrated by the fact that between 1890 and 1992, almost 6,500 of just one of these college's graduates had served as missionaries.[112] These colleges were intimately connected with the interdenominational faith missions such as the China Inland Mission. These colleges provided the major training context that informed the reviews of missionary practice and training that occurred in the twentieth century and which are referred to in Chapter 1. As such, understanding their emphases, strengths, weaknesses, and impact, helps us to build on their experience and develop more effective ways of training missionaries today.

Examples of these Bible colleges and institutes which emerged from the evangelical awakenings of the 1800s include the East London Institute for Home and Foreign Missions founded in 1872, the Missionary Training College begun by A.B. Simpson in New York in 1882, D.L. Moody's Bible Institute in Chicago in 1886, and the Boston Missionary Training School founded by A.J. Gordon 1889. These institutions and colleges were not trying to be academic. Instead, driven by love for God and a keen sense of the world's need for the gospel, they focused on preparing men and women to take the gospel to the ends of the earth. This freed them to be able to address the issues of character, spiritual formation, and practical ministry skills that are vital to missionary preparation.

These and other early Bible colleges had five distinguishing features that particularly suited them to the training of missionaries. These features were (1) that mission was central to their agenda, (2) curriculum was integrated, (3) there was a focus on spiritual formation, (4) they emphasized practical training, and (5) they maximized the accessibility of the training.

Specialist missionary training colleges were also founded in the wake of the 1910 World Missionary Conference in Edinburgh where the need for specialized missionary training had been highlighted. They notably focused on the personal life and attitudes of the missionary and emphasized spiritual resilience, faith with integrity, cultural sensitivity, and practical theology based on authentic experience.

---

112. This was Moody Bible College, as stated in Mulholland, "Missiological Education in the Bible College Tradition," 43.

Experiencing God

These early Bible colleges emphasized spiritual formation. Personal devotions and corporate worship were a key part of the curriculum, and classes often began with prayer. Missionaries on home leave visited these colleges and students listened to them and prayed for the needs of the world and for each other. Part of spiritual formation was being involved in the college community in which faculty and students supported each other through difficulties and shared their lives with each other.

Specialist missionary training colleges founded in response to the 1910 Edinburgh Conference also particularly emphasized the spiritual development of trainees, including their ability to hear God's voice and feed on his Word. The principal of one of the Selly Oak colleges in the 1920s, Edmund Morgan believed, for example, that missionary training should focus on developing the inner life of trainees so that they would be able to lean on God and hear what he was saying to them. This would prepare them, he believed, for being able to do this under the strain of cross-cultural living with all its disappointments and failure.[113]

A second emphasis that Morgan and other principals shared was that missionary trainees should be able to relate their faith to the real world and its needs. Florence Allshorn, principal of one of the Church Missionary Society's training colleges, felt missionaries needed to be real and unpretentious about their faith. She had encountered as a missionary many "silent disasters" in missionary lives underneath the hard work of ministry and was particularly concerned about hypocrisy. In the light of this, she believed that students must develop honesty about their faith in God and genuineness in their relationships with others, and focused on providing pastoral care that addressed the deeper, emotional issues in trainees' lives.[114]

Using the Bible

The Bible occupied the central place in the studies at these Bible and missionary training colleges. Mastery of the content of the Bible was central to the curriculum of all these colleges. Typical of these colleges is Mount Hermon

---

113. Harley, "Missionary Training: The History of All Nations Christian College and Its Predecessors (1911–1981)," 68.

114. Ibid., 64–66.

Missionary Training College, whose first aim was to provide students with a thorough grounding in the Bible. Its first principal stated: "The college must stand for and preach the whole Bible, the Word of God, from cover to cover."[115] Another principal felt that above all missionaries needed to have a better knowledge of the gospel and so made it a priority to redress what she saw as relatively poor knowledge of the Bible in missionary candidates.[116] Each of these colleges devoted large sections of their timetable to biblical studies. All Nations Christian College, for example, devoted just over a third of their course to the study of key biblical texts to provide a model for approaching, interpreting, and applying biblical passages.[117]

The emphasis on the Bible in missionary training colleges was married to a desire to develop in students an understanding of culture. The concern was that trainee missionaries would be able to relate the Bible to life and the issues they would face in ministry. One of the missionary training college leaders felt that "missionaries need to be trained to relate their biblical, theological and historical understanding to the task of mission."[118] Hand in hand with this emphasis on the Bible there was also a focus on practical training. A key aspect of their practical nature was that, rather than requiring the study of original languages, they focused on gaining mastery of the Bible in English. A knowledge of the original languages of the Bible was nearly always viewed in both Bible and missionary training colleges as supplementary rather than foundational to ministry.[119]

Engaging with Culture

The third emphasis of the Bible and missionary training colleges that aimed to prepare men and women for missionary service was for students to appreciate the world around them, including the culture of other peoples. Morgan argued that training must develop cultural sensitivity. He warned of the dangers of the "heinous presumption" of missionaries preaching to people when they understand nothing about their culture. One way of doing this, he believed, was

---

115. Ibid., 86.

116. Gwenyth Hubble, principal of Carey Hall from 1945 to 1960, reported in ibid., 69.

117. Ibid., 181.

118. Edmund Morgan was the warden of the Church of England's missionary training colleges and his views are briefly described in ibid., 67.

119. Mulholland, "Missiological Education in the Bible College Tradition," 48.

to teach the traditional disciplines of theological schools from a missiological perspective.[120]

Meg Foote, the principal of Mount Hermon Missionary Training College in London, was similarly concerned that students developed an appreciation for other cultures. Her approach to helping this happen was to provide practical cross-cultural ministry experience to students including interaction with the ethnic minorities then living in West London. Foote also ensured that practical ministry experience was combined with reflection on that experience. Following several months of practical experience in a local church, the students engaged in reflection and evaluation together of what they had learned, and then discussed subjects such as church unity. She felt that these discussions were "far more meaningful in the light of such experience." [121]

Ministry Skill Training

Training in the Bible and missionary training college tradition was believed to occur not only through the academic program but through all the experiences of life. These colleges therefore had a strong emphasis on practical training in the skills that are needed for Christian ministry. Courses on practical subjects such as song leading, ministering to young people, missionary medicine, or accounting were included in many programs. Most importantly, students were involved in ministry, in the afternoons and/or on weekends. They engaged in pastoral work, Sunday School teaching, youth group leading, and evangelistic work, prison visitation, tract distribution, and personal evangelism among unchurched people.[122]

KEY EMPHASES FOR TRAINING MISSIONARIES TODAY

The emphases of the training group at the 1910 World Missionary Conference as well as of the principals of missionary training colleges that were established after it continue today. There is widespread agreement among missionary

---

120. Harley, "Missionary Training: The History of All Nations Christian College and Its Predecessors (1911–1981)," 64–70.

121. Ibid., 83.

122. Mulholland, "Missiological Education in the Bible College Tradition," 51.

trainers that missionaries need training in the following key areas in addition
to biblical studies and theology:

- the personal life of the missionary as a family or single
- the biblical basis for missions and history of missions
- language and culture acquisition,
- intercultural communication and contextualization,
- cross-cultural evangelism, discipling,
  church planting and nurture.[123]

Some specific mission contexts may require additional areas of training,
such as preparation for specific religious contexts or security concerns, but
these five foundational areas should be the main focus of training along with
study of the Bible.

Hundreds of specialist missionary training institutes are currently training
many thousands of missionaries in Asia, Africa, South America, Europe, and
North America. The lessons learned from the past need to be applied to the
present, so that the strengths of the specialist missionary training continue
and the weaknesses are addressed. The lessons from the past highlighted in
this chapter continue to be emphasized by studies of missionary training today. For example, a task force composed of eight seasoned missionary trainers
from every continent, who have first-hand experience of hundreds of missionary training institutions in many parts of the world, affirmed three areas that
missionary training programs must be vigilant about: (1) selecting high quality
missionary trainers, (2) focusing on character and interpersonal skill development, and (3) providing cross-cultural ministry experience for trainees.[124]

Selecting High Quality Missionary Trainers

The first area that missionary training programs must give special attention
to is by far the most important: the quality of the training staff. Missionary
training centers need to choose their training staff carefully, as "teachers are the

---

123. Robert Ferris, "Standards of Excellence in Missionary Training Centers," *Training
for Cross-Cultural Ministries* 1 (2000): 3; William David Taylor, "Setting the Stage," in
Internationalizing Missionary Training: A Global Perspective, ed. William David Taylor
(Grand Rapids, MI: Baker Book House, 1991), 8–9; Robert Brynjolfson and Jonathan
Lewis, eds., *Integral Ministry Training: Design and Evaluation* (Pasadena, CA: William
Carey Library, 2006), 91–92, 214–16.

124. Ferris, "Standards of Excellence in Missionary Training Centers," 3.

curriculum which models obedience to Christ."[125] Since trainers must be models of what they want the trainees to become, they must above all be marked by spiritual maturity and well-developed interpersonal skills. Tite Tienou argues that the spirituality of those who train missionaries must be credible in that they should be able to relate to the world and to people.[126]

Trainers must also have extensive cross-cultural experience. They should have been missionaries themselves, just as nearly all the early principals of missionary training colleges were. Robert Ferris, who led a task force to identify qualities of effective missionary training centers, and who is familiar with many majority world programs, writes:

"Many institutions have erred gravely in this regard. Intending to provide the finest staff for their training programs, they have recruited teachers with high academic degrees, often fresh from their graduate or post-graduate studies. This is a reasonable choice, if the purpose of the institution is to develop bright theoreticians. If the purpose is to train effective practitioners, however, highly degreed recent graduates are a poor choice."[127]

Trainers who have served as missionaries themselves are able to teach with authenticity because they teach from experience.[128] They are able to illustrate their teaching with examples from real life and know from experience what kinds of qualities are most needed to survive and thrive in cross-cultural ministry.

Focusing on Character and Interpersonal Skill Development

A second area requiring special focus by missionary training programs is the development of character and interpersonal skills. This is best done, even though it is costly in terms of time and energy for staff, in the context of a genuine community in which trainers and trainees live together, eat together, pray together, and minister together. "No other setting simulates the intensity of relationships the trainee will encounter on the missionary team or the stresses of

---

125. Kenneth Mulholland, "Teaching Them All Things: Three Dots and a Pilgrimage," in *Teaching Them Obedience in All Things: Equipping for the 21st Century*, ed. Edgar J. Elliston (Pasadena, CA: William Carey Library, 1999), 13.

126. Tite Tienou, "The Training of Missiologists for an African Context," in *Missiological Education for the Twenty-First Century: The Book, the Circle, and the Sandals: Essays in Honor of Paul E. Pierson*, ed. Paul Everett Pierson, et al. (Maryknoll, NY: Orbis Books, 1996), 97.

127. Ferris, "Standards of Excellence in Missionary Training Centers," 2.

128. Harley, *Preparing to Serve : Training for Cross-Cultural Mission*, 47–48.

cross-cultural ministry. Unless the needed graces and skills are well-developed, an uncertain future awaits on the mission field."[129]

The strengths of the early Bible college movement are reflected to a varying degree in today's Bible colleges, but the pressure felt by most colleges to become more academic and to focus on intellectual development comes at the expense of the development of spirituality, character, and practical ministry skills. Ted Ward explains:

> So long as "practical experience" is stultified by treating it as a poor cousin of intellectual learning, so long as "Christian service assignments" are weekend outings divorced from distinct and relevant dialogue with one's "academic learnings," and so long as theological education is seen as preparatory to (rather than simultaneous with) ministry, a weak linkage will continue between education and the development of the church.[130]

Ward urges Christian training institutions, including Bible colleges and seminaries, to ensure that helping students grow in obedience as servants of God, rather than growing in knowledge as scholars, stays the first priority. Knowing is important, but it must not be made to be primary; it must go hand in hand with doing, and must be acted on in practical service of God and of others.

A poignant example of this kind of drift to the academic at the expense of the practical and spiritual is the story of Harley House, founded in 1872 with the specific encouragement of Hudson Taylor to prepare missionaries for the China Inland Mission. It withered and died in 1910, primarily because it had failed to keep its vision for preparing people for Christian service and especially missionary service. The course had been extended to four years, and prayer and practical ministry including evangelism had fallen into the background. As a result, graduates no longer applied to the faith missions and the faith missions stopped sending them candidates for training.[131]

---

129. Ferris, "Standards of Excellence in Missionary Training Centers," 2.

130. Ted W. Ward, "Evaluating Metaphors of Education," in *With an Eye on the Future: Development and Mission in the 21st Century*, ed. Duane H. Elmer and Lois McKinney (Monrovia, CA: MARC, 1996), 45.

131. David Cheesman, "Do Leaders Grow Colleges? Leadership, Prosperity, and Decline in Theological Education," *The Theological Educator* 6 (2013).

Providing Cross-cultural Ministry Experience

Missionary trainees need practical cross-cultural ministry experience. One researcher, Patrick, set out to determine the most effective preparation for tent-makers, and discovered that the most significant factor that seemed to promote missionaries' effectiveness was working for at least one year in cross-cultural ministry in the home country before leaving for their eventual field of service. Working in a church or attending Bible college, in contrast, did not impact their effectiveness. This research suggests that cross-cultural ministry training and experience prior to going overseas is crucial to future effectiveness.[132]

Brasher's research on the preparation of missionaries in his mission agency lends weight to Patrick's conclusion. He found that "the overwhelming evidence from the statements and ratings . . . show that actually having opportunities to do evangelism and discipleship is the best training tool."[133] The practical ministry experience that many missionary training institutes provide is a real positive, but it is often among people from the same culture and includes little engagement with people from other cultures.[134] As a general guide, at least a quarter of the training time should be devoted to actual ministry in a cross-cultural setting.[135] Ministry skills are best learned through a process of observing skilled practitioners, imitating them, receiving feedback from practitioners and recipients, and learning to reflect on individual performance in order to improve.

For effective cross-cultural ministry, missionaries need to reflect on their experience in the light of the experience of others through history as well as in the light of insights of disciplines such as intercultural communication and religious studies that are brought together in the field of missiology. Too often, missionaries remain unaware of the riches of the resources available to them in missiology beyond the basic introductions they were given in pre-field orientation. In order to engage in a deep way with the people missionaries are working with, they need to know how to become proficient in their language(s), how to

---

132. Patrick, "Tentmaking Unveiled—'The Survey Says,'" *Evangelical Missions Quarterly* April (2007).

133. Brasher, *Important Factors in Pre-Field and Field-Based Preparation of Missionaries Serving with Cross and Crescent International*, 112.

134. Harley, "Missionary Training: The History of All Nations Christian College and Its Predecessors (1911–1981)," 217.

135. Ferris, "Standards of Excellence in Missionary Training Centers," 2.

research their culture, and how to grapple positively with cross-cultural hermeneutics, critical contextualization, and indigenous theologies.

THE NEED FOR ONGOING, JUST-IN-TIME, IN-MINISTRY TRAINING

In addition to the study that most missionaries do before going to the field, they also benefit greatly from ongoing learning that is relevant to their specific context and ministry and that they continue to pursue as a missionary. Many missionaries still do not have sufficient access to just-in-time, on-the-job, accessible, in-ministry training which would help them establish effective, sustainable ministry beyond the initial years on the field. In a survey of active missionaries in WEC International in 2002 the majority of respondents considered that lack of experience or training was a significant hindrance to their work.[136] When missionaries reach the stage of trying to plant a new church, for example, often several years after they arrive in their country of service, they need accessible training in cross-cultural church planting and help in thinking through issues as they arise. The last time that many cross-cultural church planters thought about church planting, for example (if they ever did) is often at least 3 years earlier during their Bible college or seminary training.

IMPLICATIONS FOR TRAINING MISSIONARIES AND FOR MISSIONARY TRAINERS

Over the last century the emphasis on character formation and authentic, practical, cross-cultural ministry experience in institution-based missionary training has gradually weakened. However reviews of missionary training consistently stress its importance. In addition, the need for missionaries to have cross-cultural understanding and an in-depth knowledge of their Bible, alongside the ability to practically apply biblical understanding to the challenges encountered in cross-cultural ministry has been repeatedly emphasized.

---

136. Richard Hibbert and Evelyn Hibbert, "Report on Hindrances to and Needs in Reaching the Unreached and Church Planting in Wec Fields," (Rehe, Germany: WEC Intercon, 2002).

7

APPLYING BIBLICAL PRINCIPLES TO THE PROCESS OF MISSIONARY TRAINING

The Bible has a lot to say about teaching and training people. This can be divided into what it says about the purpose and goals of training and what it says about the process of training. In earlier chapters we have looked at what the Bible points out as goals of training. In this chapter we focus on what we can learn from the Bible about the process of training. In particular, the chapter focuses on key principles that should inform how trainers and training programs put their training into action. Although these biblical principles are relevant for any Christian education, this chapter will focus on their relevance to missionary training.

In the Bible, the training of God's servants is always integrated with life. Teachers, like their students, continue to learn. Learning occurs in the context of life and in the context of the trainer's ministry, which provides a living model for what the graduate trainee will be doing. Training in the Bible is a life-to-life process conducted over a number of years, usually in the context of community, with the expectation that the trainees will develop attitudes and behaviors and a whole way of being that will impact their life and ministry. In the same way, missionary training should be a life-to-life, community-based process occurring in the context of cross-cultural ministry.

CHOOSE WHO YOU TRAIN

A critical part of training that is often overlooked is the selection of trainees. The need for missionaries to be people of exemplary character requires churches and mission agencies to be careful about who they choose to endorse and send as missionaries. Missionary trainers often play a part in selecting which people should be recommended for missionary service. Churches, mission agencies, and missionary trainers all need to know what kind of people they should be looking for.

Effective training for cross-cultural ministry is quite trainer-intensive and often very challenging for the trainee. For this reason, it is sensible to do everything possible to check that trainees are ready for this type of ministry before they embark on the specific training. This approach is summarized in the saying, "Select hard, train easy." If trainers are convinced about the suitability of trainees, it is easier for them to invest in their personal growth. At the same time, if trainees are confident that this is what they should be doing, they are more likely to persevere when things get tough.

In order to be sure that potential missionary candidates are ready, churches, mission agencies and trainers all need to have clear criteria which makes it relatively easy for each party to identify whether the candidate is ready. When these criteria are clearly articulated, it not only helps with selection but it also aids those helping the potential trainee prepare. In addition, the trainee also knows what to work on. This makes the selection process itself formational for trainees as they engage with what they have to become in order to be effective missionaries.

Ideally, people should be selected for training for missionary service following the formation of foundational qualities in the missionary's home church. The selection process should involve a negotiation between the church and the cross-cultural ministry trainers. A mission agency may also be involved in this process if there has already been discussion with the agency about the potential missionary's joining the organization. The purpose of this process is to help all parties to become convinced (or otherwise) of the call, aptitude, and readiness of the candidate for missionary work. A person should only come into missionary training when their church believes that they have been called by God into this work and that they fulfill the foundational criteria for Christian leadership that are described later in this section.

What, then, are these foundational criteria that the church and missionary trainers should focus on to work out who is suitable for missionary service? At the most general level, missionaries should be good representatives of Jesus. Whether or not they hold a formal leadership role, missionaries represent Christ and act as his ambassadors, so they must be people who can be imitated as examples. Every missionary has a position of influence on other people. As such, every missionary is a leader even if they do not have a formal leadership role.

Because of the key influence they have on others and their role as Christ's ambassadors, missionaries should as a minimum have the qualities required of church leaders that are set out in 1 Timothy 3:2–7 and Titus 1:6–9. The stress in each of these lists of characteristics falls heavily on qualities of character, and in particular on having a good reputation in the wider community. According to these passages missionaries, like all Christian leaders, must have a good reputation with outsiders, be above reproach, blameless, respectable, upright, and holy, and manage family, children, and household well. Their children must also be respectful.

The intention of this listing of characteristics is to stress that every member of the community, Christian or non-Christian, should think well of the leader. For missionaries, not only does this indicate that they should have a good reputation in their churches, it also means that they should be well respected in the non-Christian community. When missionaries enter new cross-cultural communities, sending churches and agencies need to have the confidence that they will be able to act in ways that commend themselves to the local people. Just as Christians belong to the community of Christ, the community of Christ exists in the context of a wider community and leaders must be exemplars to church members of how to act in a godly way towards the wider community.

The good character and self-control of Christian leaders, including missionaries, recommends the gospel to the community. Missionaries' homes are open to others through their hospitality, and they are able to skillfully proclaim their faith and provide an answer to those who enquire or to those who seek to undermine the faith (cf. 1 Pet 3:15–16).

Although nearly all the characteristics in the two lists of leadership characteristics in 1 Timothy and Titus are qualities of character, there is one key skill that stands out. That is that elders, and missionaries by extension, must be able to teach and pass on the gospel to others. Missionaries likewise must be able to explain the gospel clearly and faithfully to people (1 Tim 3:2; Titus 1:9).

Missionaries must exercise self-restraint and be self-controlled in their relationships with others. This means that among other things they must rein in the expression of their emotions when that would otherwise harm others. Paul goes on to explain that this includes not being argumentative or quarrelsome, being quick-tempered or violent, being dependent on alcohol, or being a lover of money or pursuing dishonest gain. (I Tim 3:2–3; Titus 1:9).

In order to have self-control, leaders including missionaries must know themselves and also have some idea of how they will react in different situations. For missionaries, the challenge in self-control is the unpredictability of what they will face. Being aware of normal emotional responses and having some experience in how to manage emotions is important preparation for self-control in cross-cultural situations. Paul advises that leaders—and by implication missionaries—should not be new converts so that they can have been tested first. This testing implies exposure to the demands of ministry and the opportunity to develop godly character through the experience.

Another key characteristic of leaders, including missionaries, is being hospitable (1 Tim 3:2: Titus 1:8). Missionaries' lives and homes need to be open. They have to be ready to give themselves, and usually their families, to others as well. Missionaries need to lead transparent lives so that what they seem to be is actually what they are. Hospitality does not just mean providing a meal, it means giving self, time, and possessions to others. It encompasses being welcoming and generous regardless of how the host is feeling. This same spirit of hospitality and generosity extends to a welcoming attitude that intentionally looks for the best in people and seeks to encourage and nurture them regardless of circumstances.

A key aspect of cross-cultural ministry is that it is an exercise in practicing hospitality as much as or even more than it is the transmission of facts about our faith.[137] Conde-Frazier, Kang, and Parrett describe hospitality in this way:

> Hospitality creates a place where we are connected to one another. It is a space that is safe, personal, and comfortable. It is a place of respect, acceptance, and friendship. . . . The place of hospitality offers attentive listening and a mutual sharing of lives and life stories.[138]

Missionaries need to be able to create this kind of space in their lives and in their homes, in which people feel accepted and respected. In this space both the stranger and the missionary can share their stories, including, in the missionaries' case, how they have been transformed by Jesus.

RECOGNIZE THAT GOD IS THE ULTIMATE TEACHER

Training is ultimately God's work. We are all in God's school as he guides us into the truth by his Spirit, transforms us by the renewing of our minds, and shapes us to become more like Jesus (John 14:17; Rom 12:1–2; 2 Cor 3:18). Wisdom, understanding, and discernment come from God as his gift (Prov 2;

---

137. Benjamin D. Espinoza, "Practicing the Welcoming Gospel: Hospitality in Cross-Cultural Ministries," *Evangelical Missions Quarterly* 50, no. 4 (2014).

138. Conde-Frazier, Kang, and Parrett, *A Many Colored Kingdom: Multicultural Dynamics for Spiritual Formation*, 171, 72.

cf. 1:9). Whatever other people do to help train someone, ultimately the positive formation that happens in a person's life is the result of God working on that person (2 Cor 3:18; Rom 8:29).

> Training programs cannot cause growth. They can only set the environment and conditions for growth. Although trainers can help trainees grasp their responsibilities, guide their learning, and set conditions for growth, God causes the growth.[139]

God is the master teacher and trainer. We see this in the way he trained the whole nation of Israel throughout the course of the Old Testament. He revealed himself to them through the miracles Moses and Aaron did and through the miracle of opening up the Red Sea and the Jordan for them to cross over. He revealed his character to them through the law, and he kept calling them back to himself through the prophets. He trained Israel in a particularly intensive way through the forty years they were in the desert, in what one writer has named the "Wilderness School."[140] Using a wide variety of methods, God tested the Israelites' hearts and worked on developing their faith in his ability to look after them and accomplish his purposes.

Missionary trainers need to let God be God in their trainees' lives. It can be tempting to try to force people to change into how we want them to be, but often God has a different pathway to growth that he wants them to follow. At the same time, in our commitment to develop people as trainers, we can sometimes forget each person's uniqueness and fail to appreciate how their specific God-given qualities may have a particular contribution to make to the extension of God's kingdom, sometimes in ways that may not seem best to us. Perceiving the training group as an inclusive learning community where each member, trainee and trainer, both learns and contributes value to everyone's learning, as God directs the processes and experiences, can help to overcome this attitude.

BE A MODEL AND MENTOR TO TRAINEES

The Scriptures provide many case studies of leadership training, and in each case the mode of training was apprenticeship or mentoring on-the-job, where

---

139. Lewis, "Philosophy of Integral Ministry Training," 23.

140. Mary LeBar, "The Wilderness School," in *Education That Is Christian*, ed. Lois E. LeBar and Jim Plueddemann (Colorado Springs, CO: ChariotVictor, 1995).

the job was a 24/7 vocation. Examples include Moses' training of Joshua, Eli's training of Samuel, and Elijah's training of Elisha. New Testament case studies of apprenticeship include Jesus' training of the twelve disciples, Barnabas' training of Paul, and Paul's training of Timothy and others in his missionary teams.

Jesus trained his disciples by life-to-life apprenticeship. This involved calling them to live with him, follow him, and observe everything he did with the aim that they would imitate him, and then go out to do what he had shown them to do (Mark 3:13–15). Using this method, "truth was not taught in abstract doctrines or regulations; it was caught in the experience of their shared life."[141] This was the perfect example of holistic or integral training. Character, skills, and knowledge were modeled by the master to his disciples in the course of daily life and ministry. Jesus' approach to training was primarily as a mentor, and his mentoring method was relational, informal, oral, and mobile.[142]

Paul trained missionaries using the same apprenticeship approach. Following the way in which Barnabas had mentored him into missionary life and work, he intentionally chose and invited specific people from the churches he had planted to join his missionary team and to learn how to do missionary work as on-the-job apprentices (Acts 16:1–3; 20:4).

Since mentoring and apprenticeship is the key mode of training exemplified in the Scriptures and especially by the master trainer Jesus, our missionary training efforts should be shaped by this method. Even though our historical and social circumstances differ in significant ways from those in Jesus' time, we cannot expect to improve on his fundamental mode of training. In fact our training approaches can only be effective to the extent that we take time to build meaningful relationships with trainees. A helpful adage to keep in mind is "the closer the contact, the stronger the impact."[143]

Moses and Joshua provide another example of the normal pattern of training in the Bible. Moses modeled leadership to Joshua in the context of everything that daily life demanded of him. He showed Joshua who a leader should be, how he should act, as well as providing opportunities for Joshua to grow personally, develop his skills, and grow and develop in personal

---

141. Robert Emerson Coleman, *The Master Plan of Discipleship*, The Personal Evangelism Library (Old Tappan, NJ: F.H. Revell Co., 1987), 146.

142. Krallmann, *Mentoring for Mission: A Handbook on Leadership Principles Exemplified by Jesus Christ*, 124.

143. Ibid., 149.

confidence. Moses' life was transparent to Joshua, and Joshua was allowed to observe Moses' deep encounters with God and their impact on him.

In biblical examples of apprenticeship and mentoring, the trainee accompanies the trainer in their daily activities and service of God. The trainer is not only someone who knows things, but someone who is currently doing the role that the trainee will eventually take up and who models the character qualities and attitudes needed to fulfill that role. The trainee learns through a combination of being, doing, and knowing.[144] Trainers not only tell the trainee things, but model the qualities and skills that they want to see in the trainee. The trainee observes what the trainer does and how he does it, is given opportunities to practice those skills, listens to what the trainer explains and absorbs this understanding, and watches the way the trainer lives, imbibing his attitudes. Joshua's training under Moses followed this pattern.

Joshua's training began when he was selected as a young man as Moses' assistant and companion (Num 11:28). From then on he went where Moses went, watched what Moses did, and did whatever Moses told him to do (Ex 24:13–14; 33:7–11). He was trained in character qualities and attitudes by being with Moses and watching how Moses responded to every situation. In the incident of the Golden Calf he saw Moses' zeal for God and concern for his glory but also his genuine care for God's people and willingness to be blotted out of God's book so that they would be forgiven (Ex 32:15–35). When he tried to get Moses to stop two men prophesying, apparently worried that they might be trying to usurp Moses' position, he saw Moses' humility (Num 11:26–30). And in the incident of the spies and rebellion of the people, Joshua saw how Moses' first response was not to fight back but to turn to God and leave the outcome to him (Num 14).

Training in the Bible was always highly practical and occurred in the context of ministry. The things Joshua needed to know, for example, were taught in the context of doing things. When he was given the task of leading the Israelite army against the Amalekites while Moses held up his staff on the hill, Joshua experienced God's power and how God works through human agency—both through his doing the fighting as well as Moses' role of holding up his staff (Ex 17:8–15). It was in this context of doing the work—the "ministry" of serving Moses and God's people and therefore God as well—that Joshua

---

144. Robert J. Banks, *Reenvisioning Theological Education: Exploring a Missional Alternative to Current Models* (Grand Rapids, MI: W.B. Eerdmans, 1999), 92.

learned something God specifically wanted him to know—that is, that He would completely destroy Amalek in the future (Ex 17:14). Similarly, when he was sent as one of the twelve spies to explore Canaan (Num 13–14), he learned among other things the critical importance of trusting and obeying God for the well-being of His people.

In the same way, the ideal is for missionary training to involve life-to-life, in-ministry modeling of missionary work by a trainer to trainees. Through this, the trainer not only shows and explains to the trainee what to do, but also provides a living model that the trainee can refer to when considering what to do or how to feel in other contexts. There is no doubt that this approach to training is highly demanding for trainers, however, as it is the biblical exemplar for training, it has to be seriously considered.

ENCOURAGE TRAINEES

Apprenticeship and mentoring also address the all-important emotional aspect of learning. The trainer's role is to provide a supportive environment in which what they say and do encourages the trainee to keep learning and growing. Where relationships among trainees and with the trainer are healthy, trainees feel secure enough to try out new ways of doing things and to ask difficult questions that are puzzling them. The gospels record many instances when the disciples asked Jesus to explain things they did not understand.

Trainers should look for opportunities to directly encourage trainees. Laurent Daloz, who has written extensively on mentoring, sees the mentor's encouragement as communicating this message: "I am on your side; we are in this together." This message comes through the trainer's words that affirm the trainee when they do something right and also affirm their integrity as a person and that they are okay even when things go wrong.[145]

A second way that trainers can encourage trainees is to arrange tasks so that the trainee can experience success. Joshua's experience of being sent out as a spy to report on the land of Canaan can be seen as this kind of test. Such tests can be set by the trainer to build confidence, perseverance, and resilience. These help to build the learner's self-efficacy, which is their belief that they can do what the work requires. These tests are combined with words of encouragement

---

145. Laurent A. Daloz, "Mentorship," in *Adult Learning Methods: A Guide for Effective Instruction*, ed. Michael W. Galbraith (Malabar, FL: Krieger, 2004), 455.

from the trainer. God told Moses to encourage and strengthen Joshua in the task of leading God's people to inherit the land (Deut 1:38; 3:28). In the face of a huge task ahead of Joshua and the fact that Moses was no longer going to be with him, he told Joshua, "Be strong and courageous. . . ." (Deut 31:7).

TRAIN IN COMMUNITY

People are communal beings. We are born for relationships and need each other. In addition, we need the diversity of ideas and experience that different people bring to a group in order to make our understanding more robust, and increase our capacity to cope with the challenges of life. Even where the Bible records individual mentoring relationships, such as Moses and Joshua, Elijah and Elisha, these were not exclusive relationships. Moses and Joshua were part of a close-knit community wandering in the desert, with constant interaction with the leaders and people of Israel, as well as the other people they encountered on their journey. The hierarchy of leadership that Moses established to manage the Hebrew community must have ensured that there was constant interaction with the community leaders (Ex 18:13–26). In the same way, Elijah and Elisha were also interacting with different groups of prophets (2 Kgs 2:3,5,7,15–18;6:1–7). Although these communal interactions are often missed by readers of the Bible from individualistic cultures, they are obvious and implicit to readers from collectivist backgrounds.

Just living or participating in a communal experience is not sufficient for missionary training because it is possible to be present but non-engaged, or for the community to be dysfunctional. Missionaries need to be adept at relating to people from diverse backgrounds. They need to know what a healthy community looks like in order to be able to reproduce it. Having experienced the value of diversity will help them to be willing to invest in the effort needed to develop healthy community. In particular, they need to have seen and experienced how to manage conflict. The gospels record many instances when the disciples were in conflict with each other, and Luke is open about the conflict between Barnabas and Paul. As working in groups and with different groups of people is so intrinsic to cross-cultural ministry, the role of groups in training in the Bible can provide examples and principles that can be applied to missionary training today.

Although Moses' training of Joshua was one-on-one, the training of prophets, Jesus' disciples, and Paul's missionary band all occurred in groups. Some prophets lived, traveled, and ate together under the leadership of a senior prophet (e.g., 1 Sam 10:10; 19:20; 1 Kgs 20:35; 2 Kgs 2:1–18; 4:38–44). In this community they learned about the importance of discerning God's voice when he spoke through their peers, the extent of God's power, and how God cares for his servants (e.g. 1 Kgs 20:35–37; 1 Sam 19: 18–24; 2 Kgs 4:38–44). There was some fluidity of membership as Saul was able to join their company for a time (1 Sam 10:10, 19:23–24).

Jesus focused his training on a group of twelve disciples. At times he focused on a smaller group of three disciples—Peter, James, and John, and at another time the group was expanded to include seventy-two disciples who he sent out in pairs on a ministry practice trip (Luke 10:1). But most of the time it seems the focus was the twelve who lived, traveled, and ate together with Jesus. Together they listened to Jesus' teaching, watched his way of dealing with people, and experienced his miracles.

Although Jesus' focus was the twelve, his learning community was not exclusive. This meant that others, such as the seventy-two, the crowds, and the women who saw to the group's needs, were welcome to join in with what was going on. The more dedicated community of twelve trainees therefore had to continually interact with others who wanted to learn from Jesus. The inclusivity of Jesus' conception of this community was reinforced on several occasions when Jesus rebuked his disciples for wanting to exclude people (e.g. Luke 18:15–16; Matt 19:13–14; John 4:4–42). That is, Jesus created an open learning community where people beyond the dedicated trainees were free to participate. It seemed as if Jesus welcomed all who wanted to learn. He also used the challenges some enquirers faced in learning as object lessons for the disciples (e.g. Matt 19:16–30). The community of disciples provided belonging, security, mutual encouragement, stimulation, challenge, and a sense of accountability not only to Jesus but to the group.[146] This same picture of fluid group boundaries seems evident in Paul's traveling band.

The training community was not a set of individuals learning in parallel to each other. What happened in the group was intrinsic to their learning. Their interaction provided many opportunities for learning as Jesus responded

---

146. Krallmann, *Mentoring for Mission: A Handbook on Leadership Principles Exemplified by Jesus Christ*, 58.

to things that were happening among them. They learned, for example, from Jesus' responses to Peter when he tried to walk on water but started to drown, when he tried to turn Jesus from his pathway of suffering, and when he refused Jesus' offer to wash his feet (Matt 14:22–33; Matt 16:21–28; John 13:1–17; Luke 22:31–36). They learned from Jesus' response to James and John's request for the places of highest honor (Mark 10:35–45), and from a repeat and development of that lesson when they were arguing among themselves about who would be the greatest at the Last Supper (Luke 22:24–30). They learned from Jesus' response to Thomas' puzzlement (no doubt expressing their own) about knowing where Jesus was going and how to get there (John 14:1–14) and from how Jesus responded to Thomas' later lack of faith (John 20:24–29). This meant each participant had the opportunity to learn from each other's experiences, perspectives, and questions, as well as learning how to relate to each other and manage a group.

ENCOURAGE ACTIVE LEARNING

The book of Proverbs contains key information about the process and outcomes of training. One of the purposes of this book is to give wisdom about how to train people (1:5) and it gives us an understanding of the teaching-learning process. In particular, Proverbs chapter 2 focuses on the process of training and its various ingredients.[147]

For training to be effective, according to Proverbs chapter 2, learners must be active participants in the learning process. When learners engage actively in the process of learning, they receive wisdom from God, who is the ultimate source of wisdom and understanding. There are several ingredients in this active learning process. It begins with a father teaching his son in the form of words and commands (Prov 2:1). But to be effective, what the father says must be combined with the next ingredient—the child's active participation in the learning process by "applying your heart to understanding," "call[ing] out for insight," and "search[ing] for it as for hidden treasure" (2:2–4). Even this, though, is not enough for learning to occur. The final ingredient in the process is God stepping in and giving wisdom: "then you will understand the fear of the Lord and find the knowledge of God. For the Lord gives wisdom, and from

---

147. Michael V. Fox, "The Pedagogy of Proverbs 2," *Journal of Biblical Studies* 113, no. 2 (1994).

his mouth comes knowledge and understanding" (2:5–6). God's granting of wisdom depends on the active search for it by the trainee in response to listening to the teaching of the trainer.[148]

This approach to learning is consistent with a problem-based approach to learning in which trainees are confronted with a challenge or dilemma and have to seek out answers and apply them. When problem-based learning is related to authentic ministry issues, biblical insights can be explored and tested to try and understand their practical application to real-life problems. This lends motivation and urgency to biblical study, along with an expectation that the Holy Spirit will provide insight and maybe directly intervene to bring resolution. This affirms that the "Word of God is alive and powerful" (Heb 4:12) and builds faith in God's power to act on situations in the future.

INTEGRATE THE TRAINING PROCESS WITH LIFE

Clues about the process of training can also be found in how Israelite parents were meant to train their children. Their training was informal, holistic, and integrated. Parents would discuss God's commands with their children in all kinds of situations—"when you sit at home and when you walk along the road, when you lie down and when you get up." (Deut 6:7). Training was a continuous activity integrated with the rest of life. And far more than a list of "how tos," it gave children a comprehensive understanding of their identity and purpose as well as how to live for God. [149] This side of the Cross and Pentecost, the Holy Spirit lives in believers and is continually teaching us and guiding us into all truth, making us more like Jesus and producing the fruit of the Spirit in us (John 14:16–17; 1 John 2:27; Gal 5:22). His teaching of us is integrated with life, just as all training should be.

DEVELOP IN TRAINEES A HABIT OF LIFELONG LEARNING

God drove the lessons of the past home in a concrete and highly memorable way by instituting ceremonies for his people to remember and reflect on God

---

148. Ibid., 243.

149. cf. Walter Brueggemann, *Theology of the Old Testament: Testimony, Dispute, Advocacy* (Minneapolis, MN: Fortress Press, 1997), 682–83.

and what he had done for them. As the Israelites went to the various festivals in Jerusalem, made sacrifices, brought some of their harvest, and made shelters, children would ask their parents what they were doing. In response, parents would tell them the foundational stories that provided reasons for what they were doing or seeing. When a child asked why they were sacrificing a firstborn lamb at Passover, for example, their parents would explain the story of Pharaoh and how God killed every Egyptian firstborn but spared every Israelite firstborn (Ex 13:14–16). When children asked their parents about the pile of stones at Gilgal, they would hear about the power of God in the stories of how God dried up the Jordan and the Red Sea (Josh 4:21–24).

This process ensured not only that the stories of what God had done were passed on from generation to generation, but also that his people were continually reflecting on what God had done and was continuing to do in their lives and applying these insights to their current circumstances. Learning about God's ways and their meaning for contemporary life was therefore developed as a habit that continued throughout the lifespan and through the generations of God's people.

In the same way, missionaries should be reflective practitioners who continue to learn and apply what they learn in each context and moment of their lives. A missionary training community can also model this by having regular times for the community to formally reflect on and review their personal, communal, and ministry growth and practice. Regular formal events such as graduations can provide opportunities to create meaningful ceremonies with the purpose of helping trainers and continuing trainees, as well as graduating trainees, remember and reflect on God and what he has done for them, and the purpose of the training.

MAKE TRAINING REPRODUCIBLE

A focus on passing on what trainees have learned to oncoming generations was a key feature of both Jesus' and Paul's training of others. Jesus' last command to his own disciples was to make more disciples and to teach them to obey everything he had commanded them. This meant that the second generation of disciples would be taught to obey the command to make disciples by making yet more disciples (Matt 28:18–19). Paul similarly expected his trainees to pass on what they had learned to others (2 Tim 2:2). He did not limit his thinking to only the first generation of trainees, but told Timothy to pass on everything he had learned to the next generation, the next link in the chain, and envisaged the next link after that by requiring that the men Timothy passed things on to had to be able to teach others.

In the same way, missionary training should be reproducible. In order to fulfill the Great Commission, training missionaries to take the gospel beyond the boundaries of each people group is part of making disciples of all nations. When training missionaries, care should be taken to ensure that a reproducing ethos is built into the training and that missionaries are empowered to train new missionaries wherever they go.

IMPLICATIONS FOR TRAINING MISSIONARIES

The overwhelming priority of training according to the Bible is developing the trainee's character to become more like Jesus. The character of trainees is formed primarily through trainees emulating living models and this means that trainees should spend significant blocks of time with trainers as they together engage in ministry. Trainees need to have biblical knowledge, but the purpose of this knowledge is to apply it to life. Theology should therefore be discussed and developed in the context of and in connection to real-life issues as they come up in the course of life.

Another striking feature of training in the Bible is that it most often occurs in the context of a community. Trainees are shaped by and developed through communal interactions and the community itself develops as the members grow. The community is inclusive. The membership can be quite fluid, changing as various learners move in and out according to their questions, needs, and opportunity to engage. In contrast to many community training models being employed today, the context of the community is not static as the group should be flexible enough to move around according to the ministry of the trainer. The tasks of the trainees are determined by active ministry demands and vary according to what the group encounters. This is certainly a more authentic way of developing the flexibility needed for missionary life.

Although some churches may be able to test potential missionaries' suitability for and call to cross-cultural ministry, many will need to do this in partnership with mission agencies who have the cross-cultural expertise to assess the candidate's readiness. Some churches, and most mission agencies, will also ask the candidate to undergo psychological testing to identify areas of vulnerability which might cause problems under the isolation and stress of cross-cultural ministry. Where there are experienced missionaries in the congregation and the context of the church includes people from other cultures, churches are better able to play a greater role in the selection of their own missionaries. Much of the testing of suitability for cross-cultural ministry consists of exposing aspiring missionaries to the demands of cross-cultural ministry and helping them assess whether they feel called and suited to this type of ministry.

Training that is offered in a cross-cultural context enables the trainees to encounter unfamiliar questions, derive responses and test them in authentic ministry. This process is more robust when a group of trainees learn together as they can discuss the issues, debrief their experiences and develop responses in a way that involves a "dialectical interaction between the Christian faith and the current experience of the community."[150]

It is quite possible, though, to be in a cross-cultural context and to be surrounded by living examples and yet not grow in maturity. Growth requires active engagement and reflection on the part of the learner. The kings of Israel were expected to read God's word, meditate on it, apply it in daily practice, and respond to feedback from their advisors and the prophets. They were expected to consistently attribute honor to God and give him the worship he is due. They were also expected to follow the example of godly kings who lived before them. When they failed, they were expected to repent and make restitution to injured parties. In the same way, missionaries grow in maturity by reading God's word, meditating on it, applying it daily, interacting with people who advise and challenge them, honoring God in all circumstances, following the example of more experienced missionaries and local believers (who are the best examples of contextualized faith in the context), and being quick to repent and be reconciled with others.

---

150. Conde-Frazier, Kang, and Parrett, *A Many Colored Kingdom: Multicultural Dynamics for Spiritual Formation*, 86.

STEPS IN DESIGNING MISSIONARY TRAINING

Designing an effective training program involves a number of steps. This chapter explains seven key steps that trainers need to work through in the process of designing effective training for missionaries. These same steps can also be used to help current missionary trainers evaluate existing programs in order to improve their effectiveness. These steps are:

- Consult with stakeholders
- Define the learning outcomes
- Determine how you will know whether the learning outcomes have been achieved
- Create the learning environment
- Design the learning experiences
- Design meaningful ways to evaluate the training
- Implement the training as a reflective learning spiral

CONSULT WITH STAKEHOLDERS

Christians who are involved in supporting, sending, and receiving missionaries are the key stakeholders of missionary training programs. Stakeholders of missionary training programs therefore typically include church leaders, mission agency personnel, currently serving missionaries, and ideally, local Christian leaders in the areas that missionaries serve. Church and mission agency leaders should always be included in the process of defining the outcomes of training, and local Christian leaders from the areas missionaries serve should be included if at all possible. The aim of the process of consulting stakeholders is to be able to write a job description for, or profile of, an ideal graduate of the program.[151]

---

151. Useful resources to aid in the process of stakeholder consultation are: Ferris, *Establishing Ministry Training: A Manual for Program Developers*; Lewis, "Stakeholder Assumptions and Consensus Building"; "The Outcomes Profiling Process."

Starting with a profile of an effective missionary helps to avoid the common problem of overemphasizing knowledge at the expense of character and ministry skills. It also helps the designers and implementers of the training to address and manage any competing agendas different stakeholders may have. In well-designed programs, the competing agendas will have been worked through in the stakeholder consultation process, and the profile will represent a balanced fulfillment of all parties' needs.

DEFINE THE LEARNING OUTCOMES

The first question that should be asked of any training program is, "What is the purpose of the learning?" Explicitly defining learning outcomes is a crucial step in designing training because they determine the shape of everything else in the program. In the light of these outcomes, trainers will work out how to assess learning, create an appropriate learning environment, determine what training methods to use, and find ways of evaluating the program. Too often, the learning outcomes of training programs are defined after the program has already been set up and simply perpetuate whatever the program is already doing rather than shaping the whole program and increasing the ministry effectiveness of graduates.

Another advantage of clearly defining outcomes is that it helps to avoid the creation of unintended training outcomes. A poignant example of this is provided by Paul Gupta and Sherwood Lingenfelter in their book *Breaking Tradition to Accomplish Vision*. They describe how a Bible college in India that had been founded to train people for ministry reviewed where its graduates were going after the training. They found that none of them were becoming the evangelists, church planters, missionaries, or pastors they had hoped to train. Instead, nearly all went on to do some kind of further study, and very few ended up in full-time ministry of any sort. Deeply disappointed, the board of the college together with the new principal, shaped a new program around much more clearly defined objectives. This eventuated in thousands of church planters and other ministers of the gospel being trained and going out into ministry.[152]

---

152. Paul R. Gupta and Sherwood G. Lingenfelter, *Breaking Tradition to Accomplish Vision: Training Leaders for a Church-Planting Movement: A Case from India* (Winona Lake, IN: BMH Books).

A graduate of a missionary training program who has achieved its learning outcomes should be competent to the level defined by the outcomes. Pre-field training programs should define competence for those who are starting on their missionary journey. If graduates have proven that they are competent, stakeholders can be confident in supporting and sending them to the ends of the earth. This is helpful to offset the assumption that a specific period of learning before departing for the field is sufficient for a lifetime of missionary service. By defining competency at different stages of a missionary's life, training can be designed and delivered when needed, according to specific ministry challenges. For example, the new missionary just setting out for the field should be competent to begin studying language and culture. Once missionaries have learned the language and started ministry, they need to be competent in contextualization and cross-cultural discipleship. Competency profiles can be prepared by stakeholders according to what is needed for specific types of ministry.

The word *competency* is used as a technical term in designing educational programs to define the things stakeholders consider a competent person embodies. In training that is designed around competencies (competency-based training), in order for trainees to be assessed, learning outcomes must be clearly articulated as things that can be observed. Outcomes and assessments are therefore transparent in the sense that trainees are told exactly what trainers are expecting them to be able to do, be, and know. Subjective feedback may be given during the training program, but the grading of trainees is not based on this.

Competencies describe attitudes, skills, or knowledge. The *elements* of a competency outline the essential steps involved in performing each competency. Trainees are graded simply according to whether or not they can fulfill the performance criteria that make up each element of competency. These criteria detail what competent performance looks like in a particular area. Table 3 describes the meaning of each of these words and phrases that are used in competency-based training in terms of what the trainee or assessor must do. Table 4 illustrates these using the specific example of the competency "(Trainees) respond appropriately to a given range of cross-cultural experiences."

How well trainees fulfill *performance criteria* is not the focus of this kind of training. A trainee is either competent, or not competent, and if they are not competent, further training is given until they become competent. Personal encouragement and feedback can be used to promote excellence, but grading relates to fitness for the task rather than as a way to compare trainees. In this kind of training, it does not matter how long it takes trainees to learn to perform the criteria, nor how many times they try to achieve competency in them. For this reason, defining *performance criteria* is critical. Extra information specific to each context where training can occur is provided in the *range statement*.

Competency	The trainee demonstrates that he or she is able to do this.
Element Of Competency	The trainee shows that he or she is competent by demonstrating that he or she can do this.
Performance Criteria	The assessor determines that the trainee is competent by observing the trainee do this.
Range Statement	This defines the context and specific aspects of each performance criteria that must be fulfilled during the time that the trainee is being observed.

Table 3 Describing aspects of competency

COMPETENCY	
Respond appropriately to a given range of different cross-cultural experiences	
Element	Performance Criteria
1 Act respectfully towards speakers of other languages	• Listen without demanding translation in contexts where another language is spoken
	• Learn and use basic greetings and phrases in another language with native speakers of that language
2 Behave appropriately in different cultural contexts	• Eat unfamiliar food from another culture
	• Visit a home without causing offense
	• Wear appropriate dress with respect to gender roles and expectations
	• Behave appropriately with respect to gender roles and expectations
3 Explain another religion with respect	• Visit a mosque, temple, shrine, or other religious construction and sensitively and respectfully elicit an explanation of its function and purpose from a person who worships there
	• Respectfully give an explanation of a non-Christian religion received from an adherent of that religion
4 Develop appreciation for styles of creativity and communication which are different from the trainee's own culture	• Respectfully explain a sample of the visual arts from another culture
	• Respectfully explain an example of the performing arts from another culture

COMPETENCY	
Respond appropriately to a given range of different cross-cultural experiences	
Element	Performance Criteria

RANGE STATEMENT

Native speakers of that language are speakers of the language who have spoken that language since their early childhood.

Unfamiliar food from another culture is food prepared and served by a member of that culture and which the trainee has not previously experienced.

A home is visited without causing offense. This means without causing offense to the occupants and other visitors in the home at the time of the visit or acting or speaking offensively about the visit afterwards.

Appropriate dress is worn with respect to gender roles and expectations. In this performance criterion, the guide for appropriateness is the standards of the cultures being interacted with rather than the standards of the culture of the trainee.

Behavior is appropriate with respect to gender roles and expectations. In this performance criterion, the guide for appropriateness is the standards of the cultures being interacted with rather than the standards of the culture of the trainee.

Table 4 An example of a technical definition of a competency

There are several key differences between competency-based learning design and a knowledge-transmission model.[153] A competency-based approach is more flexible. As the key focus is on the fact that competency is attained rather than how it is attained, the training can occur anywhere and in any way that promotes developing competence. This also means that learners who come into a training program with some existing competencies can demonstrate that they already have these rather than having to participate in training for things they can already do. In addition, trainees are encouraged to help their peers achieve competence since competency-based training is non-competitive in its ethos. In fact, through helping others, trainees develop their own skills and understanding. In this way, competency-based training lends itself to communal learning situations. This kind of cooperation in learning also fosters the concurrent development of interpersonal skills.

Another difference between a competency-based training approach and traditional knowledge-focused learning approaches is the rigor with which

---

153. J. Allen Thompson, "Training Church Planters: A Competency-Based Learning Model," in *With an Eye on the Future: Development and Mission in the 21st Century: Essays in Honor of Ted W. Ward*, ed. Ted Warren Ward, et al. (Monrovia, CA: MARC, 1996).

assessment is designed to be transparent and measurable.[154] For example, if one of the outcomes of the training is that graduates are humble, competency-based trainers ask, "How can the assessors know that a person is humble? What concrete evidence of humility would we expect to see in his or her life and ministry?" Traditionally, judgments about character qualities like humility are based on subjective assessments by people who may or may not know the student well. It is not unusual for individual students to receive subjective judgments from different trainers that contradict each other. Competency-based training defines who is qualified to make the judgment, the context in which it can be made, and what, exactly, should be observed. The process is transparent in that the criteria are clear to the trainee as well as the assessor.

3. DETERMINE WAYS OF ASSESSING LEARNING

Every training program needs to work out whether trainees learn what they are supposed to—that is, whether they achieve the learning outcomes of the program. Too often, trainers use particular methods of assessment simply because that is what they themselves experienced when they were being trained. Assessment should always serve to encourage further learning. Sadly, the overused written test more often discourages adult learners than encourages them and so should be used sparingly and with caution. Good learning design begins with learning outcomes, determines how they are assessed, and then crafts the learning context and experiences around the assessments.

There are two main types of assessment: summative and formative. Written exams and driving tests are each examples of summative assessment. Students' performance determines whether or not they can proceed to a higher grade, achieve a particular job or status, or are deemed safe to practice a particular skill such as driving a car.

Summative assessment does not do much to help people learn because its focus is on telling the trainee that they have or have not done well enough. It does not, however, usually specify what the trainee needs to do to be able to perform better. In contrast, formative assessment focuses on providing feedback that helps students improve. Its aim is to help students learn.

---

154. Some good general examples of competencies and performance criteria, as well as a simple explanation of competency-based assessment can be found at http://www.batchelor.edu.au/biite/wp-content/uploads/2012/06/CBT-Overview.pdf

Philip Crooks provides a good summary of the challenges associated with using formative assessment.

Formative assessment is generally more demanding for a trainer than summative assessment because it first requires the trainer to articulate what excellence is, identify specific components that define what excellence entails and how it is achieved, and then communicate these clearly to the trainee. If a trainee does not perform well, the trainer needs to be able to articulate the specific steps the trainee needs to take in order to improve performance.[155]

Summative assessment should be used sparingly. One situation it is well suited for is as a filter for selection into a training program. If, for example, the graduate profile requires graduates to be able to share the gospel effectively with people they do not know, but the training program does not help trainees engage with strangers or share the gospel with them, it would be better to set this criterion as a pre-selection test. This would also help to allay false expectations of the training program and clarify exactly what it does offer.

As selection tests, like all summative tests, involve high stakes for participants, it is very important that the nature of the test, where and who administers it and the qualifications of the assessors are clear and transparent. This is even more important in intercultural contexts where trainers and trainees are from different cultural backgrounds as assessors' ethnocentric assumptions may inadvertently prejudice them. An example of this would be a white Australian conservative evangelical who fails a Gypsy (Roma) Christian on the basis of not giving a linear, three point sermon based on a propositional statement, when the most effective form of preaching in the Roma Christian's context is a narrative style mirroring local Roma story rhetorical constructions.

Assessment is often colored by competitive overtones. Many education systems are highly individualistic and pit students against each other along hierarchies of achievement. Trying to encourage group work in settings where learners are used to individual assessment can be very difficult because students have been trained by experience that their individual performance and therefore results will be strongly affected by the composition of the group and the engagement of each member. Learning for Christian ministry, though, is for the common good and should therefore reinforce and reward collaboration.

In Western college systems, trainers often find it very difficult to set group assessment tasks. Students resist these because they are very aware that their

---

155. Philip Crooks, personal email, 24th February, 2015.

individual marks are affected by the amount of effort contributed by each group member. They rarely feel any responsibility for others' learning and resent others receiving good marks based on another person's work. Western assessment moderation systems also usually resist the same marks being awarded to all members of a group, insisting that marks be distinguished between individuals.

In group cultural contexts, it is often the individualistic trainer who has a problem. The group can be so committed to each member doing as well as possible that they will actively support weaker and lazier members and protest against the trainer who presumes to differentiate marks according to individual effort. For us this became very evident during an exam when one student copied from another, and we wanted to penalize the person who "cheated." From the group's perspective, we were being unreasonable, as they wanted the person who "cheated" to benefit from the others' work and could not bear the thought that one member's progress might be delayed while the rest of the group moved on.

Another important characteristic of assessment is its authenticity—how closely the assessment task resembles what graduates will do in their place of work or ministry. Assessment should be as authentic as possible from as early in a training program as is feasible. This helps training programs to avoid teaching content as abstract knowledge blocks unrelated to outside life. For example, if students are studying world religions and the purpose is to help students interact well and share the gospel with people from other religious backgrounds, students should spend time speaking with people from other religious backgrounds and be assessed on the quality of their interaction with them. If trainees are learning about counseling, a semi-authentic assessment would be to role play a counseling scenario and an authentic assessment would be to counsel someone in need.

Assessment should be designed in such a way that it is valid and reliable. Validity refers to whether or not the assessment is measuring what it is supposed to be measuring. For example, a student may know the gospel well and be able to give a good testimony in an informal conversation with a peer who is not threatening. When the same student is required to write an essay about the gospel, however, he or she may fail because of poor writing skills. If the purpose of the assessment was to determine whether or not the student knows the gospel, the written essay was not a valid assessment as it actually assessed the student's writing skills rather than his or her knowledge of the gospel.

In the same way, the ability to write a good essay about teamwork would not be a valid way of assessing a trainee's ability to work in a team.

A reliable assessment is one which, when taken by the same set of students but in different contexts and assessed by different assessors, returns the same results consistently. Reliability is strongly affected by the context. Trainers often unconsciously assume reliability in different contexts when it is not appropriate. This is particularly the case when assessments designed in one context are applied uncritically in other contexts, especially different socioeconomic and cultural contexts. Assessments often have implicit cultural assumptions built into their design. As a result, an assessment that is reliable when used by two trainers from a similar cultural background can be unreliable when trainers from different backgrounds administer it. A classic example of this is intelligence testing. Most intelligence tests assume the sociocultural and literacy training which are common among white, middle-class, educated families. When the same tests are used with children from different backgrounds they may not perform as well even if they are more "intelligent" than their white, middle-class peers.

In missionary training, an assessment of a trainee's ability to relate to people from other cultures performed by a trainer observing the interaction may be unreliable if the assessors or trainees are from different cultures. For example, if the trainee and the assessor are both from individualistic, task-focused cultures, the trainee who spends ten minutes with a local person from another culture and only discusses a list of jobs to be done might be assessed as having interacted well with the local person. However, an assessor from a collectivist, people-oriented culture might consider the trainee as having been "cold" and be appalled that the trainee did not first ask about the health and well-being of the person's family and spend at least an hour with the local person, including sharing a drink or meal together.[156] In order to increase the reliability of assessments, all the possible variables need to be defined or controlled.

In the context of designing missionary training it can be useful to ask the following questions about assessments:

---

156. This type of intercultural misunderstanding is common and is described as occurring between "hot" and "cold" cultures by Lanier and poignantly portrayed between bride and groom's parents in the film, "My Big Fat Greek Wedding." Lanier, *Foreign to Familiar: A Guide to Understanding Hot- and Cold-Climate Cultures*; *My Big Fat Greek Wedding*, directed by Joel Zwick (New York: HBO Home Video, 2001), DVD.

- Are exams and tests necessary? Why? Could they be replaced by formative assessment tasks?
- Are written assessments necessary? What are they assessing? Are there more authentic forms of assessment that could be used instead?
- Why give grades and what do they mean?
- Why have time frames on assessment tasks?
- Do your program's assessment tasks communicate any para-messages to the trainees? Is there an implicit curriculum in association with assessments? If so, and it is intentional, could you make it explicit?
- Can you articulate the specific steps involved in producing an excellent result for each assessment?

Sometimes teachers and students get so focused on assessments that it seems as if nothing else matters. A by-product of making assessment expectations more explicit is that it sometimes seems as if anything else that is covered in a course is superfluous. This can be offset by careful attention to assessment design and integration of assessment components with course content and delivery methods. The more time-poor adult students are, and the more they are focused on receiving the certificate rather than learning for its own sake, the more assessment can unhealthily and unhelpfully dominate learning. Trainers are responsible to engage students beyond wanting to get their certificate or degree. Both training institutions and trainers should reflect on the purpose of their training and whether what they are offering embodies that purpose. If, on reflection, they are convinced that their training really does help to achieve their purpose, the next step is to examine the processes of learning and the implicit curriculum.

4. CREATE THE LEARNING ENVIRONMENT

Training does not occur in a vacuum. People are affected by the physical environment of the training. The nature of that environment will communicate different things to trainees based partly on their past experiences. Learning contexts that resemble what trainees experienced in schools will evoke the feelings and expectations associated with school. Learning environments that resemble homes are more likely to evoke the feelings and expectations of home. The physical setting provides cues for how people should behave.

The physical environment includes not only the classroom but also the whole context in which the classroom is situated. Even the relative placement of teachers, peers, and objects will affect the learning dynamic, as will the various aids and resources that are used during the learning activities. Before any specific learning activities are designed, the overall configuration and meanings of the learning environment and how they relate to the learning outcomes should be carefully thought through.

The learning environment for missionary trainees should include significant exposure to cross-cultural ministry as part of their training. As much of their training as possible should be done in contexts where they have to relate to people from other cultures. This should go beyond having students from different cultural backgrounds in the classroom to include experiences of relating to other people outside the classroom from different cultures. Exposure to cross-cultural ministry grounds the training in the realities and challenges of cross-cultural interaction and enables trainees to develop competence and confidence in relating to people from cultures different to their own. Engaging in supervised ministry with people with different worldviews can also help trainees to recognize their own ethnocentrism and to develop skills in communicating their faith to followers of different religions.

A Positive Learning Environment

A positive learning environment helps learners learn. Positive emotions are facilitated by physical comfort, good relationships, respect, safety, and success. An increasing amount of research is being conducted on the relationship between emotional climates of learning and the way this affects students' motivation and ability to engage with learning. It is clear that where students feel respected, included, and safe, they are happier and both students and teachers feel more confident.[157]

Relating to people from different cultures can make trainees feel quite anxious, especially where their prejudices make them feel threatened.[158] Trainers

---

157. Sue Roffey, *Positive Relationships: Evidence Based Practice across the World* (London: Springer, 2012).

158. This is emphasized and helpfully explained in detail in William B. Gudykunst, "Managing Anxiety and Uncertainty," in *Bridging Differences: Effective Intergroup*

therefore have to work hard to support the trainees through their anxiety and debrief their experiences. Trainees may also be anxious about the learning process as a result of negative past experiences of learning. If, for example, school was a place of anxiety due to poor performance in tests or a history of being bullied, these feelings will be transferred to the adult learning situation. The teacher therefore needs to manage the students' feelings as part of the process of teaching. Building a positive learning environment means generating positive feelings in association with learning. This needs to be done intentionally by attending to both the physical and the emotional environment, as well as the spiritual and intellectual well-being of each student. In most cases this will involve actively looking for opportunities to encourage trainees and affirm their strengths. Creating a positive learning environment will not only benefit the current learning but will foster positive feelings towards future learning.[159]

The curriculum of a training program includes both the planned and unplanned experiences that learners interact with in the program. This goes far beyond what teachers say in classes to include all the informal interactions between teachers and learners and among learners, the physical context of the training program, practical and ministry tasks and responsibilities given to students, and written and unwritten rules. In many cases, there is a written, or explicit, curriculum and a hidden or implicit curriculum. The implicit curriculum is conveyed in the way things are done, the messages given by leaders and the stories that are created and perpetuated by the trainers and trainees. In a positive, healthy learning environment the implicit curriculum closely matches the explicit curriculum. In more open and transparent training environments, trainers can freely disagree with each other, conflict is not hidden, negative experiences are worked through collectively rather than ignored or hidden, and feedback from trainees is actively sought and valued.

A Communal Learning Environment

Learning in a community with experienced missionaries who are still involved in ministry and continuing to read, reflect, and apply what they are learning is

---

Communication (London: Sage Publications, 2004), 18–35.

159. For a good overview of the relationship between emotion and learning in adults read the chapter by John M. Dirkx, "The Meaning and Role of Emotions in Adult Learning," in *The Jossey-Bass Reader on Contemporary Issues in Adult Education*, ed. Sharan B. Merriam and Andrâe P. Grace (San Francisco, CA: Jossey-Bass, 2011).

a particularly powerful approach to missionary training. Not only do trainees have the opportunity to engage with real-life ministry issues, they also benefit from the role modeling of missionaries who are continuing to learn.[160]

Communal learning is a specific approach to learning in which all members of the community are actively learning and committed to helping each other learn. Communities do not just happen because people are grouped together; they need to be intentionally developed around a common purpose or identity. In a learning community, the resources and experience that each member brings to the group is recognized and valued. This orientation is one of the best ways to overcome the insidious effect of competitiveness that is inherent in many Western educational structures. A communal learning ethos means that novice learners are appreciated and respected as much as advanced learners, and the skills of the advanced learners are utilized for everyone's learning. In contrast with the competitive ethos of Western individualistic learning, this approach accords more closely with collectivist values that consider resources, including individual personal resources, as existing for the common good.

The more diverse the backgrounds of the members of the learning community, the richer the potential is for learning due to the greater diversity of perspectives on the issues being examined. But with this diversity comes the need for trainers to support, encourage, and provide as safe a learning environment as possible so that learners can ask questions and talk about the things that are puzzling or troubling them.

Jack Mezirow, a highly influential educational thinker, described learning as a process of relating what is being learned to an internal meaning framework. He proposed that when learners encounter ideas that do not fit into their existing framework, they are quick to reject them. If the ideas are too similar, they may not engage with them because they consider they already know them. He suggested that learning is often triggered by a disorienting dilemma that requires the learner to search for a new way of seeing the problem. The process of being confronted by such dilemmas, having to give up old ways of thinking and integrate new ideas into their meaning frameworks is uncomfortable and challenging. In order to support learners through this process of learning, it is important to provide a safe social network in the form of a learning

---

160. Hibbert and Hibbert, "Nurturing Missionary Learning Communities."

community.[161] When the community is healthy, people feel safe to take risks, ask questions, and experiment with new ways of doing things as members feel accepted and respected as they are. The group is also able to debrief difficult experiences and engage with failures as learning opportunities that everyone can learn from.

Mezirow's widely embraced theory of learning implies that we should increase group learning in our training programs. In communal learning situations that are comfortable for participants, multiple perspectives on issues can help people to critically evaluate their assumptions, adjust their way of thinking, and develop their meaning frames. Group members draw each other into learning things that they could not have achieved on their own.

Being a trainer in a communal learning context requires different skills than being a traditional lecturer or teacher. Parker Palmer describes learning as having the subject rather than the teacher or the students at the center of the learning process. Putting the subject at the center means that both teachers and students are held accountable to the subject rather than their arbitrary desires or biased perspectives. The task of the teacher is to let the subject—in this case the Bible and the insights of missiology—speak for itself.[162] In a community of learners where the subject is at the center, the trainer's role is primarily as a facilitator of learning rather than a director of activities. The trainer must begin by intentionally working on developing relationships within the community and developing a clear sense of group identity and belonging.

Techniques for promoting communal learning focus on enabling each member to participate freely in the group, supporting those who are more timid, modeling mutual respect, creating opportunities for equal participation, and helping members discover and share insights rather than having them presented by the teacher. This kind of learning is less under the control of the trainer. Trainers will have to let go of the need to control and be ready to gently steer the group towards the learning outcomes, appreciating that some of the diversions on the journey to the learning outcomes may end up being the most

---

161. Jack Mezirow, "Learning to Think Like an Adult: Core Concepts of Transformation Theory," in *Learning as Transformation: Critical Perspectives on a Theory in Progress*, ed. Jack Mezirow (San Francisco, CA: Jossey-Bass, 2000).

162. Parker J. Palmer, "Teaching in Community: A Subject-Centered Education," in *The Courage to Teach: Exploring the Inner Landscape of a Teacher's Life* (San Francisco, CA: Jossey-Bass, 1998).

important lessons the group engages with. At the same time, the trainer also needs group management skills, including being able to help the members of the group resolve conflict.[163]

Another important aspect of the learning environment is the degree to which it is accessible to learners and flexible so that it can change with learner needs and situational demands.[164] A flexible and accessible training program will allow as many suitable trainees as possible to access the training. It will therefore consider using a variety of possible delivery options such as intensives, night classes, part-time training, short-term blocks of training interspersed with time on the field, mentoring and coaching in ministry, and online learning as potential components of the training program. Instead of thinking primarily of delivery modes that are the most convenient for trainers and the training institution, a flexible, accessible approach will think through what will most help potential missionaries be trained.

In all learning design it is important not only to think about maximum flexibility and accessibility but to keep the purpose of the learning at the forefront. Learning outcomes that are focused on interpersonal skills, for example, cannot be achieved primarily through online means. We must use all the resources that the modern world offers, but use them critically, evaluating whether they achieve the intended outcome in relation to actual ministry practice.

5. DESIGN THE LEARNING EXPERIENCES

Once outcomes and ways of assessing them have been defined, the next step in designing training for missionaries is to choose the most helpful methods of training. To do this, trainers need to understand the characteristics of adult learners, cater for various different individual and cultural learning styles, and choose the best methods for achieving each outcome.

---

163. For those who are interested in reading more about communal approaches to learning in Western education, we recommend reading about communities of practice: Etienne Wenger-Trayner and Beverly Wenger-Trayner, "Communities of Practice: A Brief Introduction," http://wenger-trayner.com/theory/; Etienne Wenger, *Communities of Practice: Learning, Meaning, and Identity*, Learning in Doing (New York, NY: Cambridge University Press, 1998).

164. Elliston and Kauffman, *Developing Leaders for Urban Ministries*, 150, 59–60, 69.

Understand Adult Learners

Sometimes people forget that life involves continual learning and act as though learning stops at the end of childhood and their time in school. When this happens, people think of learning mainly in terms of school classrooms, the teaching methods used in them, and the feelings they experienced when they were in school. But there are major differences between children's schooling and how adults learn.

Children, in most contexts of the world, have no choice about having to go to school and very little choice about what they learn. They are not responsible for the outcomes of the schooling process. Instead, teachers and governments set these and bear the responsibility for their fulfillment. Children have relatively few responsibilities during school hours and outside them. They do not generally question their teacher's right or qualifications to teach them. Their lack of experience of life and minimal familiarity with academic discourses make it easy to perceive children as empty vessels waiting to be filled up, or dormant machines waiting to be prepared for work. Life is ahead of them, and children are usually open to being directed by others about what they should do.

In contrast to children, adults have life experience and multiple responsibilities. They have proven themselves through various culturally prescribed rites of passage and expect to be respected for what they have achieved. They have acquired a level of maturity and skills through negotiating each stage of life, such as finding a life partner, raising children, finding meaningful work, and managing conflict. Adults have also developed an advanced understanding of the world around them.

Because of their prior experience and the skills, maturity, and understanding that they have developed through them, adults are able to identify many of their own learning needs and are capable of directing themselves to fulfill those needs. Given a choice, they intentionally avoid engaging in activities that they do not think will be useful to them. This is particularly the case because most adults are time-poor and therefore have to prioritize what they give their attention to. Adults also expect their teachers to be more expert than they are. They expect their teachers to not only have appropriate certification but also to have credible experience in what they are teaching others to do.

Many teaching and training programs that are aimed at adults (including missionary training programs) unhelpfully replicate the approaches used in children's schooling. Both education providers and adult learners contribute to this problem, as adults embarking on training programs tend to hand over responsibility for their learning to their teachers.

The principles of adult learning or andragogy have changed very little since they were first promoted by Malcolm Knowles in the 1970s. Knowles' major insight was that adults differ from children in their approach to learning and that this difference should be taken into account when planning education for adults. He stressed five key aspects of adults as learners. He proposed that adults: (1) need to know why they are learning something before they start to learn it; (2) naturally feel responsible for their own learning and want to have a say in how they learn; (3) have a rich background of life experience that should be recognized as a resource for their learning by teachers; (4) become ready to learn something new when they face a real-life situation needing new skills, insights, or attitudes; and (5) are motivated to learn when they perceive the learning as relevant and practical, enabling them to perform tasks or deal with problems they face.[165]

Many education and training programs still use methods of teaching that fail to take into account these characteristics of adult learners. Designing missionary training that is clearly practical and relevant to the tasks missionaries face, that builds on previous life and ministry experience, and helps trainees take responsibility for their learning will make the learning experience much more beneficial to potential missionaries and contribute to them being more effective in the field.

Training institutions sometimes respond to adult learners taking responsibility for their own learning with punitive measures rather than addressing the underlying issues. For example, when students do not attend lectures or tutorials because they find them unhelpful, some institutions respond by making them compulsory for passing the course. This does not help students to engage with learning nor address why students do not attend. It can also cause students to disengage or even drop out. It would be much better to talk with students about how to make the course more useful and relevant.

Adults have a wealth of life experience that they bring with them to their training. This means that they have a great deal to contribute to any learning experience they engage in. Additionally, adults expect to be treated like adults

---

165. Malcolm S. Knowles, in *The Adult Learner: A Neglected Species* (Houston, TX: Gulf Publishing, 1990), 54–65, 77–87; For a succinct overview of Knowles' key ideas, see http://www.learningandteaching.info/learning/knowlesa.htm

and have their experience respected. The non-recognition of students' experience has recently been noted as a significant problem in Australian theological education.[166] Not only would including participants' experience in class discussions increase the relevance of course content, it would also help to keep the content grounded in real life. Sometimes there will be content areas that students are more expert in than the trainer. It is wise, and less work for the trainer, to hand over these areas to the students to teach. This approach will model the respect that every missionary should have for people with different backgrounds than themselves.

Adults are usually also busy with work and providing for their families. They choose to do further training often at considerable personal cost. Because of the cost of learning both in time and money they often feel they do not have time to waste on non-essentials. They find it difficult to engage with material or activities that they do not see as being directly related to the purpose for which they are studying. Trainers should therefore constantly be helping trainees to see the connections between what they are learning and its purpose. If a learning activity does not have a clear connection to why adults are learning, trainers should seriously question its inclusion.

Adults are able to manage their lives. They have jobs, families, children, mortgages, homes, bills—multiple responsibilities. There is no reason for them to revert to being children when they take on the role of student except for their prior conditioning in school. Adults are more motivated when they have control over their own learning and are used to learning how to manage multiple, often conflicting, demands. As they are juggling so many priorities, they will tend to choose those activities that they perceive as meaningful or which they consider to be more interesting or enjoyable. It is good practice, therefore, to give adults choice about what and how they learn so that trainer and trainee can be working together to maximize trainee engagement and motivation.

When designing education for adults, it is important to find out why potential students want the training being offered. The high status associated with being awarded a certificate or degree ensures that some people will pursue them regardless of the nature of the learning involved. Many teachers complain that adult students pursue pieces of paper—certificates—with little regard for the content being "taught." In practice, these adult students are clearly

---

166. Ball, *Transforming Theology: Student Experience and Transformative Learning in Undergraduate Theological Education.*

demonstrating that they value the certificate in terms of what it will offer them in life, however they can see little benefit in what is being "taught" in order to obtain the certificate. The students' perspective is very legitimate and should alert the trainers to the need to discuss with the students whether it is possible to make the learning experiences on the way to the certificate more relevant.

A final characteristic of adults is that they are accomplished learners, as attested to by their having negotiated many of life's challenges. But many feel inadequate in formal learning contexts. Their feelings of inadequacy are often reinforced when they receive low grades on academic papers. Academic writing and thinking is a specific skill set which has many valuable aspects, but it is not the only, or even the most important skill set that people wanting to work in cross-cultural ministry situations need to master. Feeling inadequate exacerbates adults' feelings of helplessness in training situations and can lead to them wanting trainers to assume the primary responsibility for how much they learn. If the trainer is aware of these feelings of inadequacy and adopts more appropriate methods of teaching that draw on the strengths adult learners bring to their learning, trainees will not only learn more but also engage more in the learning experience.

Adjust for Different Learning Preferences

The concept of individual learning styles developed as a response to research done by Howard Gardner on multiple intelligences. Gardner identified seven distinct intelligences and suggested that individuals differ in the degree to which they use each one. The impact of Gardner's work on education was to raise awareness that as different individuals process information in different ways they therefore also learn in different ways. This being the case, if learning programs predominantly use just one method of presenting information, this will disadvantage the learners who are not strong in this area. Gardner's seven areas are visual-spatial, bodily-kinesthetic, musical, interpersonal, intrapersonal, linguistic, and logical-mathematical.[167]

Many educators use a simpler approach to understanding learning styles than Gardner's. One model describes just three main learning styles: visual,

---

167. Howard Gardner, *Frames of Mind: The Theory of Multiple Intelligences* (Basic Books, 1993). A brief overview of Gardner's learning styles can be found at infed.org, "Howard Gardner, multiple intelligences, and education," http://infed.org/mobi/howard-gardner-multiple-intelligences-and-education/.

audio, and kinesthetic. Most people can quickly identify themselves as predominantly preferring to learn using one of these three styles. Most training programs overuse the audio style, give some minor concessions to visual style (for example, by using PowerPoint slides), and have virtually no kinesthetic elements. A quick search of the internet generates many websites on learning styles and online surveys that learners can use to explore their own preferences. These websites also offer suggestions about ways of teaching or learning that best suit each style.[168]

The main implication of learning styles is that trainers need to use a variety of methods of instruction in each training session in order to ensure that the needs of all learners are catered for. It can be a good idea for trainers to discuss learning styles with trainees and identify the main learning style of each student so that if a training group has a preponderance of a particular set of learning preferences, the trainer can spend proportionately more time using an approach that suits that learning style. Another technique that can be used to address differing learning styles is to offer multiple options of different learning tasks and assessments so that trainees can choose the activity that they feel best suits their preferences. A further extension of this idea is to use individual or group learning contracts in which the learners can negotiate with the trainer how they will approach the task. This gives the learners control over their learning but also ensures that the learning outcomes are still fulfilled.

Cultural background also affects the way people learn in a number of different ways. Different societal structures result in different attributions of authority, perceptions of wisdom, ways of processing and communicating information and experiences, and views of the roles of teachers and learners. Although outsiders are quick to stereotype the learning of different cultures, each culture has a vested interest in ensuring that its people learn what is important in ways that are valued. The process of learning can be as powerful as or even more important than the content or skill that is transferred. In fact, the attitudes or affective elements of learning are more commonly communicated through the processes of learning than its products.

In multicultural or cross-cultural learning contexts where the trainees and trainers are from different cultural backgrounds, missionary trainers need to

---

168. A brief overview of VAK learning styles with links to self-assessment tools can be found at "Visual, auditory, and kinesthetic (VAK) learning style model," http://www.jcu.edu.au/wiledpack/modules/fsl/JCU_090460.html

be aware of and adjust their training in response to all these aspects of learning and be careful not to stereotype either the students or their ways of learning. Trainees from other cultures will enrich the learning experience if they are allowed to participate in ways in which they feel comfortable, and if they feel safe to contribute. The onus is on the trainer and/or learning designer to learn as much as possible about the cultures involved and to negotiate ways of providing learning experiences that facilitate learning. In some cases, the best way will be to work through mediators or local trainers.

Select Methods Appropriate to Outcomes

The kind of training and teaching methods that are appropriate to each kind of learning outcome differ. Methods that best develop character qualities are different in emphasis than those that develop ministry skills, and those that best develop knowledge are different again. These differences are discussed in this section.

The best approaches to helping someone develop character qualities and attitudes are modeling and mentoring.[169] Trainees preparing for cross-cultural ministry who need to develop in the areas of respect, trust, and openness to those from different backgrounds to themselves, for example, need to observe good role models. They need to see people who embody these qualities interacting with people from other cultures. They also need to relate to people who are very different than themselves and be able to debrief those experiences so they can work through their personal responses. The "working through" is not simply an intellectual exercise but involves identifying emotional responses and learning how to control them.

The principle for learning how to do something is very simple: trainees need to do it. Doing is learned by doing. The medical profession teaches doctors that the process of training in doing is summarized by: see one, do one, teach one. Ideally, trainees should first be shown how to do a particular task by someone who has some expertise in it. After observing others do the task, trainees practice doing it themselves and ideally should be given specific feedback about how well they performed and how to improve. When feedback is not provided it is possible for trainees to develop and perpetuate unhelpful practices. After practicing and feeling confident about performing the task, teaching

---

169. Evan H. Offstein and Ronald L. Dufresne, "Building Strong Ethics and Promoting Positive Character Development: The Influence of HRM at the United States Military Academy at West Point," *Human Resource Management* 46, no. 1 (2007).

someone else how to do it reinforces the learning and often also provides added insight concerning how to do it better.

Sometimes the parts of a more complex task need to be broken down into smaller components and each component modeled and mastered separately before they are tacked together. Some very complex tasks such as interpersonal negotiation or musical performance cannot easily be broken down into their various components. There is an element of "art" or "tacit knowledge" in the task that is developed through observing master performers and receiving their feedback on the trainee's own performance.[170] Master performers develop their skills in increasingly complex areas through having experience in related tasks over long periods of time. This is also true of highly effective missionaries.

When a trainee masters a skill, their learning can be deepened even further if they teach others what they have mastered. This passing on of skills serves to reinforce what has been learned and often helps the trainee understand and develop further nuances of understanding about and skill in the task.

There is a place for practicing interpersonal skills in a safer setting than in real life. This is particularly the case when dealing with issues that may provoke a strong emotional response in the trainee or the person they are interacting with. For these situations, role plays and simulations are helpful. These role plays and simulations must be well-constructed to ensure that the appropriate emotional response is evoked and can then be debriefed. It is not simply about developing scripts and practicing them, nor about providing varied learning experiences.

Emotional responses can be unpredictable and powerful and in order for a missionary trainee to prepare for effective ministry, they need to encounter emotionally difficult situations and be able to manage their personal responses. After practicing in the more controlled setting of a role play, trainees will still need supervision in a real-life setting as their response in a real context may be more than they expect and the needs of the people they are interacting with also need to be cared for. For this reason it is valuable to have a training situation which is removed from where the graduate will eventually work, so that their ministry is not unnecessarily hindered by mistakes made in the novice phase.

---

170. This development of tacit knowledge in professional training is explored by Donald Schön in his book *Reflective Practitioner: How Professionals Think in Action*, new ed. (Aldershot, England: Arena, 1995).

The Brazilian educator Paulo Freire once described the traditional approach to education as "banking."[171] In this paradigm, students come as empty vessels. Information is poured into them and then, it is believed, they will be able to access that information when they need it in the future. This is a common but false assumption of many training programs. Very little of the hundreds of lecture-delivered and textbook knowledge that students hear and see is retained. Research into learning approaches other than lecture has demonstrated that students learn far more, and retain much more of what they learn, when they have to seek out knowledge for themselves in relation to relevant, real-life problems.[172]

Using a problem-solving approach to teaching and learning instead of an information-transmission approach helps students learn how to access relevant knowledge, engage with its content, and also understand its application to real-life problems. They also learn additional skills in how to seek out resources to solve other problems they might encounter in their future ministry. This approach to learning more strongly focuses on learning how to learn and how to evaluate and apply the overwhelming amount of information that is available in the contemporary world.

There are occasionally situations in which there are good reasons for knowledge to be "downloaded" to students. Examples of this include where an expert is sharing about recent research that has not yet been published, or an expert provides a "digestible" summary of multiple views for a novice audience. In these cases, it is recommended that the content is delivered in bite-sized portions of under twenty minutes that can be absorbed by students and that the lecture is made available as text or an audio/video recording so that students can listen to it or watch it again and repeatedly refer to it. This ensures that the rich resources of academia for which God has gifted some people are made available to everyone.

In contexts where trainees are less highly educated, are oral learners, or are unable to read, knowledge can still be made available through leveraging the expertise of more educated group members and through the use of oral summaries prepared by the trainer. More literate or educated group members

---

171. Freire, *Pedagogy of the Oppressed.*

172. Richard Yates Hibbert and Evelyn Catherine Hibbert, "Assessing the Need for Better Integration in Theological Education: Proposals, Progress, and Possibilities from the Medical Education Model," in *Learning and Teaching Theology: Some Ways Ahead*, ed. Les Ball and James R. Harrison (Sydney: Morning Star Publishing, 2014).

can read and explain texts to their less literate peers and will learn through the process of interacting with the content in this way. At the same time, if group members are allowed to question and discuss the texts, especially their relevance to their own experience, the whole group will develop skills in critical thinking and in thinking about how to think (metacognition). Literacy is not a pre-requisite for critical thinking.

6. DESIGN MEANINGFUL WAYS TO EVALUATE THE TRAINING

Evaluative exercises are often simply performed as part of a bureaucratic process, or to fulfill accreditation requirements, or for teaching staff to demonstrate reasonable student satisfaction. If these are the only reasons to gather feedback data, then perfunctory student surveys are more than adequate. But if trainers are serious about developing and delivering training that helps their graduates be effective in ministry, a more rigorous and engaged evaluative process is needed.

The most common approach to program evaluation is to get students to fill in feedback surveys at the end of a unit of teaching. Although this may give helpful information on whether students enjoyed the subject or think it might be helpful in the future, it is not a very useful instrument for determining the effectiveness of training. This is because in most cases the students will not have had any opportunity to apply what they have learned to their work. In cases where a subject is being taught to students who are already in ministry and are able to apply what they are learning immediately, though, this kind of feedback is highly relevant.

Most institutions carry out regular reviews of their programs in response to external requirements, especially those set by accreditation bodies. Internal and external reviews tend to concentrate on the consistency between learning outcomes, performance criteria, and assessment tasks. This is an important part of evaluation, but only a start. Program evaluators should also observe the quality of teaching to evaluate how much of what is on paper is reflected in practice.

Good program evaluation involves stakeholders in the process and looks especially closely at how well graduates of the training function in their ministry roles. This is the crux of effective evaluation. It is what the stakeholders think that ultimately reflects how helpful the training program is and expresses what matters most.

Stakeholder feedback should be utilized to continually improve the training program. An example of this would be for teachers to liaise with stakeholders about the kind of things they would like the training program graduates to be able to do. If the stakeholders say that they would like the graduates to be effective in building relationships across cultures, teachers and stakeholders could research how effective graduates are in doing this at various stages after graduation and what difficulties they are encountering. They could use their findings to modify the training program to help graduates be more effective in this skill. The effect of any modifications to the training and its outcomes would continue to be researched and an ongoing evaluative feedback loop be built into the course design and delivery.[173]

Achieving excellence takes time. This means that it will usually take at least ten years to know the extent to which graduates are effective as missionaries because there needs to be time to evaluate the long-term effectiveness of graduates in their places of ministry and for evaluative loops to be established between ministry practice and training. The major impact of the learning falls outside the normal immediate timeframe of student feedback at the end of each semester. This means that if institutions, organizations, or individual trainers want to effectively evaluate their training, they need to have a long-term commitment in mind.

7. IMPLEMENT AND EVALUATE THE TRAINING

Designing an excellent training program requires time, commitment, and courage. Courage is needed because excellence in teaching and learning is associated with a commitment to do whatever it takes to ensure that learning outcomes are achieved in a way that is most meaningful to trainees and stakeholders. This usually involves innovation and doing things differently than the way they have always been done.

---

173. An excellent guide to doing this kind of evaluation of training programs can be found in Perry Shaw, *Transforming Theological Education: A Practical Handbook for Integrative Learning* (Carlisle, UK: Langham Partnership, 2014), 56–60.

9

PUTTING THE STEPS INTO PRACTICE

A Case Study

This chapter describes the design and implementation of a program of training for cross-cultural church planters which spans the time from their initial interest in becoming a missionary to their involvement in church planting on a field. There are five major stages: missions call assessment in their home church, pre-field preparation, language and culture study, ministry planning, and ongoing involvement in a learning community. Figure 7 summarizes the stages of this training process. Trainees are part of the training community throughout this process. This chapter describes and outlines the steps involved in the design and implementation of this program.

The training described in this chapter was developed over a period of six years. In 2005, based on the principles outlined in the earlier chapters of this book, we began to develop a missionary training program that focused on training cross-cultural church planters. We began by researching and defining the needs of cross-cultural church planters and defining competencies. A group of experienced missionaries, including cross-cultural church planters with many years of experience, reviewed the program and gave advice f or its improvement. The program was then put into practice in Sydney, Australia in the context of a highly multicultural neighborhood. It was then submitted to the education authorities in Australia and received accreditation by the Australian government as a Certificate IV, Diploma, and Advanced Diploma in Cross-Cultural Church Planting.

The training was implemented by a small team of experienced missionaries who live in rented homes in a multicultural suburb in Western Sydney, Australia. Further development and fine tuning of the program occurred as it was put into practice. This meant that the training could be evaluated and improved as a result of feedback from applying it. Trainee feedback and experience were also incorporated into the development process.

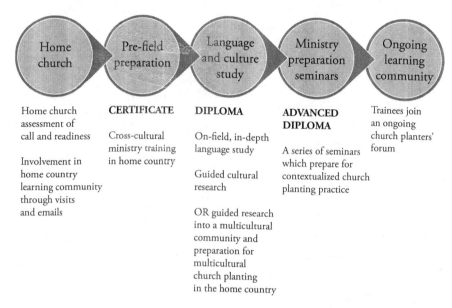

Figure 7 Five stages of Journey Training

This training is designed to intentionally instill and nurture a life-long commitment to learning and to encourage trainees to develop learning communities wherever they find themselves. We believe that the training of missionaries begins in their churches with their foundational spiritual formation and ministry training, and that it then continues through more specialized pre-field missionary training. But missionaries' learning and becoming more effective in their ministry must not stop there. Learning and training should continue on the field with language and culture learning followed by further learning related to the specific kind of ministry the missionary is involved in. This conceptualization of learning and training as a journey that continues through all of life led us to name this training program, *Journey Training*, and the training team, the *Journey Team*.

Trainers from various mission agencies are experimenting with approaches that resemble the Journey Training in many ways, particularly with the aim of retaining younger missionaries who first go to a field with a short-term commitment. One example is TIMO,[174] the Africa Inland Mission's two-year training

---

174. AIM USA, "Timo (Training in Ministry Outreach)," http://www.aimint.org/usa/serve/timo.

program. The challenge of these ways of training has always been the transition from short-term to long-term and the requirement that many agencies have for graduates of these programs to go to a Bible college or seminary before embarking on long-term missionary service. This usually requires the missionary to leave the field just when they have gained a reasonable working knowledge of a local language and culture in order to study in their home country for two or three more years. Some missions such as WEC have tried using distance education options for at least some of the training, but the demands of early cross-cultural adaptation and language learning have usually proven too heavy for most new workers to also be able to cope with tertiary level study by distance at the same time.

RECOGNIZING THE NEED FOR A DIFFERENT WAY OF TRAINING MISSIONARIES

The Journey Training was developed in response to a felt need for specific training for cross-cultural church planters in WEC International. WEC's focus is on taking the gospel to the world's least reached people groups and planting churches among them. The need for better training for cross-cultural church planters was first formally recognized in the year 2000. As WEC's International Directors for Equipping and Advance, we conducted a survey of active WEC missionaries working in evangelism and church planting in Africa, Asia, Latin America, and Europe. Of the sixty-three respondents, 59% listed "lack of experience or training" as one of the top two hindrances to their work. In the same way, of the respondents who were members of church planting teams, 89% reported that "lack of training in evangelism and church planting" was the second most significant hindrance to their ministry.[175] Herbert Brasher's research into his mission agency similarly found that lack of preparation for evangelism and discipleship was a major obstacle to missionary effectiveness.[176]

One of the major challenges that WEC faced and that needed to shape any training that was developed was that, after their initial period of language and cultural learning on the field, few missionaries seemed able to develop

---

175. Hibbert and Hibbert, "Report on Hindrances to and Needs in Reaching the Unreached and Church Planting in Wec Fields."

176. Brasher, *Important Factors in Pre-Field and Field-Based Preparation of Missionaries Serving with Cross and Crescent International*, 115.

contextualized strategies for evangelism and church planting. Some fields were doing a better job of providing guidance and some input for new workers than others, but many missionaries were left to struggle on their own. This often led to a major crisis after the initial two or three years of language learning in which missionaries wondered how to approach the task of pioneer church planting.

As in Patrick's study of missionaries from many agencies, few WEC missionaries had relevant practical experience of cross-cultural ministry in their home countries.[177] Many felt at a loss about how to start the work of church planting. Others attempted to replicate methods of evangelism or discipling used in their home countries but were often frustrated by the lack of response or apparent lack of comprehension they encountered from local people. It seemed clear that a way of intentionally supporting and guiding new missionaries through in-depth culture study, advanced and focused language study and the development of contextualized ministry strategies could be a real help in increasing the effectiveness of these missionaries. It might also help to increase missionaries' satisfaction with their ministry and decrease missionary attrition.

Our research into existing training programs being offered in Bible colleges both in Australia and overseas failed to discover, at least in the mid-2000s, any programs that were specific to cross-cultural church planters that could be used in other contexts. The closest thing to meeting the need we were faced with were programs offered by some Bible colleges in Asia that require their trainees to plant churches during their degree programs or in parallel to them.

STEP 1: CONSULTING WITH STAKEHOLDERS

The process of developing the training began with an internal review process involving a group of experienced church planters and trainers in WEC International over a period of approximately two years. Drawing on profiles for effective missionaries and church planters developed by other agencies this group developed an integrated profile for pioneer church planters. This led to a list of competencies arranged according to three stages of cross-cultural work: pre-field preparation, on-field language and culture learning or multicultural church planting in the home country, and initial ministry on the field after completing language study.

---

177. Patrick, "Tentmaking Unveiled—'The Survey Says.'"

This extensive review process involved the input of a wide range of experienced church planters who had worked in the Middle East, the Turkic world, Thailand, Ethiopia, Europe, Japan, China, India, Pakistan, Korea, Vietnam, Papua New Guinea and Australia. Each of the missionaries involved in the review of competencies had at least eight years field experience and had been involved in cross-cultural church planting themselves as well as in training people.

STEP 2: DEFINING THE LEARNING OUTCOMES

Experienced cross-cultural church planters currently serving in three mission agencies (OMF International and SIM International and WEC International), as well as in Australian churches and Bible colleges formed an Advisory Committee. This group gave detailed feedback on each competency over a period of six months. The review process included receiving detailed feedback on the profile and incorporating suggestions in its re-writing to ensure each competency was clearly expressed and relevant to a wide range of cross-cultural church planting situations.

The final step in the process, necessitated by the Australian government's educational accreditation requirements, involved forming a second Advisory Committee. This committee was also comprised of experienced cross-cultural church planters (from New Tribes Mission, Church Missionary Society, Interserve, Wycliffe Bible Translators, Australian Christian Churches World Missions, and Global Interaction), two mission agency leaders (including the former World President of the Christian Missionary Alliance), Australian church pastors, and the vice-principal of a Bible college.

Discussions with the Advisory Committee led to more clarity about the awards that should be given once various levels of training had been completed. Three awards were agreed on to correspond with three levels of training at different stages of cross-cultural church planters' journey of learning.

The Certificate enables a trainee to develop the hands-on knowledge, skills, and attitudes necessary for planting churches in a cross-cultural context. It facilitates the development of sensitivity towards speakers of another heart language, but the trainee does not develop any significant understanding of another culture. Graduates are considered qualified to begin church planting among people from other cultures who are living in the home cultural context of the trainee under the supervision of experienced cross-cultural workers.

Diploma trainees develop an in-depth understanding of a culture other than their own and are able to relate sensitively to people from other cultures. Graduates of the Diploma are considered qualified to begin church planting in another culture, or in a multicultural context, without supervision.

In the Advanced Diploma, trainees acquire the hands-on knowledge, skills, and attitudes necessary for planting churches in a cross-cultural context. They develop significant understanding of another culture and approaches which enable indigenous control and the development of reproducing churches. Graduates are qualified to plant churches in another culture and to supervise new cross-cultural church planters. According to the Australian Qualifications Framework (AQF), the Advanced Diploma is considered as equivalent to the first two years of a Bachelor degree and can count as credit towards this degree.

STEP 3: DETERMINING WAYS OF ASSESSING LEARNING

As part of preparing for accreditation, what is to be assessed in order to prove competency is thoroughly defined. Each performance criterion is repeatedly reviewed to ensure it is clear and also achievable at the level it is allocated. Who is qualified to assess the criteria, any limitations, and a specific range of contexts for assessment are defined. In addition, lists of examples of the type of evidence that can be gathered to prove competency also have to be provided.

In order to illustrate the level of detail involved, the following example is taken directly from the accreditation documents.

COMPETENCY: Works effectively in a multicultural church planting team	
Element of Competency	Performance Criteria
Manages conflict on the team	• Familiarity with the methods *other cultures on the team* use to resolve conflict is demonstrated
	• Biblical principles of conflict resolution are defined
	• A team approach to conflict resolution is negotiated
	• Common areas of conflict in multicultural church planting teams (including the role of women, discipline of team children, and theology) are discussed and resolved
RANGE OF VARIABLES	
Every culture, each culture, and other cultures represented on the team refers to each ethno linguistic culture represented on the team.	

EVIDENCE GUIDE

Overview

A person who demonstrates competency in this unit must be able to provide evidence that they can work with others to form a team and achieve a team task, understand the cultures, personalities, and team roles represented on the team and manage conflict on the team.

Critical Aspects of Evidence to Demonstrate Competency in This Unit Are:

Assessment requires evidence of the following products or processes to be collected:

Products

• Outline of the normal stages of team life

• A team covenant

• Summaries from each team member of the main features of each culture on the team

• List of biblical principles for conflict resolution

Processes

• Achieving a specific team task together

• Demonstration of familiarity with the different methods of conflict resolution used by each culture on the team

• Negotiation of a team approach to conflict resolution

• Discussion of common areas of conflict in multicultural church planting teams

Resource Implications

It is essential for the assessment of this unit that there is a team to work with and that there are at least two different ethno linguistic cultures represented among the membership of the team.

Consistency in Performance (Methods of Assessment)

Assessment should involve:

• Observation of the team and its processes of formation, function, conflict management, and work

• Observation of discussions and negotiations

• Observation of the products of the team's work

• Inspection of written products

• Assessment by intermittent checking at various stages of each task application or at the completion of each task in accordance with the performance criteria is recommended

Context of Assessment

This unit must be assessed in a cross-cultural church planting context.

Assessor Competencies

Cross-cultural church planting competency needs to be assessed by experienced cross-cultural church planters. Appropriate and relevant industrial experience for assessing Certificate IV competencies requires at least three years continuous experience learning another language and working in another culture.

Table 5 Assessment information and evidence guide

As can be seen from Table 5, who can assess, where the assessment can occur, what the trainees must do to fulfill the performance criteria, and the kind of evidence to be gathered has been thought through and documented. In practice, trainees formed a multicultural team and were introduced to theory about intercultural conflict management, observed while they discussed how they would manage conflict as a team, and in some cases, how they actually did manage conflict, as well as each team providing the trainers with a statement about their agreed-upon process for managing conflict which was included in their written team covenant.

STEP 4: CREATING THE LEARNING ENVIRONMENT

Preparing the Training Team

Finding suitable members of the training team was a process that took over a year. Members of the Journey Team needed to be people with significant cross-cultural missionary experience who had a passion for investing in the lives of new missionaries and who were willing to move into a multicultural suburb of Sydney and be actively involved in ongoing cross-cultural church planting work there. This way of training was quite different to what people were used to, and it was therefore important to invest this time in helping people in our organization understand what the training involved.

Potential new members of the training team meet with the current team to make sure they understand the different approach to training, are committed to it, and are also willing to be involved in ongoing ministry in-context. Potential team members usually spend some time living with the team to experience what Journey Team life is like and, after deciding to join, have a one-year trial period. New team members must ascribe to the Journey Team vision and values and complete a certificate in vocational training and assessment, which is part of the Australian accreditation requirements for assessors of this type of training.

As the Journey Team is part of a mission agency that is committed to the planting of reproducing churches among unreached people groups, its focus is on preparing missionaries who are equipped to do this work. The team clarified its vision, goals, and strategies by following the team development process outlined in the book, *Leading Multicultural Teams*.[178] Expectations of the team

---

178. Hibbert and Hibbert, *Leading Multicultural Teams*.

and of ministry were also discussed in this process. This meant that all team members had been through exactly the same process that trainees would go through in their pre-field training.

Journey Team

The vision of the Journey Team is to empower missionaries to effectively plant multiplying churches cross-culturally, and to help them empower others to do the same (2 Tim 2:2). In keeping with the multiplication ethos of church planting movements, we are intentional about making the training reproducible by equipping trainees to continually work to reproduce themselves in others (Phil 4:9).

Vision: What we want to see

We want to see empowered workers who are:

1. Effectively planting multiplying/reproducing churches cross-culturally, and

2. Empowering others to do the same (2 Tim 2:2)

Mission: What we do

• Provide a 2 Tim 2:2 model of training which is church-centered, reproducible[1] and highly relational

• Model what we want to see

• Mentor life-to-life

• Select hard, train easy

• Prioritize the unreached

• Provide a training and church planting model that is non-extractional[2]

• Work with the culture not against it[3]

Values: The beliefs that drive our actions

• Everyone should keep on learning.

• Hands-on experience with reflection is the best way to learn.

• People and building relationships are more important than programs.

• Process is as important as product.

• God values culture and is already at work within it.

[1] Reproducible applies to both the outcome in cross-cultural church planting among the unreached as well as reproducing of the training itself. This drives us to create a training movement in contrast to a centralized institution. The reproduced Journey identities are movement-like in that they are built on principles which are expressed differently in different contexts and are not subject to central control. Resources are freely available but also non-copyrighted in the sense that they may be freely adapted to meet local contextual needs.

[2] The training and church planting strives to keep people in the community where church planting is occurring and actively encourages local people to stay within their social networks.

[3] Culture is the God-ordained way in which society maintains order and communicates and lives out its values. We actively encourage the development of patterns of church life that honor, respect, and utilize local ways of doing things that do not compromise biblical values.

Table 6 Journey Team vision, mission, and values statement

In the teambuilding process, team members made suggestions regarding what they wanted incorporated into a vision, mission, and values statement. We discussed these together, collated and negotiated until the whole team agreed. This statement is shown in Table 6. The footnotes in the statement explain some of the terms. This document became a key reference point which enabled the trainers to make decisions regarding program adjustment on a day-to-day basis. Its content is explained to trainees at the beginning of their training so that they can understand why the training happens in the way it does and what principles underpin it. It also is used to help keep the training team on track with its original purpose.

Selecting Trainees

Journey Training starts in the churches of the trainees and in consultation with them. We stress to each potential trainee's church that what Journey Training offers is *cross-cultural* expertise. We do not replace the church as the primary spiritual and ministry formation agent in a missionary candidate's life. When potential trainees express an interest in becoming cross-cultural church planters we talk not only with them but also with their church. We ask the church to take the responsibility to help the potential trainee meet some basic requirements. These basic requirements that we ask the church to work with the trainee to fulfill are that the trainee:

- Has read the whole Bible.
- Is growing in maturity and responsibility so that the church leadership would be happy to have the trainee in the leadership team of the church. (This does not mean that the trainee is ready to be the sole leader of a church, but simply that the current leadership would be happy to have the trainee working with them in the leadership team of the church.)
- Has demonstrated a vibrant quality of spiritual life and has demonstrated the discipline necessary to sustain it. (The church is free to assess this in whatever way best accords with their denominational orientation and heritage.)
- Has had experience in evangelism and discipleship in the local church's secular community context.

- Has an idea of where he or she believes God is calling
  him or her to go and that the local church leadership (or
  church community) has tested this calling and affirm it.

At the same time that trainees are working with their churches towards meeting these criteria, WEC Australia works with the church to help it understand what missionary life and work involves and how the church can support its missionaries well. A contract is negotiated between the agency and the church that helps to articulate and clarify the expectations the church and the agency have of each other.

Churches are free to help the missionary candidate fulfill the requirement for entry into Journey Training in whatever way seems best to them, including recommending they go to Bible college. A helpful resource that churches can use to help mentor their potential missionaries has been developed by Greg Carter.[179] It is a workbook that guides the reader through the different steps involved in preparing to be a missionary.

During the time it takes them to fulfill the basic requirements for embarking on Journey Training, trainees are encouraged to have exposure to cross-cultural ministry, either in their own context under the supervision of experienced missionaries in their own congregation, or through engagement with the Journey Team in multicultural Western Sydney. This provides an opportunity for the trainee and their churches to test the trainee's call and suitability for cross-cultural ministry in a safe environment and without major dislocation from their normal context. The involvement of the home church in the testing of the missionary's call and preparation for service helps to build a good relationship with the home church and enhance the church's understanding of the missionary task.

Training Occurs in the Context of Authentic Cross-cultural Ministry

Journey trainers are both practitioners and mentors who embody the values of the training and put into practice what they are training others to be and do. Journey trainers not only have past experience—a minimum of six years field experience—but they also have ongoing involvement in cross-cultural church planting in the training context. Trainers engage in cross-cultural ministry

---

179. Greg Carter, *Skills, Knowledge, Character: A Church-Based Approach to Missionary Candidate Preparation* (Valparaiso, IN: Snowfall Press, 2010).

with the trainees both to model being a missionary and also so that they can assess the specific areas trainees need to develop in and give feedback to trainees about how they are developing as cross-cultural church planters. By living in a cross-cultural context and engaging in ongoing cross-cultural church planting among unreached peoples, the trainers model the reality of the challenges of this type of work and how to respond to and persevere through them.

Trainees form into ministry teams, live in rented housing in the community, and experience the normal stresses of both relating to other team members and maintaining healthy relationships with their families. Relating to missionary co-workers and maintaining healthy family relationships are the two most significant areas of stress that are repeatedly mentioned in missions research as leading to people leaving the field.[180] Trainees begin to experience these stresses during their training and can be debriefed to help them understand themselves and interpersonal dynamics better. They can also try out new strategies to manage stress and gain experience in forgiving others and resolving conflict in God-honoring ways.

Trainees Become Part of a Learning Community

While they are doing initial preparation in their home church, trainees are invited to become part of the Journey Team learning community. They are invited to seminars, informal get-togethers, and opportunities for hands-on involvement in cross-cultural church planting. Members of their churches are also welcome to participate in Journey learning community activities. It has so far proved difficult, though, for trainees to get much involved in the community because they are busy with other life commitments.

There is no competitive learning in the Journey Training. Trainees learn from each other and with each other. Those who have more expertise in different areas are encouraged to use that expertise for the benefit of their fellow trainees. For example, in a seminar where trainees have to engage with academic texts, those who are able explain those texts even to those who are non-literate. Through doing this, those who have more academic experience learn how to articulate difficult concepts simply and teach and communicate clearly. In this way, they act as living models for developing critical thinking

---

180. E.g., Blöcher, "What ReMAP I Said, Did, and Achieved," 15; Brasher, *Important Factors in Pre-Field and Field-Based Preparation of Missionaries Serving with Cross and Crescent International*, 81.

for the rest of the group. Through this approach, all are empowered to think critically about the issues and to learn how to work with a group to empower all members of the group to learn.

Journey Training intentionally develops lifelong learners. As trainers continue to be vitally interested in the issues the trainees are exploring, they attempt to embody what Parker Palmer describes as the subject being in the center of the learning exercise, rather than the teacher.[181] Trainers reach out to the unreached and continue to learn "on-the-job," using the same approaches as those they are advocating. Trainees see trainers evaluating their own practices, reflecting on theory in the light of experience and engaging in ongoing learning. In this way, trainers also seek to embody Donald Schön's concept of being a reflective practitioner.[182] Journey Trainers are also part of an ongoing missiological reading community which meets to discuss missiological texts with other missionaries and missions lecturers.[183] Journey Trainers therefore continue to learn and reflect on their practice in the light of theory. They model this process of ongoing reflective learning to their trainees. Trainees engage in the same process with missions texts during their training. This becomes a model for trainees to adopt in their own lives.

New missionaries tend to underestimate the complexity of cultural learning and the time it takes to learn to be effective in ministry.[184] Most of the missionaries that Herbert Brasher interviewed had not grown in the way they did evangelism and discipleship beyond the things they were able to do before coming to the field.[185] Yet missionaries should ideally be continually honing their approaches to evangelism and discipleship as their understanding of their context deepens. In order to overcome this ministry stasis or fossilization, missionaries need to develop a habit of reflective learning practice. This can be stimulated by instilling an ethos of ongoing learning and by providing trainees with practical experience in how to keep on learning.

181. Parker J. Palmer, *The Courage to Teach: Exploring the Inner Landscape of a Teacher's Life*, 1st ed. (San Francisco, CA: Jossey-Bass, 1998).

182. Schön, *Reflective Practitioner: How Professionals Think in Action.*

183. This learning community embodies what is recommended in the paper: Hibbert and Hibbert, "Nurturing Missionary Learning Communities."

184. Brasher, *Important Factors in Pre-Field and Field-Based Preparation of Missionaries Serving with Cross and Crescent International*, 42.

185. Ibid., 107.

There is an inherent expectation continually communicated through Journey Training that trainees will become trainers of others. Journey Training is not a product that is forgotten or placed on a shelf and never referred to again once the training is completed. It is a process that aims to produce trainers of others and equips them to do this. The steps in the training, the activities, its structure and assessments are each transparent and can be openly questioned so that everyone understands what principles inform them. Trainees are encouraged to ask questions and to examine why things are done the way they are. The aim is that trainees feel confident not just in what to do but also in how to replicate the training in their own ministry contexts.

Journey Training aims to create a community which follows the Apostle Paul's instructions to Timothy in 2 Timothy 2:2 to pass on the things he had heard to reliable men who will be able to teach others. Reproducibility applies to both the outcome of cross-cultural church planting among the unreached as well as reproducing the training itself. This drives us to create a training movement in contrast to a centralized institution.

Journey Training is built on principles that can be expressed differently in varying contexts. Training resources are simple and can be freely adapted to meet local contextual needs. Training is conducted in the homes of trainers and in local community contexts, such as parks and cafes, demonstrating that the training can be easily delivered anywhere, without the need for expensive buildings or equipment.

STEP 5: DESIGNING THE LEARNING EXPERIENCES

Journey trainers focus on developing a facilitative approach to teaching which involves supportive listening, encouragement, making suggestions, and asking stimulating yet sensitive questions at relevant times. It also involves modeling life and ministry, including interpersonal and intercultural relationship-building. Finally, it involves holding trainees and teams accountable for what they need to do. The focus is not on just teaching about, or leading or doing things for the team members, but actively building trainees' capacity to do things for themselves so that they are better prepared for less supportive environments in the future.

Developing an Integrated Curriculum

In order for the training to be delivered in a meaningful way, the learning outcomes or competencies that need to be fulfilled are organized around ministry activities. Team-related competencies, for example, were grouped around activities relating to teambuilding which was coupled with the competencies related to developing an initial church planting strategy. As a team has to have a specific focus in order to form, trainees needed to engage with cross-cultural church planting theory and practice in order to inform their planning together. As the training teams are multicultural, a number of performance criteria related to cross-cultural communication might also be addressed.

Using this approach, several competencies can be assessed at the same time as trainees work on one ministry task such as building a team. Trainees can therefore progress at the rate that they achieve their tasks rather than according to a set lesson-timed structure. As trainees engage in the task of building a multicultural team, for example, they learn about teams, intercultural communication, conflict management, and their own personalities. In this way, skills training and knowledge input are delivered just when trainees need them. This motivates them to engage with the content.

In other cases, subject content is distributed across a number of ministry tasks. Cross-cultural church planting theory is explored, for example, not only as the team develops its strategy and planning sessions, but also in a missiology reading group focused on the biography of a cross-cultural church planter, as well as when trainees research the experience of missionaries for the sake of personal spiritual development.

Training is done in homes, cafes, and parks, so the training program is easily adjustable if visitors arrive unexpectedly, or circumstances arise in ministry that make it better to explore a particular issue at that time rather than having a pre-specified session. As the competencies are pre-defined and specified, there is little risk of some areas being neglected as all the performance criteria have to be achieved before the training is completed. Fulfillment of performance criteria is monitored by using work books or databases which match the performance criteria, allowing for the provision of evidence or trainers signing observation checklists.

Experiencing God

Journey Trainers are accessible to trainees. Trainees live either in the trainers' homes or nearby. They have learning sessions in the trainers' homes or other informal settings and do ministry together with them. Trainers share their lives with the trainees, including their weaknesses and frustrations. Trainers are vulnerable, transparent, and invest personally in the lives of trainees. They intentionally provide an authentic living model of a missionary for trainees and spend time with trainees, relaxing and working together, making the most of spontaneous opportunities to build into trainees' lives rather than relying on formal appointments.

In this way, trainees closely observe trainers' lives, the way they pray, maintain fellowship with God, and refer to the Bible and its commands in everyday life and ministry. At the same time, trainers mentor trainees and can be intentional about their spiritual formation and respond to the challenges trainees face during their training. Any concerns are openly discussed with trainees. At the same time, the challenges of being holy in different cultural contexts can be modeled, experienced, and debriefed. Trainers intentionally build relationships with trainees that extend beyond the training time so that they can continue to have input into their lives.

Using the Bible

The importance of knowing the Bible's content and experiencing the impact it has on a believer's life devotionally, through hearing God speak and through the effect obeying it has on life, is reinforced in different ways through Journey Training. The home church of the trainee has the initial responsibility for ensuring that the trainee has read through the whole Bible and relates to it in a way that the church considers a leader should. The Journey Team recommends different aids for reading through the whole Bible,[186] and expects all trainees to gain over 80 percent in a basic Bible content exam by the end of the Advanced Diploma.[187] Trainees can do various versions of the exam as many times as they

---

186. e.g. Selwyn Hughes, Trevor J. Partridge, and Robert Backhouse, *Cover to Cover Complete* (Farnham, Surrey, UK: CWR, 2012).

187. The set of Bible content exams that the Journey Team uses can be found at http://www.whitneyhq.com/biblecontent/

need to. It is intended as a guide to help trainees assess their own Bible knowledge and to identify gaps, rather than as a barrier per se.

As well as being familiar with the Bible as a textbook for their own lives, trainees develop their ability to search through it for answers to questions that arise in the course of their ministry experience. They learn how to access different reference tools and to critically engage with cross-cultural hermeneutical and theological issues. This means not only that trainees have to keep growing in their understanding of the Bible throughout their training period, but trainers also have to keep on learning themselves to be able to demonstrate how to tackle the complex biblical and theological issues that cross-cultural encounters raise. As these questions are explored in a supportive learning community, trainees ideally feel free to express doubts, raise troubling questions, and challenge one another. In the same way, trainers transparently express their own struggles and things they are still resolving, and feel free to say when they do not have all the answers. In this way, they model an authentic faith and healthy and practical ways of accessing resources to help solve contextualization and other cross-cultural ministry quandaries.

Relating to People

Journey Training sets relationships as a priority. If there is relationship breakdown in the training group, it is addressed before the training program moves on. If local people visit during a training session, they are included or the session halts until further notice. Journey Trainers actively model the priority of people over the programs and all the training is conducted in the community, in homes, and in other informal settings.

In their pre-field training, trainees form teams that are often multicultural and engage in cross-cultural ministry to people in the neighborhood as a team. They are introduced to possible differences in personalities, team roles, and cultures and helped to think through how these can affect team relationships. They are also exposed to methods of managing intercultural conflict and are supported as they work through any conflict that arises in their team. Trainees also visit different ethnic churches in the region and are expected to participate in at least one secular community activity each week, as well as other evangelistic tasks which their team may decide to do. They also observe and hear about the personal relationships that Journey trainers have with people in their local community.

Engaging with Culture

Journey Training occurs in the context of cross-cultural ministry. Journey trainees are exposed to different cultures by living among people from different cultures and intentionally working on building relationships with them. By working to fulfill the different performance criteria, specific intercultural skills are developed. Through interaction with people from different cultures, missiological readings, and input from experienced missionary trainers and guided research, trainees are exposed to both the practicalities and theory of intercultural engagement. Their ability to develop a deeper understanding of culture is further developed by specific training in ethnographic research methods. Through this they learn how to observe, continually ask questions, identify their own assumptions, and test assumptions by asking locals before coming to any conclusions. The importance of asking local people about their culture is emphasized by one missionary interviewed by Brasher:

> I guess Ahmed understood that I wanted to learn, and he was willing to help me, so I learned an awful lot from him. And asking—I heard more than once from Africans, "Why did no missionary ever ask me this question?" . . . Which is strange—I think we should all be asking people.[188]

During their language and culture learning on the field, trainees reflect on readings that relate to the things they are researching and experiencing. By the time of the ministry preparation seminars, trainees should have enough biblical and anthropological background to begin the process of integrating their insights in order to engage in effective contextualization. In the seminars trainees engage with missiological readings. The integrative process is facilitated by discussions which both help to build understanding but also help to ground the concepts in the varying experience of participants. Their varying experience provides insights which help new missionaries explore the different perspectives that different cultures have on specific biblical and theological areas. After the seminars, trainee-prepared contextualized strategies and tools are given to local believers for feedback and then tested in the ministry context.

---

188. Brasher, *Important Factors in Pre-Field and Field-Based Preparation of Missionaries Serving with Cross and Crescent International*, 175.

OVERVIEW OF THREE LEVELS OF TRAINING

The competencies of Journey Training are grouped into three award levels—Certificate, Diploma, and Advanced Diploma. These build on each other. The Certificate is the first and foundational level of training that is designed to be completed before the missionary trainee goes to their eventual field of service. The Diploma is designed to be completed during the missionary's first three years on the field while they are getting to know the culture and language. The Advanced Diploma focuses on developing more advanced skills for cross-cultural church planting and is designed to be worked through after missionaries' initial period of language and culture acquisition.

The competencies associated with each award are listed in Table 7. The training is flexible in that if trainees can demonstrate that they already have the competencies associated with the Certificate, they can begin at the Diploma, and if they have the competencies for the Diploma, they can start with the Advanced Diploma. Similarly, if trainees can demonstrate that they fulfill any of the competencies without the training, they do not have to do the training associated with those competencies and can focus on developing other competencies. All the competencies for the Journey Training are listed in the table below, organized according to the essential elements for missionary training. More details for each competency, including their performance criteria, can be found in Appendix 1.

Level 1: Certificate	Level 2: Diploma	Level 3: Advanced Diploma
Experiencing God		
	Maintain personal well-being (CCP21)	
Using the Bible		
Articulate Christian principles effectively using storytelling (CCP1)	Develop a practical Christian response to spiritual practices (CCP11)	Describe cultural themes and prepare a biblical response (CCP29)
Create a repertoire of stories and articulate these appropriately for selected audiences (CCP2)		Explore indigenous theologies and apply principles of indigenous theologizing to a specific cross-cultural context (CCP36)
Enable others to interpret Bible passages using a communal, reproducible, inductive method (CCP3)		Explain, analyze, and put into practice the process of contextualization (CCP38)

Level 1: Certificate	Level 2: Diploma	Level 3: Advanced Diploma
Articulate a biblical response to contemporary theological issues in mission (CCP10)		
Relating to people		
Work effectively with others (BSBWOR203A)	Behave and communicate appropriately cross-culturally (CCP13)	Acquire vocational proficiency in the language of the people where the trainee will be doing cross-cultural church planting (CCP35)
Work effectively in a multicultural church planting team (CCP9)	Acquire basic vocational proficiency in the language of the people where the trainee will be doing cross-cultural church planting (CCP17)	Communicate a contextualized gospel (CCP30)
Communicate Christian principles with people from other cultures, identify key challenges in cross-cultural communication, and articulate a Christian response to the beliefs and practices of different cultures (CCP7)	Develop proficiency in using the language in vocationally relevant ways (CCP18)	Develop a cross-cultural church planting strategy (CCP32)
Outline the principles of cross-cultural church planting (CCP4)	Communicate concepts in another language (CCP23)	Develop a reproducible strategy for discipling all believers (CCP33)
Prepare and put into practice a beginning cross-cultural church planting strategy (CCP5)	Engage with a multicultural community, design a multicultural church planting strategy and begin to implement it (CCP19)	Develop a culturally appropriate strategy for leadership development (CCP34)
	Articulate the challenges of developing and promoting biblical multiculturalism (CCP20)	
Engaging with culture		
Research and describe aspects of another culture using ethnographic methods (CCP6)	Research everyday life using ethnographic methods (CCP14)	Examine history to derive principles for cross-cultural church planting practice today (CCP37)
Respond appropriately to a given range of different cross-cultural experiences (CCP8)	Research and describe social systems (CCP16)	Explore leadership in different cultures and the impact of intercultural interaction on leadership of new churches (CCP39)
	Describe the religious system and beliefs (CCP12)	Articulate the challenges of facilitating reproducibility and preventing dependency in cross-cultural church planting (CCP31)
	Investigate the formal teachings and practice of a religion (CCP22)	Perform and write drama in a different culture's drama style (CCP40)

Level 1: Certificate	Level 2: Diploma	Level 3: Advanced Diploma
	Collect data for worldview analysis using ethnographic methods (CCP15)	Perform and choreograph dance in a different culture's dance style (CCP41)
		Perform and compose music in a different culture's musical style (CCP42)
		Create visual art in a different culture's artistic style (CCP43)

Table 7 Listing of all Journey Training competencies according to the essential elements for missionary training

In preparing this table it quickly became clear that many competencies include two or more of the essential elements for missionary training. Therefore in classifying the competencies, we have tried to highlight the primary focus of the competency. For example, those competencies requiring trainees to engage in church planting obviously incorporate every essential element however, as trainees must be able to relate to people as a very foundational step, these are classified under "Relating to people." In the same way, although contextualization requires engagement with culture, as well as using the Bible, it is the ability to relate the Bible across cultures which is most critical.

Another thing that quickly becomes apparent is the lack of specific competencies relating to *Experiencing God*. Partly this reflects the fact that competencies cannot be quantified and compared in terms of equivalent content in the same way as knowledge courses can and also the difficulty of defining measurable outcomes for character qualities. In practice, the unit BSBWOR203A, which is from a business vocational course and is focused on working effectively with others, requires obedience to biblical commands to respect, love, and forgive one another in order to be fulfilled in the team training context. Many specific character and spiritual growth measures will be found in the performance criteria for the competencies, but this is a level of detail too great to include in this table.

Specific Descriptions of Each Level of Journey Training

In this section, each award is outlined with a list of competencies covered in that award followed by a brief description of the training program. Each of the statements of competency can be prefaced with "By the end of the training the trainee will be able to. . . ."

Certificate: Cross-cultural church planting orientation

COMPETENCIES

Using the Bible

- Articulate Christian principles effectively using storytelling (CCP1)
- Create a repertoire of stories and articulate these appropriately for selected audiences (CCP2)
- Enable others to interpret Bible passages using a communal, reproducible, inductive method (CCP3)
- Articulate a biblical response to contemporary theological issues in mission (CCP10)

Relating to people

- Respond appropriately to a given range of different cross-cultural experiences (CCP8)
- Communicate Christian principles with people from other cultures, identify key challenges in cross-cultural communication, and articulate a Christian response to the beliefs and practices of different cultures (CCP7)
- Outline the principles of cross-cultural church planting (CCP4)
- Prepare and put into practice a beginning cross-cultural church planting strategy (CCP5)
- Work effectively with others (BSBWOR203A)
- Work effectively in a multicultural church planting team (CCP9)

Engaging with culture

- Research and describe aspects of another culture using ethnographic methods (CCP6)

The certificate is offered as a pre-field 12-week residential program that is conducted in Western Sydney. This region is highly multicultural and many suburbs have large numbers of Muslims, Buddhists, and Hindus from the Middle East, Southeast Asia, and the Indian subcontinent. The trainees live either in trainers' homes or in nearby rental accommodation.

The trainees form a team, research the area and its people and begin to get to know them, develop the first stages of a church planting strategy, and put their strategy into practice. They read and reflect on the work of effective cross-cultural church planters.[189] They learn to tell and contextualize Bible stories, as well as other stories that communicate biblical principles, and develop their skills by using these stories in their cross-cultural outreach. By the end of the twelve weeks the trainees have engaged in a minimum of one hundred hours of cross-cultural church planting activity, which includes communicating with their home church and other supporters.

During this pre-field training, trainees also get involved in local community activities such as sport, craft, or adult education courses so that they can develop the ability to relate to local people in their own contexts. They visit different ethnic churches in the region and participate in a house church. Towards the end of this residential program they are introduced to ethnographic study through doing practical ethnographic research tasks in the local context. This prepares them for the next (diploma) level of their training. A draft timetable is included in Appendix 2 to give some idea of how this learning experience is organized.

Diploma

The Diploma is offered as two different options. The first option is for those who go overseas as more traditional missionaries and are immersed in another language and culture. The second option is for trainees who stay at home and are engaged in cross-cultural outreach in multicultural contexts.

Option 1: Learning Language and Culture through Immersion in Another Language and Culture

COMPETENCIES
Experiencing God
- Maintain personal well-being (CCP21)

Using the Bible
- Develop a practical Christian response to spiritual practices (CCP11)

Relating to people
- Behave and communicate appropriately cross-culturally (CCP13)

---

189. e.g. Vincent J. Donovan, *Christianity Rediscovered*, 25th anniversary ed. (Maryknoll, NY: Orbis Books, 2003).

- Acquire basic vocational proficiency in the language of the people where the trainee will be doing cross-cultural church planting (CCP17)
- Develop proficiency in using the language in vocationally relevant ways (CCP18)
- Communicate concepts in another language (CCP23)

Engaging with culture

- Describe the religious system and beliefs (CCP12)
- Research everyday life using ethnographic methods (CCP14)
- Collect data for worldview analysis using ethnographic methods (CCP15)
- Research and describe social systems (CCP16)
- Investigate the formal teachings and practice of a religion (CCP22)

Over the two to three year period of language acquisition and getting to know the culture(s) on the field, trainees are in regular contact with either an on-field mentor or a Journey Team Trainer who guides them through a process of ethnographic research of the local context and culture. If there are enough trainees in a particular geographical area, a regular face-to-face group meeting allows for communal discussion of their findings and missiological readings. We experimented with blogs and e-learning forums with little success, mainly because of the added demands this places on the trainee as they are adjusting to the demands of life on the field. The most effective interaction has occurred through email and Skype calls with the Journey trainer.

The ethnographic study is guided by a list of questions designed to stimulate trainees to think about and explore areas that they otherwise may not be aware of. The questions are grouped by subject areas such as family relationships, the spirit world, and death and dying, and sequenced according to the level of language and cultural understanding needed. By the end of the two to three year period missionaries are tackling more complex areas such as wisdom, epistemology, and beauty. At the same time, language use skills are developed with concrete markers in both general and ministry areas. A Field Supervisor, who is a more experienced missionary on the field, acts as an assessor of competency. A list of resource questions are found in Appendix 3.

This process ensures that trainees have gone deep enough into the culture to prepare relevant and appropriate strategies for evangelism, gathering, discipleship, and leadership training. It provides a systematic way of developing a lifelong learning attitude and habit of being open and asking questions about language and culture. This approach can be adapted to the rate and difficulty of the missionary's language study. An outline of the progression of tasks and Field Supervisor assessments is included in Appendix 4.

Option 2: Multicultural Church Planting in the Home Country

COMPETENCIES

Experiencing God
- Maintain personal well-being (CCP21)

Using the Bible
- Develop a practical Christian response to spiritual practices (CCP11)

Relating to people
- Behave and communicate appropriately cross-culturally (CCP13)
- Engage with a multicultural community, design a multicultural church planting strategy, and begin to implement it (CCP19)
- Articulate the challenges of developing and promoting biblical multiculturalism (CCP20)

Engaging with culture
- Describe the religious system and beliefs (CCP12)
- Research everyday life using ethnographic methods (CCP14)
- Collect data for worldview analysis using ethnographic methods (CCP15)
- Research and describe social systems (CCP16)
- Investigate the formal teachings and practice of a religion (CCP22)

Trainees who stay in their home country also do guided anthropological study and ethnographic research focused on the different cultures and religions of the peoples represented in their specific multicultural context. This type of church planting is very complex and demanding. As the trainers for Journey Training are involved in church planting in multicultural contexts, it is a natural extension of the training to train others to work sensitively and effectively in these contexts.

The major differences between this approach to church planting and the pioneer cross-cultural church planting among the unreached is that the church planter does not learn another language and is usually dealing with multiple minority people groups. The church planting is often occurring as a daughter church being planted by a well-established and dominant church based on cultural patterns and assumptions inherent to the dominant culture. Seminars relating to multiculturalism, power, and minority groups are offered as part of this diploma.

As trainees do not have the advantage of the personal experience of learning another language and culture in depth, great effort is made to help trainees appreciate differences in cultural values and the dynamics of intercultural interactions. Issues related to the complexity of building and supporting community in the context of multiple cultures are explored.

Advanced Diploma: Starting cross-cultural church planting

COMPETENCIES

Using the Bible

- Describe cultural themes and prepare a biblical response (CCP29)
- Explore indigenous theologies and apply principles of indigenous theologizing to a specific cross-cultural context (CCP36)
- Explain, analyze, and put into practice the process of contextualization (CCP38)

Relating to people

- Communicate a contextualized gospel (CCP30)
- Develop a cross-cultural church planting strategy (CCP32)
- Develop a reproducible strategy for discipling all believers (CCP33)
- Develop a culturally appropriate strategy for leadership development (CCP34)
- Acquire vocational proficiency in the language of the people where the trainee will be doing cross-cultural church planting (CCP35)

Engaging with culture

- Articulate the challenges of facilitating reproducibility and preventing dependency in cross-cultural church planting (CCP31)

- Examine history to derive principles for cross-cultural church planting practice today (CCP37)
- Explore leadership in different cultures and the impact of intercultural interaction on leadership of new churches (CCP39)
- Perform and write drama in a different culture's drama style (CCP40)
- Perform and choreograph dance in a different culture's dance style (CCP41)
- Perform and compose music in a different culture's musical style (CCP42)
- Create visual art in a different culture's artistic style (CCP43)

In-ministry Seminars

After completing the guided ethnographic study and acquiring a good level of proficiency in the local language, trainees attend a series of seminars. These seminars are offered in ways that are accessible to the trainees involved and may be conducted as a residential block in the sending country, on the field, or in a region. The Advanced Diploma seminars are conducted as interactive discussions in informal settings and are consistent with normal Journey communal learning. Seminar attendees are encouraged and supported to pass on what they learn to their fields. Seminar content is based on the ethnographic study and reflection that workers have done over their language study period.

Foundational Seminar: Analyzing Worldview and Preparing a Contextualized Gospel

This foundational seminar is intellectually and spiritually challenging and requires fairly deep reflection and critical thinking. It addresses the following competencies:

- CCP29 Describe cultural themes and prepare a biblical response
- CCP30 Communicate a contextualized gospel
- CCP36 Explore indigenous theologies and apply principles of indigenous theologizing to a specific cross-cultural context.

In this seminar trainees analyze the worldview of their people in order to identify their key felt needs. They then research biblical answers to these needs. Contextualized gospel messages are prepared, and culturally appropriate methods of communicating the messages are examined. Issues of cross-cultural hermeneutics and the development of local theologies are also explored. On their return to their field, trainees check their analysis with the local people they are working among and with more experienced missionaries. They also communicate the contextualized presentations of the gospel and empower local Christians to do the same.

Seminar 2: Prepare a Cross-cultural Church Planting Strategy

This seminar addresses the following competencies:

- CCP31 Articulate the challenges of facilitating reproducibility and preventing dependency in cross-cultural church planting
- CCP32 Develop a cross-cultural church planting strategy
- CCP37 Examine history to derive principles for cross-cultural church planting practice today

Building on their cultural analysis, trainees consider what culturally appropriate churches in their ministry context would look like. They then design church planting strategies that could facilitate church multiplication. They examine the approaches of other cross-cultural church planters and evaluate their own strategy in the light of these. The seminar is followed up by trainees implementing their strategy and evaluating their tools and methods in their own ministry context.

Seminar 3: Prepare a Cross-cultural Discipleship Strategy

This seminar focuses on these competencies:

- CCP33 Develop a reproducible strategy for discipling all believers
- CCP38 Explain, analyze, and put into practice the process of contextualization

In this seminar trainees explore the content and methods of discipleship for church multiplication that are appropriate for their cultural context. They evaluate approaches to discipleship in other contexts and prepare a strategy for discipleship in their own ministry context. Indigenous methods of education, training, and the development and recognition of wisdom and character maturity are examined. This seminar is followed up by implementation and evaluation of some of the elements of their prepared discipleship strategy on the field.

Seminar 4: Prepare a Cross-cultural Leadership Development Strategy

This seminar covers the following competencies:

- CCP34 Develop a culturally appropriate strategy for leadership development
- CCP39 Explore leadership in different cultures and the impact of intercultural interaction on leadership of new churches

In this seminar trainees analyze the cultural data they have collected about leadership and leadership selection, development, and recognition. Different methods of leadership development used in their local context and other contexts are examined and evaluated with respect to cultural relevance and the potential for reproducibility. The trainee is helped to develop a blueprint for leadership training that is then taken back to local believers and more experienced missionaries for feedback.

Timing and Sequencing of Seminars

The four seminars can be taught together as a ten-week residential block for missionaries on home leave or as three two-week field-based seminars with time for implementation and reflection in between. It is best when their delivery is timed to correspond with ministry needs. The church planting strategy seminar, for example, is best conducted just before workers are ready to start church planting. The seminars can be offered as a planned sequence for new workers, but are also equally relevant for more experienced workers who want to evaluate their current practice or move into new areas of ministry. The most critical factor is that the seminar participants have previously invested time in doing in-depth research of the culture of the people they work with. In the process of doing the research, they also should have learned to question and test their assumptions about why local people do the things they do. Examples of seminar outlines and post-seminar follow-up are provided in Appendix 5.

STEP 6: DESIGNING MEANINGFUL EVALUATION

The Certificate, Diploma, and Advanced Diploma in Cross-Cultural Church Planting have been fully accredited by the Australian Skills Quality Authority of the Australian Government. The Australian education system allows for these awards to build on each other and then be credited towards a degree. The advantage of having government accreditation is that it ensures that the whole training process is educationally sound in its design and consistent with best practices in the field of cross-cultural church planting as defined by experienced cross-cultural church planters. The periodic review of the program that maintaining accreditation requires provides a good structure for helping to ensure that the program is continually aligned with best missionary and educational practice.

STEP 7: IMPLEMENTING AND EVALUATING THE TRAINING

The Journey Training was implemented using the reflective learning process described at the end of Chapter 5. Practical experience of doing the training informed the development of how it was delivered, incorporating both trainee and trainer feedback. Trainers engaged in peer review of their training practice among themselves and by inviting other educators in to observe and give feedback. They also participated in a two-week course on adult educational methods required by the Australian government for accreditation, and incorporated these insights into their practice. After each training course the trainers continue to gather for a day to review the program, and modifications are made to the next course in response to this review as well as trainee feedback and feedback from graduates and other missionaries observing them on the field.

REFLECTIONS ON THE CHALLENGE OF IMPLEMENTING THIS TYPE OF MISSIONARY TRAINING

Missionary trainers who want to implement a training approach similar to the Journey Training face two key challenges. The first is to overcome the assumption that only a two to three year Bible college program adequately prepares people for missionary service.

The second challenge is to find the right trainers. The training is highly demanding for trainers, because they are involved in ministry as well as being highly involved in the lives of the trainees. In the program in Sydney, for example, trainees live in the homes of the trainers for the pre-field training, learning community weekends and for seminars. The trainers should also have a good network of supportive friends in order to be able to cope with the demands of the training and have the emotional energy to invest in trainees and the local people. This makes the quality of the training team very important for the well-being of the trainers. It is essential to invest the time necessary to establish a healthy and effective team.

In traditional sending countries where mission agencies and churches are very well established and have been sending out missionaries for centuries, the path to the mission field through Bible colleges is strongly established and alternative pathways have generally not proved to be viable. This means that for this type of training to succeed, the most viable option is for it to be integrated into existing Bible college programs. Missionaries who have returned from the field could act as trainers by continuing to be involved in cross-cultural ministry in their home countries.

In non-traditional sending countries, where there are more informal movements of church members into missions, this type of training provides a flexible method for equipping lay Christians to be missionaries wherever they go to work in the world. Utilizing a 2 Timothy 2:2 approach, more experienced workers can train new missionaries in relevant knowledge, skills, and attitudes as needed. The training can be conducted in-ministry and just-in-time, and then passed on to others. The competency profiles can help church leaders to know who is ready to be sent and what those in training need to work on.

10

IMPLEMENTING
MISSIONARY TRAINING

The Great Commission imperative to make disciples of all nations creates an urgency to equip Christians to understand the culture of the world outside the church and to relate their faith to it. In each of the four major places that equipping for long-term mission takes place—Bible colleges and seminaries, churches, specialized pre-field non-formal missionary training courses, and on the mission field through on-the-job training—the curriculum needs to be integrated with life and ministry experience so that trainees develop key skills for cross-cultural ministry and Christian character qualities that will enable them to represent Jesus well.

As represented in Figure 8, missionary training needs to address all four essential elements described in Chapters 2 to 5 in order that trainees develop in their experience of God, their ability to relate and apply the Bible to the contexts they are engaging with, and their ability to build relationships and communicate the riches of the Christian message to people from all different walks of life. The best context for trainees to encounter and engage with these elements is authentic cross-cultural ministry.

The steps for designing missionary training that are explained in Chapter 8 and illustrated in Chapter 9 can be applied to any training program that intends to train missionaries. Consulting with stakeholders, defining learning outcomes, determining assessment, creating the learning environment, designing learning experiences, and establishing meaningful review and evaluation processes are essential for ensuring effective learning in any situation.

Wherever people are learning about missions, they will benefit from being part of a learning community. Learning from each other and together, being able to manage conflict, and benefiting from the diverse perspectives of community members all reinforce vital aspects of any missionary's work. The critical ingredients for a missions learning community are open trainers and trainees who are engaging in cross-cultural ministry, as well as access to resources which provoke and explore relevant questions, such as missiological articles, books, or multimedia presentations.

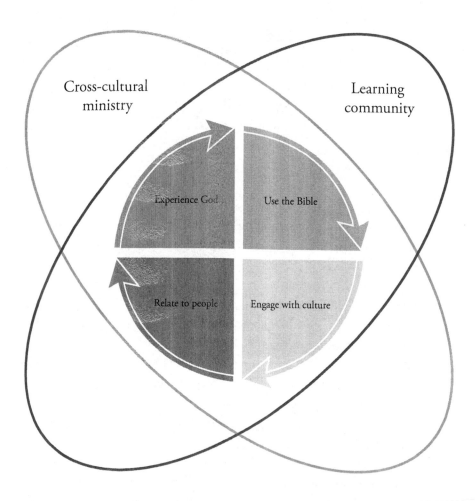

Cross-cultural ministry

Learning community

Experience God

Use the Bible

Relate to people

Engage with culture

Figure 8 Essential elements and contexts for missionary training

As there is no requirement for a specific venue, a learning community can be flexibly created wherever learners gather. The more regularly learners are able to meet, the more they will be able to foster a sense of collective commitment to learning. Online learning communities are more likely to foster sustained engagement if they are founded on face-to-face relationships. They are also nurtured by regular face-to-face interaction, such as can occur at conferences.

Any expertise—in terms of experience or formal study—which exists in the group, becomes a resource to use for the benefit of everyone's learning and development. The learning community should provide ample opportunity for members of the group to discuss and reflect on what is presented or studied in the light of each member's experience. In order for this to happen, the group has to be a safe place where participants feel free to ask questions, challenge assumptions, have conflict, and experiment with different ways of applying what they are exploring in their own ministry, even if they fail.[190]

THE IMPERATIVE OF TRAINING IN A CROSS-CULTURAL MINISTRY CONTEXT

Two key features of missionary training distinguish it from training for Christians planning to work in their own cultural context. The first is that missionary trainees need to be given practical experience in ministry among people from different cultures. Missionary trainees must encounter the challenges of cross-cultural work in a holistic way, including the spiritual and affective dimensions of crossing cultures.

Some recent writing on missional Christianity and missional churches draws on missiological theory to rethink how to share the gospel and be the church in a way that is relevant for the Western world.[191] But missionary work encompasses a far more demanding and specific commitment to cross-cultural engagement and to taking the gospel to unreached peoples wherever they are than being missional does.[192] Without significant personal immersion in another culture and language environment, it is extremely difficult to grasp the profound difference culture makes on all aspects of human experience. It is also virtually impossible to overcome the inherent human ethnocentric tendency

---

190. For an in-depth biblical study of how early Christian communities functioned as learning communities, refer to Claire Smith's book, *Pauline Communities as 'Scholastic Communities': A Study of the Vocabulary of "Teaching" in 1 Corinthians, 1 and 2 Timothy and Titus* (Tubingen, Germany: Mohr Siebeck, 2012).

191. For a good example of the helpful application of missiological theory to the West see M. Frost and A. Hirsch, *The Shaping of Things to Come* (Peabody: Hendrickson Publishing, 2003).

192. See Ed Stetzer, "Missions Vs. Missional? We Really Need Both," *Christianity Today*, 9 September 2013.

to judge according to inherited cultural values and to seek to impose inherited ways of thinking and doing things onto people from other backgrounds.

The more free members from different cultural backgrounds of a local church feel to express their authentic identity, the more suited that church will be to facilitate the training of potential missionaries. In churches, as in all social organizations, the dominant culture's ways of thinking and doing things tend to dominate. In contrast, missionaries are compelled to adopt and adapt to other cultures, rather than to impose their own ways on others. Multicultural churches that are committed to reaching out to their diverse cultural neighbors, especially if their membership includes one or two experienced missionaries who are active in outreach, provide an ideal training context for potential missionaries. These trainees can experiment while still being supported by people who know them well and care for them.

Where churches are situated in less diverse communities, they will need to send their members to other contexts in order to gain the cross-cultural experience they need. This may mean partnering with multicultural or other-culture churches, with a training team in a cross-cultural setting, or with experienced missionaries who are willing to take missionary trainees with them on specific training trips to other suburbs, cities, or countries.

This principle of training in the context of cross-cultural ministry is no different for missionaries on the field who are training local believers to be missionaries. The dynamic between the expatriate missionary trainer and the local people who are training to be missionaries is not sufficient as cross-cultural ministry exposure. The missionary trainer needs to find a way to provide cross-cultural ministry experience for trainees, whether it is among people from another cultural group in the local context, or by taking or sending trainees to a different context.

Enrolling students from different cultural backgrounds into training programs is a good way to expose them to other cultures, but it by no means adequately addresses students' need for cross-cultural exposure. Few institutions seriously engage with the assimilationist tendencies of the dominant culture of the institution that impacts institutional values, ethos, training, and administrative processes, and how the power dynamics of this affects intercultural relationships within the institutional environment. If the model of training being adopted is an institution-based residential program, the only way to effectively address the need for exposure to cross-cultural differences is to actively recruit a diverse faculty and arrange cross-cultural ministry experiences for students in multicultural teams. Since it is unrealistic to expect the dominance of the majority culture to be overcome in a training institution, trainers should openly recognize and discuss this reality in their teaching and in institutional decision-making.

SELECTING THE RIGHT TRAINERS

The second feature of missionary training that distinguishes it from training for Christians planning to work in their own cultural context is that it relies on trainers who have been missionaries themselves. Training programs are only ever as good as the trainers involved in them. Compromise at this point damages the integrity of everything the program stands for or intends to achieve. While it may be convenient and comfortable to employ recent graduates who have done well in the course, credibility as a missionary trainer can only be proven through field experience. Trainers need to fit the profile that the training seeks to produce, so that they can become role models who embody the values and goals of the training.

The best missionary trainers are those who have had long-term experience in cross-cultural ministry. This includes learning at least one other language and in-depth learning of culture over many years of residence among people from a different cultural background. It is even better if trainers have ongoing involvement in cross-cultural ministry. Head knowledge about missions is simply no substitute for the holistic, challenging, and often overwhelming experience of being immersed in and doing ministry in another culture.

At the same time, missionary training programs should aim to have a diverse group of trainers in terms of their ethnic, denominational, and mission agency backgrounds, as well as a balance of genders that reflects the world's missionaries. The modeling of biblical community in diversity is an important aspect of missionary spiritual formation. The ability of missionaries to work with and relate to diverse others affects both their cross-cultural outreach and their ability to work with other missionaries.

In training situations where the majority of trainers do not match the profile of effective field missionaries, two strategies could be employed to gradually address this. The first is to begin a more focused and disciplined recruiting strategy for future trainers. Secondly, training programs could actively encourage as many missionaries from diverse backgrounds and working situations as possible to join the training program for anywhere from a few hours to several weeks. These missionaries could be provided with opportunities to formally share and informally interact with trainees, as well as participate in regular teaching sessions. Their participation should not just be in missions subjects but also biblical and theological subjects where they could be allowed to raise issues and questions related to the real challenges they face in their ministry. This would not only expose students and teachers to the dilemmas of communicating faith across cultures, but it would also foster a stimulating, faith-developing environment within the program. An added benefit of this would be the exposure of students to a diverse range of role models. Trainees with different backgrounds, strengths, and personalities might find mentors and role models among these visiting missionaries. In addition, it is likely that greater exposure to missionaries would result in higher recruitment of new missionaries, as our recent research has indicated that, at least for new Australian missionaries, contact with missionaries is the single most important factor in their path into missions.[193]

SELECTING THE RIGHT TRAINEES

In order to enroll the right trainees, criteria for accepting people into the training need to be well-defined. Not everyone is suited or able to become a missionary. The challenge for training programs is to determine what their selection criteria should be. Whatever criteria are agreed on, they and the reasons for them need to be clearly communicated to applicants and their churches. There is always a need for some degree of compromise between giving people a chance and accepting people who are so good that they do not really need the training.

The clearer the outcomes of the training are, the easier it will be to determine entry criteria and to involve stakeholders in active recruitment and referral of suitable trainees. Clear outcomes can also help churches to better prepare their members for further, specific missionary training and be more involved in the assessment of their suitability for cross-cultural ministry.

The selection of missionary trainees should be a negotiated process between church, trainers, and sending agency. Having more active involvement by the

---

193. Richard Yates Hibbert, Evelyn Catherine Hibbert, and Tim Silberman, "The Journey Towards Long-Term Missionary Service: How Australian Missionaries Are Being Called and Choose Mission Agencies," *Missiology: An International Review* (forthcoming).

home churches in the process will benefit the long-term viability of training programs in terms of student numbers and financial support. At the very least, training program staff should talk with church leaders about their members who are potential trainees and explain what the training hopes to achieve.

POSSIBLE WAYS BIBLE COLLEGES, SEMINARIES, AND OTHER PROGRAMS COULD ENHANCE THEIR TRAINING FOR MISSIONARIES

Consulting Stakeholders

The first step in reviewing an existing training program is to consult with the stakeholders. The primary stakeholders are sending churches and mission agencies. Missionaries who are currently serving with those agencies or who have recently left the field are particularly important to consult with as they are the people who receive, look after, and support new missionaries through the challenging first few years on the field. They are also the people most aware of the limited resources and practical realities of what missionary work involves on a day-to-day basis. Much of the work of consulting current missionaries and missionary trainers to develop profiles of effective missionaries has already been done. Existing profiles such as those in Chapter 1 can be used as starting points for review and/or discussion. Other areas that stakeholders should be asked about include the timing of training, pathways to completion of the training, and the cost to the participants.

In order to achieve its purpose of bringing change to existing programs that will help missionaries become more effective, consultation with stakeholders has to be more than just gathering their opinions. It should allow the stakeholders to have a genuine influence on training program design. It is important to gather as diverse a range of stakeholders as possible, rather than simply gathering like-minded people, or graduates of the existing program, as this helps to stop a perpetuation of the way things have always been done. Although this will make the discussions more difficult, the outcomes will be more robust and broadly representative. In addition, if stakeholders perceive that their concerns are being taken seriously, it will increase their support for the program.

Stakeholder consultation should be an ongoing feature of program review, not simply something done at the outset. Evaluative loops that examine graduate performance and allow employers or supervisors to have an input into a continually developing program result in a program that is more responsive and relevant to current needs.

Accreditation

Training institutions have often been set up and run as independent agents with little accountability to those who support them. Although they may have advisory boards that include a few missionaries with current or recent experience, these boards often have little say concerning the curriculum or its methods of delivery. Whether or not graduates are suitable for the jobs they will do is not considered practically relevant to the running or governance of the program. A good way to change this is by developing an accreditation system that specifically endorses programs that prepare missionaries well.

Accreditation means that the program has been given a stamp of approval by a group with vested interest that evaluates programs based on well-defined criteria. As a normal part of the accrediting process, different aspects of the program are evaluated and the program has the opportunity to work on areas that are weak. Where the training group is an open learning community, the accreditation process is welcomed as an opportunity to review progress, reflect on outcomes, and improve the quality of teaching and learning.

An important outcome of accreditation is that potential trainees and their supporters are more likely to choose programs that are accredited. The more prestigious and credible the accrediting body, the more impact the accreditation will have. Those colleges and training groups that state that they focus on missionary training would actively seek the accreditation, which would provide an avenue for introducing change into established programs. Training groups and institutions that achieve accreditation would have the right to include the accreditation endorsement on their websites and advertising material. Potential trainees will preferentially choose those programs that have the accrediting body's stamp of approval. Once students start preferentially attending these programs, stakeholder influence increases and further program adjustments in response to changing ministry needs is easier to achieve.

Mission agencies have a strong vested interest in the quality of training for their candidates and should play the major role in establishing a missions training accreditation body. At the moment, when potential missionaries contact a mission agency, they are usually directed by that agency towards the agency's preferred training program. However, mission agencies have little influence on the content of the program or the way it is delivered. If mission agencies became more active and chose to exert their influence, it would have a significant, positive effect on missionary training. Our recommendation would be that mission agencies band together to form a missions training accrediting body that would approve certain programs for missionary training and encourage others to meet their criteria. This would help distinguish programs that provide excellent missionary training according to specific missions criteria determined by stakeholders.

Integrating Theology with Cross-cultural Life and Ministry

There have been many calls over the past century for a more holistic approach to biblical and theological education that integrates character and spiritual formation and the development of practical ministry skills with a deep understanding of the Bible, but unfortunately these calls have rarely been acted on. Many recent books urge theological institutions to focus on training the whole person, not just their minds.[194] This call is cogently expressed in The International Council for Evangelical Theological Education's (ICETE) Manifesto on the Renewal of Theological Education:

> Our programmes of theological education must combine spiritual and practical with academic objectives in one holistic integrated educational approach. We are at fault that we so often focus educational requirements narrowly on cognitive attainments, while we hope for student growth in other dimensions but leave it largely to chance. Our programmes must be designed to attend to the growth and equipping of the whole man of God.[195]

---

194. Edward Farley, *Theologia: The Fragmentation and Unity of Theological Education* (Philadelphia, PA: Fortress Press, 1983); Bernhard Ott, *Beyond Fragmentation: Integrating Mission and Theological Education: A Critical Assessment of Some Recent Developments in Evangelical Theological Education* (Irvine, CA: Regnum Books International, 2001); Banks, *Reenvisioning Theological Education: Exploring a Missional Alternative to Current Models*.

195. International Council for Evangelical Theological Education, "ICETE Manifesto on the Renewal of Evangelical Theological Education," http://www.icete-edu .org/manifesto/index.htm.

The failure of much theological education to develop students holistically as servants of God was also evident in a recent, wide-ranging study of theological education in Australia. It revealed a "disconnect" between theological education and the life and ministry of graduates from Bible and theological colleges in Australia. Students reported little personal change over the course of their college education, and the changes they did report were primarily intellectual. More than a tenth of final year students felt that their college experience reflected an "over-intellectual approach to theology" and a "lack of practical connection to life or ministry, with virtually no connection with the secular world which is a large part of the context of lived Christianity."[196] Perry Shaw provides an excellent example of how one traditional Bible seminary went through a curriculum review process to develop a more integrated program. His book outlines both principles and practical steps that others could apply in their own situations.[197]

Missionary trainees would benefit from a more integrated theological education curriculum that connects the issues they face in cross-cultural life and ministry with their engagement with the Bible, theology, Christian history, and missiology. They also need to develop character, a spiritual resilience that will enable them to thrive in isolated situations, faith with integrity in the face of the real world, cultural sensitivity through prolonged interaction with people from other cultures, and expertise in relating their faith to the issues and experiences of life for people who live in very different circumstances than that which the missionary has grown up with. These things can only be developed in authentic cross-cultural ministry situations.

Possible Ways to Integrate This Training Approach into Bible Colleges and Seminaries

The approach to missionary training described in this book could be integrated with an existing institutional program or implemented as a parallel certificate that runs alongside the existing program. Integration is the better option as it protects against the unspoken message that missions is an optional extra.

---

196. Ball, *Transforming Theology: Student Experience and Transformative Learning in Undergraduate Theological Education*, 55, 67–69.

197. Shaw, *Transforming Theological Education: A Practical Handbook for Integrative Learning*.

Our current systems of theological education have mostly tended to marginalize mission.[198] Ken Gnanakan sees the inclusion of missions into the core curriculum as a vital need in Asia: "In fact, unless and until mission training is seen as part of overall seminary training, the division between missions and theology will itself continue to grow to damaging proportions."[199] This need to integrate cross-cultural mission training into existing Bible and theological colleges is echoed by graduates in the UK, according to a recent multi-college survey conducted by the UK evangelical missions network Global Connections.[200]

Cross-cultural ministry practical experience

One way of integrating the kind of training advocated in this book with a traditional institutional training program is through a mixture of practical and theoretical blocks of missions learning spread throughout the degree program. Medical, nursing, and teaching courses use this approach. During the teaching blocks at a college or university that is training doctors, nurses, or teachers, students learn according to traditional higher education methods. In the practical blocks that are interspersed among the theoretical ones, students have to demonstrate skills and attitudes that are then signed off by their supervisors who are usually experienced practitioners. Bible colleges and seminaries that do not have a nearby cross-cultural ministry context for trainees to engage in could adopt a similar approach.

Another possible way of integrating this kind of training into existing programs is for students intending to become missionaries to live in multicultural areas and spend two or three days of each week in cross-cultural ministry and two or three days on campus for the duration of their degree. To do this they would need to be released from monocultural church ministry commitments so that they can focus on cross-cultural ministry. They should be held accountable for specific

---

198. William Taylor points this out with regret based on his and others' broad experience of trying to foster change in formal educational institutions in William Taylor, "Foreword," in *Integral Ministry Training: Design and Evaluation*, ed. Robert Brynjolfson and Jonathan Lewis (Pasadena, CA: William Carey Library, 2006), x.

199. Ken Gnanakan, "The Training of Missiologists for Asian Contexts," in *Missiological Education for the Twenty-First Century: The Book, the Circle, and the Sandals: Essays in Honor of Paul E. Pierson*, ed. Paul Everett Pierson, et al. (Maryknoll, NY: Orbis Books, 1996), 117.

200. Brynjolfson, "Mission Training Review: Piecing Together the Puzzle; Executive Summary Report," 203.

ministry activity as guided by the requirement to fulfill specific practical ministry expectations such as those described in the Journey Training competencies.

Many Bible and theological colleges have practical ministry requirements for students to fulfill, primarily in established churches. Cross-cultural ministry placements would be a better option for students who are planning to become missionaries overseas or church planters in multicultural contexts in their home countries. If it is not possible to find opportunities for intercultural interaction in the institution's local context, a two to four week cross-cultural practicum could be conducted every year in a multicultural area or city. Another option would be to offer cross-cultural ministry as a residential block for a semester of the institutional program perhaps with one or two traditional missions subjects being offered concurrently to deepen the students' engagement with missiological issues connected to the kind of ministry they are engaged in. Advantages of conducting cross-cultural training in the same region as the institution include that it provides an alternative to expensive overseas trips for cross-cultural exposure, allows students to experience different cultures in an environment where support is readily available, and increases their skills in relating to immigrants.

To achieve their purpose, practicums, field ministry units, and extra-curricular or co-curricular cross-cultural ministry activities need to be intentional in what they seek to achieve. If the institution has ministry weeks or practicums, for example, instead of these being relatively unstructured and ad-hoc in terms of outcomes, they should be reviewed and redesigned to ensure that specific competencies are developed.

A major challenge of implementing this approach is finding, training, and supporting people who can supervise and mentor trainees/students in cross-cultural ministry. These ministry supervisors are key to this kind of training. They are of enormous benefit to Bible college and seminary training, though, not only because of the vital practical wisdom and ministry skills they teach, but also because they help to form connections between the churches or para-church ministries and the training institution.

A disadvantage of this approach is that it could perpetuate a division between knowledge and practice. Ministry skill and personal character development could be perceived as an add-on rather than the heart of effective ministry. One way to address this is to ensure that ministry debriefing sessions explicitly relate cross-cultural ministry experiences to the knowledge curriculum and that connections with cross-cultural ministry experiences are intentionally created in classes.

Reorganizing the curriculum around a problem-based learning approach

A common and helpful approach to integrating theory and practice is problem-based learning. Through the process of solving practical problems in small groups, students learn the process of how to learn together with others and this becomes as important as the products such as essays, reports, exams, and clinical skills that they produce. A problem-based approach to learning design enables learning and its products to be more authentic, motivating and life-impacting. If communal learning experiences are designed well they can also facilitate learning to help others learn rather than learning as competition.

A problem-based learning approach integrates practical competencies and knowledge outcomes as they are addressed together in the same learning activities. This approach has transformed medical training in recent decades and is also being adopted by other professions including the health sciences and teaching.[201] This involves more complex curricular design that interweaves professional outcomes (or competencies) and normal content (knowledge) delivery, and increases the authenticity of learning activities and assessments.

This more integrated approach to curriculum design utilizes curriculum mapping to regroup outcomes, including competencies, around themes, professional tasks, or practical problems rather than traditional content arrangements. In curriculum mapping, all outcomes—traditional degree learning outcomes and practical outcomes—are collated and then rearranged into an integrative whole. Curriculum mapping also enables assessment to be more efficient as a single assessment may be able to simultaneously address competencies and traditional learning outcomes from a number of different areas.

One way that Bible colleges and seminaries could reorganize their curricula using a problem-based approach is to modularize subjects so that each module is configured around specific ministry challenges. If each subject is broken down into six to ten component modules, these can be flexibly rearranged and integrated with modules from other subjects according to the different ministry configurations that are chosen in alignment with a guided path. Figure 9 illustrates the way in which different modules, depicted by light boxes, could be created from traditional subject areas (dark gray peripheral boxes) and applied to a specific cross-cultural ministry problem (central dark box).

---

201. Hibbert and Hibbert, "Assessing the Need for Better Integration in Theological Education. Proposals, Progress, and Possibilities from the Medical Education Model."

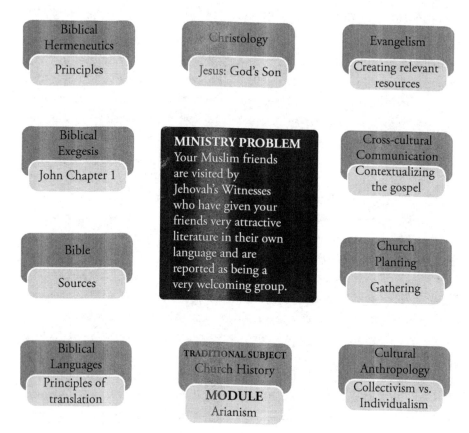

Figure 9 Example of modularization applied to a specific ministry problem

For missionaries, a Bible college degree provides a repository of tradition, a record of the way people in the past, in their various cultural contexts, have encountered God and agreed together on what he expects of them. As such, a Bible college can offer significant help to people in their current contexts by explaining the problems and questions Christians encountered through the centuries and how they have solved them, and by helping students get a better grasp of the Scriptures. These insights are found in the disciplines of biblical studies, theology, and church history. In order to make use of the treasures in this repository in their own lives and ministries, however, missionaries need to be able to make connections between biblical, theological, and historical insights and what they are encountering in the contemporary world in the culture(s) in which they are working. Problem-based learning focused around the specific challenges of intercultural ministry is a powerful tool in helping to make these connections.

A LEARNING PATHWAY APPROACH
TO MISSIONARY TRAINING

Missionaries need to become lifelong learners, so it is helpful to think of their training as an ongoing process that instills and perpetuates a commitment to continuing to learn. In today's world, more and more people are pursuing higher degrees and need to receive recognized credit for any learning they do. This means that degrees and certificates need to be considered not as standalone entities, but rather as building blocks towards further study.

One way that flexible, in-ministry training can be part of promoting lifelong learning is to specifically design it to build on previous accredited learning experiences and ensure that it leads to further accredited learning. Even in the most isolated corners of the world, graduates request certification. This is an inevitable consequence of the educational enterprise that invests value in any education and promotes opportunities for those who can prove they have studied. It is unfair to exclude graduates from these opportunities on the basis of personal ideals. If you believe the training you offer is worth doing and that your graduates have something to offer the world, then you need to find a way to recognize this through gaining some kind of recognized accreditation for your program. For this to happen, programs need to be educationally well designed. This building block approach to study enables less experienced students to gradually build their academic skills and promotes an ethos of continual learning, especially if each learning experience is perceived as valuable and relevant.

Some Bible colleges are running gap year programs that follow high school and precede college or university courses to try and recruit future students. Mission agencies are similarly running short-term programs with the hope of recruiting future missionaries. Where these short-term programs are accredited and offer credit for part of a degree, they not only become more attractive to trainees, but also provide a feasible pathway for further study even if the young person is not initially intending to continue on to college. Basically, it is easier to take a path that has already been prepared than to forge your own. In the world of higher education today, most students expect to receive credit for learning activities they have already done, and most colleges have systems in place for assessing the relative value of previous study.

Often, academic colleges are reluctant to offer credit for practical learning. However, where the practical learning has been well designed and its outcomes carefully specified, it is easier to establish its credibility as a valuable and relevant learning experience. The Australian education system has recognized this by formally defining the pathways from vocational (or practical) to higher education (academic) and specifying the relative values and possible credit from one to the other. This allows vocational missionary training programs, such as the Journey Training, to be integrated into a missions career pathway involving a range of different levels of learning over time.

An increasing challenge faced by missionary training in the West over the past few decades has been that people are going to the field later and later. Getting young people to the field before marriage or at least before they have children, when they are free to maximize their time in language study, is becoming more and more difficult. Short-term ministry opportunities get people out to the field for a few months to one or two years but then those who want to transition to long-term missionary service are usually dislocated for several years in order to obtain a Bible or theological degree.

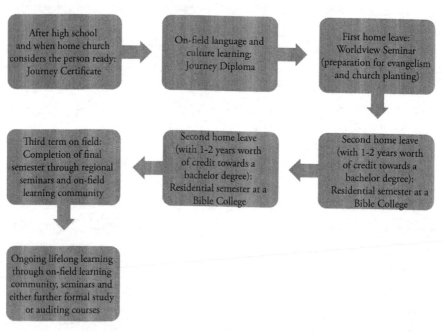

Figure 10 A pathways approach to missionary training

A pathway approach to training allows for more flexible and incremental training options without either a long delay in getting to the field or interrupting their time on the field with long periods at home. A pathway approach also has the potential to tailor what is studied to the needs of the ministry context. Mission agencies may find it beneficial both for recruiting and for improving missionary effectiveness to intentionally develop alliances with different training groups in order to be able to offer specific pathways and credit for their missionaries. Figure 10 provides an illustration of a pathways approach using the Journey Training as an example.

KEEPING THE PURPOSE IN FOCUS: HELPING MISSIONARIES BECOME EFFECTIVE

The overarching purpose of missionary training is to prepare people to effectively communicate Christ in cultures different to their own so that churches come into being and grow among them. This means that trainees must become comfortable and competent in cross-cultural settings and have the resilience to cope and thrive in ministry in unfamiliar environments. In order to grow in these areas, they need to have intentional and supported exposure to cross-cultural ministry.

The most important factors in training are the trainers and a context in which cross-cultural ministry is intrinsic to the learning experience. Churches in multicultural areas and in-ministry training programs are well situated to embed these critical ingredients into their training. Institutions and churches in situations where one culture dominates will have to work harder to provide authentic cross-cultural ministry experience and to ensure it is integrated into the overall learning experience.

Competency-based training has well-defined outcomes and is particularly appropriate for missionary training as it can be easily adapted to different venues and contexts. This makes it well suited for missionary training. Church members who are working at their normal jobs and who are preparing for future cross-cultural mission work would not have to leave their work to study but could be involved in outreach among a local minority group alongside missionary trainers as part of their normal Christian ministry.

How the competencies are addressed could be adjusted according to the normal patterns of ministry they encounter. Reflection on missiological theory could occur in small groups at times that suit trainees and trainers. Participants do not have to be highly literate or have a college degree (even though this would be an advantage), as oral learning strategies that are familiar in trainees' cultures could be employed. More literate participants can help less literate ones learn by teaching them what they have been reading, and they themselves would learn how to enable others to grasp the content of texts. This approach is also more likely to be reproduced by the missionaries in their new ministry context due to its greater flexibility and accessibility.

AFTERWORD

This book records a different way of training. There are people who want to do missionary training in a different way but the old methods persist and the tendency to privilege knowledge in training situations seems inexorable. Colleagues have encouraged us to passionately urge people to take up these principles and to develop a community of people who will enact them and support each other in the process. We have discovered, however, that passion alone is not a strong enough force to bring about change.

Change comes when people acknowledge that there is a real need for it, and when leaders support it. So we leave the reader with a question: "Do you think there is a need for change in missionary training?" If so, and you are a leader, "What are you going to do about it?" The single most influential thing you can do is to start and support an inter-mission group which accredits and therefore endorses missionary training on the basis of what is needed for effective field ministry.

For all of us, the first step towards effective missionary training is to become learners and to create learning communities around ourselves. These communities will reproduce their DNA in the people they influence. We encourage you to start a chain of learning by becoming a reflective, 2 Timothy 2:2 missions practitioner wherever you are.

TECHNICAL DESCRIPTION OF A UNIT OF COMPETENCY

A technical description of a unit of competency (which refers to one specifically defined competency) includes the following:

Code and Title

The title is active in that it states what the competent trainee does or knows, or what he or she is like.

Descriptor

The competency descriptor describes what the trainee has to do in order to achieve competency.

Application

The application of a competency outlines how this specific competency helps the trainee to fulfill what cross-cultural church planters do as their work in their specific context.

Elements

The elements of a competency are the specific, essential steps that must be progressed through in order to achieve competence. These are written in active language stating what the trainee has to do.

Performance Criteria

The performance criteria are descriptions of observable evidence that indicate to an assessor that the trainee has completed each step that is essential as part of fulfilling a competency. They are stated actively so that both trainee and assessor have no doubt about what is being assessed and in such a way that the assessor (and trainee) can easily agree that each criteria has been completed or achieved, or not. Where the performance criteria might be performed differently in different contexts (e.g. "boil hot water" would be performed differently in a Tibetan mountain village without electricity than in a European apartment) the range of acceptable variance in approach should be clarified in a range statement. As these competencies were designed specifically for the training of cross-cultural church planters, the performance criteria are specifically limited in the range statement to performance that is appropriate for these contexts. If the same competencies were re-applied to a rural, monocultural church planting context, the range statements would need to be modified.[202]

Required Knowledge and Required Skills

This describes the essential skills and knowledge required for fulfillment of the competency and the level of knowledge and skill. Skills are listed first, followed by the knowledge necessary to perform the skill. Skills are given prior importance to try to avoid knowledge eclipsing the importance of the skills and to provide a context for the knowledge.

Evidence Guide

The evidence guide states specifically what the trainee has to demonstrate to an assessor in order to be judged competent. Evidence can be in the form of specific products or indicators that a specific process has taken place. The evidence guide also specifies the context in which the assessment will take place and any specific resources that must be used in the process or preparation of the product. If the competency is interdependent with other competencies, they can be concurrently assessed and this would also be stated in the evidence guide. The evidence guide should also state the different things an assessor should do in order to be sure that competency has been achieved.

Please note: Due to the limited space available for publication, the Range Statements, Required Knowledge and Skills, and Context and Methods of Assessment have been deleted from the Competencies in Appendix 1. If you would like the full competencies, please write to the authors.

---

202. Due to space limitations, the range statements have not been included in this book. If you would like copies of these much more detailed documents, please write to the authors.

CERTIFICATE

Assessor Competencies

Cross-cultural church planting competency needs to be assessed by experienced cross-cultural church planters. Appropriate and relevant industrial experience for assessing Certificate IV competencies requires at least three years of continuous experience learning another language and working in another culture.

Units of Competency

CCP1—Articulate Christian principles effectively using storytelling

Unit Descriptor

This unit covers the communication of biblical narratives, commands, principles, and themes using storytelling.

Application of the Unit

To articulate Christian principles effectively using storytelling involves being able to understand different styles of biblical material and Christian principles and communicate them in a storying format. The focus of the unit is the process of articulating the material or principles into story format. As this process requires both an ability to interpret biblical literature and to craft stories, it is recommended that CCP2 (Create a repertoire of stories and articulate these appropriately for selected audiences) and CCP3 (Enable others to interpret Bible passages using a communal, reproducible, inductive method) are covered together with this unit or are pre-requisite to it. The aim of the unit is the development of the ability to spontaneously craft stories that communicate relevant Christian principles in response to the normal questions and events of daily life. These stories should be so natural and contextualized that they can be incorporated into normal interpersonal conversation. As such, it is a relevant skill for any Christian worker who is involved in evangelism, discipleship, or counseling in either a monocultural or cross-cultural context.

Element	Performance Criteria
1 Articulate biblical narrative using storytelling	• Articulate three historical biblical narratives using storytelling • Articulate three non-historical biblical narratives using storytelling
2 Articulate given biblical requirements for Christian living using storytelling	• Illustrate three biblical commands using storytelling • Communicate three biblical principles for Christian living using storytelling
3 Articulate key salvation concepts using storytelling	• Articulate three biblical narratives communicating salvation concepts using storytelling • Articulate three key salvation concepts using storytelling
4 Articulate key theological concepts using storytelling	• Illustrate three key biblical themes using storytelling • Articulate three key theological concepts using storytelling

Evidence Guide

Overview

A person who demonstrates competency in this unit must be able to provide evidence that they can articulate biblical narratives, biblical principles for Christian living, and key salvation and theological concepts using storytelling.

Critical Aspects of Evidence to Demonstrate Competency in This Unit

Assessment requires evidence of the following products or processes to be collected:

Products

- A minimum of three historical biblical narratives told as stories
- A minimum of three non-historical biblical narratives told as stories
- A minimum of three biblical commands illustrated as stories
- A minimum of three biblical principles for Christian living communicated as stories
- A minimum of three biblical narratives communicating salvation concepts told as stories
- A minimum of three key salvation concepts explained as stories
- A minimum of three key biblical themes illustrated as stories
- A minimum of three key theological concepts illustrated as stories

Processes
- The articulation of themes and concepts in story form
- The telling of stories

CCP2—Create a repertoire of stories and articulate these appropriately for selected audiences

Unit Descriptor
This unit develops skills in telling a variety of stories to a variety of audiences.

Application of the Unit
Creating a repertoire of stories and articulating them appropriately for different audiences involves the processes of crafting stories, telling stories, modifying stories for different audiences, and changing the forms of stories to match the different styles of storytelling found in other cultures. The focus of the unit is on the telling of stories and how the telling needs to be adjusted according to the differing backgrounds and expectations of different audiences. The context of the unit is cross-cultural church planting, so therefore its emphasis is on the communicating of biblical principles using stories and the adjusting of the storytelling for cross-cultural contexts.

Communicating biblical principles using stories requires both an ability to interpret biblical literature and to articulate biblical content into stories, it is recommended that CCP1 (Articulate Christian principles effectively using storytelling) and CCP3 (Enable others to interpret Bible passages using a communal, reproducible, inductive method) are covered together with this unit or are pre-requisite to it. The aim of the unit is the development of the ability to spontaneously craft stories that communicate relevant Christian principles in response to the normal questions and events of daily life, particularly in cross-cultural contexts. These stories should be so natural and contextualized that they can be incorporated into normal interpersonal conversation. As such, it is a relevant skill for any Christian worker who is involved in evangelism, discipleship, or counseling in cross-cultural contexts. It is also a relevant skill in monocultural contexts due to the need to consider the differing profile of any audience for effective communication to occur.

Element	Performance Criteria
1 Create stories and tell them to others	• Present the narrative content of the story in correct sequence
	• Identify the story climax
	• Craft the storytelling to build towards the climax
	• Identify the main point of the story
	• Repeatedly reinforce the main point during the storytelling
	• Communicate the teaching points of the story through the storytelling rather than through extra explanation or preaching
	• Use questions to enhance the narrative rather than to check information transfer or as preaching opportunities
	• Use reproducible props appropriately
	• The form of delivery engages the audience in a culturally appropriate way
2 Articulate stories appropriately for selected audiences	• Identify the significant cultural and demographic features of the audience
	• Change a set story to suit different audiences
3 Contextualize Bible stories in the form of stories from other cultures	• Tell a story from another culture in its original form
	• Analyze a story from another culture with respect to content, characterization, sequencing, meaning, and delivery
	• Identify a Bible story illustrating the same meaning as a story from another culture
	• Craft a Bible story in the same form as a story from another culture
	• Tell a contextualized Bible story to a person from the culture for which the story is being contextualized

Evidence Guide

Overview

A person who demonstrates competency in this unit must be able to provide evidence that they can create stories and tell them to others, articulating the stories appropriately for selected audiences. As part of the appropriate articulation they must provide evidence that they can contextualize Bible stories into the forms of other cultures.

Critical Aspects of Evidence to Demonstrate Competency in This Unit
Assessment requires evidence of the following products or processes to be collected:

Products
- A story told in which:
  - The narrative content is presented in correct sequence
  - The story is crafted towards its climax
  - The main point is repeatedly reinforced
  - There is no extra preaching or explanation
  - Questions are used to enhance the narrative
  - The form of delivery is appropriate to the audience
  - The form of delivery engages the audience
    in a culturally appropriate way
- An outline of the demographics of an audience
- A story told that has been changed to suit different audiences
- A story told from another culture
- Analysis of a story from another culture
- A contextualized Bible story told to a person from the culture for which
  the story has been contextualized

Processes
- Craft a story
- Identify the demographics of the audience
- Change a story to suit different audiences
- Analyze a story from another culture with respect to:
  - Content
  - Characterization
  - Sequencing
  - Meaning
  - Delivery
- Craft a Bible story in the same form as a story from another culture

CCP3—Enable others to interpret Bible passages using a communal, reproducible, inductive method

Unit Descriptor

This unit gives practical experience of a simple method of understanding and applying different genres of biblical literature which can be used in a cross-cultural church planting context.

Application of the Unit

Enabling others to interpret Bible passages using a communal, reproducible, inductive method involves facilitating a group to use a simple, reproducible method of biblical interpretation. This unit also covers an exploration of the nature of truth and how it is derived, defined, and propagated with particular reference to cross-cultural church planting contexts. The focus of the unit is particularly on the communal process of interpretation of the different genres of biblical text and the development of an appreciation for what each individual can bring to the discovery of meaning and application. The aim of the unit is to familiarize trainees with a simple method of biblical study which can be used in oral and literate cultures and which is not dependent on a professional teacher for its employment. The intent is that this method is used in cross-cultural church planting contexts with the intentional empowering of local people to interact with the Bible from early in their Christian experience. It is a relevant skill for all Christian workers who are involved in discipling and teaching. It is a critical skill for cross-cultural church planters who are intending to facilitate multiplying churches.

Element	Performance Criteria
1 Use a simple, reproducible method of inductive Bible study	• Read and comprehend a Bible passage
	• Note the context of the Bible passage
	• Analyze a Bible passage and divide it into meaningful sections
	• Ask questions of the Bible text
	• Compare the events, themes, and meanings of the Bible passage with other similar Bible passages
	• Derive a concrete, specific application with respect to daily life in the contemporary world
	• Apply the above steps successfully to different genres of biblical literature

Element	Performance Criteria
2 Lead a group in deriving a communal understanding of meaning from biblical texts	• Apply the above steps in a group setting • Derive meaning communally • Agree on application collectively
3 Articulate the challenges of defining and applying truth cross-culturally	• Discuss epistemology and the nature of truth • Discuss the roles of tradition, experience, the Bible, the Christian community and the Holy Spirit in defining and enforcing Christian truth • Discuss three cross-cultural case studies illustrating different cultural perspectives on Christian truth

Evidence Guide

Overview

A person who demonstrates competency in this unit must be able to provide evidence that they can use and lead a group in using a simple, reproducible method of inductive Bible study. They must also provide evidence of articulating the challenges of defining and applying truth cross-culturally.

Critical Aspects of Evidence to Demonstrate Competency in This Unit

Assessment requires evidence of the following processes to be collected:

Processes

Use of a simple, reproducible method of inductive Bible study including:

- Reading and understanding a Bible passage
- Noting the context of the Bible passage
- Analyzing and dividing the passage into meaningful sections
- Asking questions of the Bible text
- Comparisons being made with other similar Bible passages
- Deriving a concrete, specific application of the Bible passage with respect to daily life in the contemporary world
- The above method being applied to different genres of biblical literature
- Leading a group to use the above method as a communal exercise
- Discussion of the nature of truth
- Discussion of the roles of tradition, experience, the Bible, the Christian community, and the Holy Spirit in defining and enforcing truth
- Discussion of at least three different cross-cultural case studies illustrating different cultural perspectives on Christian truth

CCP4—Prepare and put into practice the initial steps in a cross-cultural church planting strategy

Unit Descriptor

This unit covers the process of preparing and putting into practice the initial steps of cross-cultural church planting.

Application of the Unit

The purpose of this unit is to provide hands-on experience of the designing and implementation of the initial steps in cross-cultural church planting. It covers the preparation of a strategy and the putting of that strategy into practice. Its focus is on doing church planting in a cross-cultural context and is specifically designed with the intention that when trainees move into another context they will know what to do to start cross-cultural church planting work. It provides the foundational steps, principles, and experience necessary for any Christian who is planning to work as a church planter in a culture other than their own and would also have relevance for monocultural church planters who are working in unfamiliar contexts.

Element	Performance Criteria
1 Prepare and implement a beginning strategy for cross-cultural church planting	• Research the geography, social demography, and spiritual state of a specific geographical area
	• Devise and implement three prayer strategies
	• Devise and implement three strategies for evangelism
	• Identify, source, and collect appropriate tools for evangelism
2 Articulate principles for establishing churches in cross-cultural contexts	• Describe the biblical essentials of church
	• Visit three different ethnic expressions of Christian church and reflect on the experiences
	• Create or experience house church
	• Formulate principles for cross-cultural church planting based on biblical data and the above experiences

Evidence Guide

Overview

A person who demonstrates competency in this unit must be able to provide evidence that they can articulate principles for establishing churches in cross-cultural contexts, prepare a beginning strategy for cross-cultural church planting and put it into practice.

Critical Aspects of Evidence to Demonstrate Competency in This Unit

Assessment requires evidence of the following products or processes to be collected:

Products
- A research report on the geography, social demography, and the spiritual state of a specific geographical area
- A minimum of three prayer strategies
- A minimum of three strategies for evangelism
- Examples of appropriate tools for evangelism
- Information concerning the sources of the appropriate evangelistic tools
- A log of the implementation of the beginning cross-cultural church planting strategy
- A description of the biblical essentials of church
- A reflective log of visits to at least three different ethnic expressions of church
- A list of principles for cross-cultural church planting

Processes

The beginning cross-cultural church planting strategy is implemented including:
- A minimum of three prayer strategies
- A minimum of three evangelism strategies
- Visits to a minimum of three different ethnic expressions of church
- Creating a simulation of house church or experiencing an established house church

CCP5—Outline the principles of cross-cultural church planting

Unit Descriptor

This unit explores the principles informing the practice of effective cross-cultural church planting.

Application of the Unit

In this unit the principles of cross-cultural church planting are outlined. The biblical bases, different models of church planting, and missiological issues in cross-cultural church planting are covered. The aim of the unit is to provide a theoretical foundation by which cross-cultural church planting strategies can be developed and church planting practice can be evaluated. Its focus is church planting in cross-cultural contexts. This unit provides essential knowledge for cross-cultural church planting practitioners which is derived through interaction with biblical, historical, and contemporary sources.

Element		Performance Criteria
1	Derive and articulate biblical theologies that inform cross-cultural church planting	• Outline a biblical theology of church planting • Derive a biblical theology of suffering and persecution
2	Evaluate different models of church planting with respect to their effectiveness in cross-cultural contexts	• Evaluate three different models of church planting with respect to their effectiveness in cross-cultural contexts • Explain the strategy of one effective cross-cultural church planter
3	Outline key principles for effective cross-cultural church planting	• State the principles of church planting movements • Describe obstacles to effective cross-cultural church planting • Explain the principle of reproducibility • Explain the role of the cross-cultural church planter

Evidence Guide

Overview

A person who demonstrates competency in this unit must be able to provide evidence that they can derive and articulate biblical theologies in relation to cross-cultural church planting, evaluate different models of church planting with respect to their effectiveness in cross-cultural contexts, and outline key principles for effective cross-cultural church planting.

Critical Aspects of Evidence to Demonstrate Competency in This Unit

Assessment requires evidence of the following products or processes to be collected:

Products

- A biblical theology of church planting
- A biblical theology of suffering and persecution
- An explanation of the strategy of at least one effective cross-cultural church planter
- A list of principles of church planting movements
- A description of the obstacles to effective cross-cultural church planting
- An explanation of the principle of reproducibility
- An explanation of the role of the cross-cultural church planter

Processes

- Evaluation of a minimum of three different models of church planting with respect to their effectiveness in cross-cultural contexts

CCP6—Research and describe aspects of another culture using ethnographic methods

Unit Descriptor
This unit covers the skills of observation and interview integral to the discipline of ethnographic research.

Application of the Unit
To research and describe aspects of another culture using ethnographic methods involves the processes of participant observation, ethnographic interview, disciplined recording of research, and the evaluation of the researcher's assumptions leading to further questions about what has been learned. This unit provides experience in doing ethnographic research and examining the assumptions an outsider makes about another culture. The aim of the unit is to provide experience in ethnographic research methods particularly as preparation for the extensive ethnographic research required in the Diploma in Cross-Cultural Church Planting. As a standalone unit it has application for any person wanting to learn about another culture in a disciplined way.

Element	Performance Criteria
1 Write an ethnographic description of a cross-cultural experience	• Observe the geographical, physical, and social context
	• Describe all events and interactions
	• Record observations as soon as possible after the event
	• Record observations without making judgments or interpretations
	• Describe the feelings of the observer during the experience
	• Identify things that are not understood by the observer
	• Identify assumptions made by the observer
	• Explore the reasons why those assumptions were made
	• Formulate questions to further understand what was observed
2 Conduct an ethnographic interview	• Introduce the interviewer
	• Explain the purpose of the interview to the interviewee
	• Ask permission to record the interview
	• Ask a "grand tour" question
	• Ask a "mini tour" question
	• Ask two "probe" questions
	• Write up or transcribe the interview
	• Analyze the transcript for key themes
	• Write an ethnographic report of the interview according to key themes and use the interviewee's own words to illustrate points being described

Evidence Guide

Overview

A person who demonstrates competency in this unit must be able to provide evidence that they can write an ethnographic description of a cross-cultural experience and conduct an ethnographic interview.

Critical Aspects of Evidence to Demonstrate Competency in This Unit

Assessment requires evidence of the following products or processes to be collected:

Products

A written ethnographic description of a cross-cultural experience including:

- A description of the geographical, physical, and social context
- A description of all events and interactions that occurred during the experience
- A record of the time of the cross-cultural experience and the time of writing the description
- Feelings experienced by the observer during the cross-cultural experience are recorded
- A list of things not understood by the observer
- A list of assumptions made by the observer about the cross-cultural experience
- Explanations for reasons why assumptions were made
- A list of questions to be asked
- An ethnographic interview is conducted including:
  - An introduction to the interviewer
  - An explanation of the purpose of the interview
  - A request for permission to record the interview
  - A "grand tour" question
  - A "mini tour" question
  - At least two "probe" questions
  - A transcript of the ethnographic interview
  - A list of key themes derived from the ethnographic interview
  - A written report of the interview arranged according to key themes and using the interviewee's own words to illustrate points being described

Processes

- Observations are recorded without making judgments
- Analysis of the transcript of the interview for key themes

CCP7—Communicate with people from other cultures about Christian principles

Unit Descriptor

This unit covers the steps necessary to develop a practical theology for a specific cross-cultural context.

Application of the Unit

Communicating with people from other cultures about Christian principles involves understanding the challenges of cross-cultural communication, comprehending the beliefs and practices of people from other cultures, articulating a Christian response and being able to communicate the response respectfully and sensitively. This unit requires trainees to listen to and converse with people from other cultures without causing offense. It also involves deriving Christian responses to unfamiliar questions and issues and being able to articulate these into conversation. The aim of the unit is to develop the skills involved in listening and understanding people from other cultures and preparing relevant and communicable biblical responses. This unit is relevant for any Christian intending to work among people from other cultures.

Element		Performance Criteria
1	Articulate the key challenges of cross-cultural communication	• Describe three models of cross-cultural communication
		• Explain the process and obstacles to cross-cultural communication
		• Give practical examples of cultural baggage
		• Give practical examples of possible receptor distortion
		• Explain the impact and development of alienization in intercultural interactions
		• Explain the concept of form and meaning in relation to cross-cultural communication
2	Identify the beliefs associated with a specific practice	• Identify beliefs associated with a specific practice
		• Describe the trainee's assumptions concerning the identified practice and its associated beliefs
		• Research and explain the assumptions of the people relating to the identified practice and its associated beliefs
3	Prepare a Christian response to the identified practice and its associated beliefs	• Derive biblical principles relating to the identified practice and its associated beliefs
		• Articulate a Christian response to the practice and its associated beliefs
4	Communicate Christian principles with non-Christians from other cultures	• Converse with non-Christians from other cultures
		• Communicate Christian principles sensitively to non-Christians from other cultures

Evidence Guide

Overview

A person who demonstrates competency in this unit must be able to provide evidence that they can articulate the key challenges of cross-cultural communication, identify and prepare a Christian response to the beliefs and practices of a specific culture, and communicate Christian principles to non-Christians from other cultures.

Critical Aspects of Evidence to Demonstrate Competency in This Unit

Assessment requires evidence of the following products or processes to be collected:

Products

- Explanations of at least three different models of cross-cultural communication
- Explanation of the process and obstacles to cross-cultural communication
- List of practical examples of cultural baggage
- List of practical examples of receptor distortion
- Explanation of alienization in intercultural interactions
- Explanation of the concept of form and meaning in relation to cross-cultural communication
- A list of a minimum of three beliefs and practices from a specific culture
- A description of the trainee's assumptions about the identified beliefs and practices
- An explanation of the assumptions of the people within the culture concerning the identified beliefs and practices
- A list of biblical principles relating to the identified beliefs and practices from another culture
- A written or otherwise presented Christian response to the identified beliefs and practices of people from another culture

Processes

- Research into the assumptions of the people within the culture concerning the identified beliefs and practices
- Derivation of biblical principles in relation to the identified beliefs and practices of people from another culture

- Preparation of a Christian response to the identified beliefs and practices of people from another culture
- Conversations with non-Christians from other cultures
- Sensitive communication of Christian principles to non-Christians from other cultures

Methods of Assessment
- Inspection of written or otherwise reported products
- Questioning related to the underpinning knowledge
- Observation of participation in discussion
- Observation of conversations with people from other cultures

CCP8—Respond appropriately to a given range of different cross-cultural experiences

Unit Descriptor
In this unit trainees are exposed to a number of typical cross-cultural situations and demonstrate an ability to behave appropriately in the different contexts

Application of the Unit
Responding appropriately to a given range of different cross-cultural experiences involves interacting with people from other cultures in the context of normal community life. The focus of the unit is on being out among people from other cultures—talking with them, working with them, learning with them, visiting them, and learning to understand and appreciate their lifestyle, religion, and creative arts. The aim of the unit is to expose trainees to a range of different cross-cultural interactions which are normally encountered when working cross-culturally and to evoke the discomfort that normally is felt in these situations. Having experienced cross-cultural discomfort together with an experienced mentor, it is then possible to develop the increased self-understanding which is necessary for effective cross-cultural work. This unit provides relevant, experiential training for any person (Christian or non-Christian) who is intending to work with people from other cultures.

Element	Performance Criteria
1 Act respectfully towards speakers of other languages	• Listen without demanding translation in contexts where another language is spoken
	• Learn and use basic greetings and phrases in another language with native speakers of that language
2 Behave appropriately in different cultural contexts	• Eat unfamiliar food from another culture
	• Visit a home without causing offense
	• Wear appropriate dress with respect to gender roles and expectations
	• Behave appropriately with respect to gender roles and expectations
3 Explain another religion with respect	• Visit a mosque, temple, shrine, or other religious construction and sensitively and respectfully elicit an explanation of its function and purpose from a person who worships there
	• Respectfully give an explanation of a non-Christian religion received from an adherent of that religion
4 Develop appreciation for styles of creativity and communication which are different from the trainee's own culture	• Respectfully explain a sample of the visual arts from another culture
	• Respectfully explain an example of the performing arts from another culture

Evidence Guide

Overview

A person who demonstrates competency in this unit must be able to provide evidence that they can act respectfully and behave appropriately in different cultural contexts, respect other religions and appreciate different cultural styles of creativity and communication.

Critical Aspects of Evidence to Demonstrate Competency in This Unit

Assessment requires evidence of the following products or processes to be collected:

Products

A respectful explanation of:

- a non-Christian religion
- a sample of visual arts from another culture
- an example of the performing arts from another culture

Processes

- Listening without demanding translation in other language contexts
- Using basic greetings and phrases in another language with native speakers of that language
- Eating unfamiliar food from another culture
- Visiting a home without causing offense
- Dressing appropriately
- Behaving appropriately
- Visiting a mosque, temple, shrine, or other religious construction and sensitively and respectfully eliciting an explanation of its function and purpose from a person who worships there
- Receiving an explanation of a non-Christian religion from an adherent of that religion
- Finding and understanding a sample of visual arts from another culture
- Finding and understanding an example of the performing arts from another culture

CCP9—Articulate a biblical response to contemporary theological issues in mission

Unit Descriptor

This unit introduces trainees to a number of contemporary theological issues in mission practice and requires trainees to articulate biblical bases for engaging in mission.

Application of the Unit

Articulating a biblical response to contemporary theological issues in mission involves interacting with the biblical text, inherited Christian traditions, and contemporary missiological theory to prepare a personal response to the different issues commonly faced by cross-cultural church planters. The intention of the unit is to develop reflective practitioners who are aware of current issues in missions and competent to work with others to create responses to difficult questions. This unit is relevant for any Christian intending to work in missions, not just as a cross-cultural church planter.

Element	Performance Criteria
1 Articulate a biblical basis for cross-cultural church planting	• Explain the biblical story of God's interaction with the nations from Genesis to Revelation
	• Outline a biblical justification for the exclusive claim of Jesus as Savior
	• Give a biblical response to the different beliefs about life after death found in three different religions and among Christians
	• Explain the relationship between the role of the Holy Spirit and the missionary in cross-cultural church planting
2 Explain current theological vocabulary and issues in contemporary mission discourse	• Explain the meanings of mission, missional, and missionary and their relationship with each other
	• Articulate the relationship between the kingdom of God, the church, and the activity of cross-cultural church planting
	• Articulate a biblical response to holism in mission
	• Give a biblical description of the inter-relationship between church and mission agency
3 Discuss the interaction between the inherited traditions of the cross-cultural church planter and the development of indigenous theologies and practices	• Explain the concept of Christendom and its implications for cross-cultural church planting in today's world
	• Explain the concept of indigeneity in missions
	• Articulate the relationship between indigenous concepts of God, truth, and righteousness, the development of indigenous theologies, and the inherited theologies of the cross-cultural church planter, and discuss the implications for cross-cultural church planting

Evidence Guide

Overview

A person who demonstrates competency in this unit must be able to provide evidence that they can articulate a biblical basis for cross-cultural church planting, explain current theological vocabulary and issues in contemporary mission discourse, and discuss the interaction between the inherited traditions of the cross-cultural church planter and the development of indigenous theologies and practices.

Critical Aspects of Evidence to Demonstrate Competency in This Unit

Assessment requires evidence of the following products or processes to be collected:

Products

- An explanation of the biblical story of God's interaction with the nations from Genesis to Revelation
- An outline of the biblical justification for the exclusive claim of Jesus as Savior
- A biblical response to the different beliefs about life after death from at least three different religions
- An explanation of the relationship between the role of the Holy Spirit and the missionary in cross-cultural church planting
- An explanation of the meanings of "mission," "missional," and "missionary" and their relationship with each other
- An articulation of the relationship between the kingdom of God, the church, and the activity of cross-cultural church planting
- A biblical response to holism in mission
- A biblical description of the inter-relationship between church and mission agency.
- An explanation of the concept of Christendom and its implications for cross-cultural church planting in today's world
- An explanation of the concept of indigeneity in missions
- An articulation of the relationship between indigenous concepts of God, truth, and righteousness, the development of indigenous theologies, and the inherited theologies of the cross-cultural church planter

Processes

- Discussion of implications for the cross-cultural church planter of the relationship between indigenous concepts of God, truth, and righteousness, the development of *indigenous theologies* and the *inherited theologies* of the cross-cultural church planter

CCP10—Work effectively in a multicultural church planting team

Unit Descriptor
This unit covers the steps necessary for effective formation and the initial stages of working together as a multicultural church planting team.

Application of the Unit
This unit is specific to cross-cultural church planting in a team whose members come from more than one culture. It covers the steps involved in forming a

team and working together on cross-cultural church planting tasks. The focus of the unit is on being a team and working through the processes and conflicts of team in the context of cross-cultural church planting. The intention of the unit is to provide authentic experience of multicultural team in a real cross-cultural church planting context. This unit can be applied either as true team formation for a team that will continue after the unit has been completed, or as an experience which will inform future team formation and life for trainees who are moving to other cross-cultural church planting contexts. Much of the content of the unit is applicable to all teams, monocultural or multicultural, but the intention of this unit is to provide specific experience for Christians who are intending to work with mission agencies overseas and who will very likely find themselves in church planting teams with workers from different cultural backgrounds.

Element	Performance Criteria
1 Work with others to form a team and achieve a team task	• Outline the normal stages of team life • Agree on a common definition of team • Agree on a team covenant • Agree on team vision, goals, and strategies • Achieve a team task together
2 Understand the cultures represented on the team	• Each team member summarizes the main features of every culture represented on the team • Demonstrate an understanding of the leadership and decision-making styles of each culture represented on the team • Discuss the expectations of leaders in each culture on the team
3 Describe the impact of personality and team role differences on team life and function	• Demonstrate familiarity with personality typing and the way it impacts team life and function • Describe team roles and their relationship to team function
4 Manage conflict on the team	• Demonstrate familiarity with the methods other cultures on the team use to resolve conflict • Define biblical principles of conflict resolution • Negotiate a team approach to conflict resolution • Discuss and resolve common areas of conflict in multicultural church planting teams (including the role of women, discipline of team children, and theology)

Evidence Guide

Overview

A person who demonstrates competency in this unit must be able to provide evidence that they can work with others to form a team and achieve a team task, understand the cultures, personalities, and team roles represented on the team and manage conflict on the team.

Critical Aspects of Evidence to Demonstrate Competency in This Unit

Assessment requires evidence of the following products or processes to be collected:

Products

- Outline of the normal stages of team life
- A common definition of team
- A team covenant
- A vision, goals, and strategy statement for the team
- Summaries from each team member of the main features of each culture on the team
- A description of team roles and their relationship to team function
- List of biblical principles for conflict resolution

Processes

- Achieving a specific team task together
- Demonstration of understanding of the leadership and decision-making styles of each culture on the team
- Discussion of the expectations of leaders in each culture on the team
- Demonstration of familiarity with personality and its impact on team life
- Demonstration of familiarity with the different methods of conflict resolution used by each culture on the team
- Negotiation of a team approach to conflict resolution
- Discussion of common areas of conflict in multicultural church planting teams

DIPLOMA

Assessor Competencies

Cross-cultural church planting competency needs to be assessed by experienced cross-cultural church planters. Appropriate and relevant industrial experience for assessing Diploma competencies requires the trainer to have had at least five years of continuous cross-cultural experience in another language context and to have started church planting in that same context.

Units of Competency

CCP11—Develop a practical Christian response to spiritual practices

Unit Descriptor
In this unit the trainee researches the cultural views and practices relating to the spiritual world of the culture and develops a practical Christian response.

Application of the Unit
Developing a practical Christian response to spiritual practices involves investigating biblical and missiological theory concerning the spirit world, in-depth ethnographic research into spiritual beliefs and practices in the culture, and preparing a practical Christian response. The aim of the unit is the development of an awareness of the spiritual dimension of a culture and the formulation of a specific and practical Christian response to a particular spiritual power practice in the culture. The context of the unit is cross-cultural church planting and its intention is to develop competency in relation to dealing with spirits and spiritual power. All cross-cultural workers need to have an understanding and recognition of the nature and control of spiritual power in the culture they are working in and to feel competent to deal with spiritual power when it is encountered. This unit helps in the development of competence in relating to this dimension of life.

Element	Performance Criteria
1 Prepare a biblical response to the world of spirits and spiritual power	• Explain the concept of the excluded middle • Conduct a biblical survey of the spiritual world and its interaction with the material world • Develop a practical theology of the supernatural
2 Research the views and practices in the culture relating to spiritual power	• Research cultural views and practices concerning sickness and healing using ethnographic methods • Research cultural views and practices concerning evil spirits, deliverance, and mental illness using ethnographic methods • Research cultural views and practices concerning blessings and curses using ethnographic methods • Use ethnographic methods to research cultural views and practices concerning charms, spells, and other means of manipulation using spiritual power to fulfill needs or desires • Research the role, methods, and means of power of spiritual power practitioners in the culture using ethnographic methods
3 Develop a practical response to a spiritual power practice in the culture	• Prepare a biblical response for each belief and practice outlined in CCP 11 Element 2 which is encountered in the culture • In collaboration with local believers and more experienced cross-cultural church planters, develop and put into practice a Christian practical alternative to one non-Christian power practice

Evidence Guide

Overview

A person who demonstrates competency in this unit must be able to provide evidence that they can prepare a practical biblical response to spiritual beliefs and practices in the culture.

Critical Aspects of Evidence to Demonstrate Competency in This Unit

Assessment requires evidence of the following products or processes to be collected:

Products

- An explanation of the concept of the excluded middle
- A biblical survey of the spiritual world and its interaction with the material world
- A practical theology of the supernatural

- A biblical response for each belief and practice from Competency Element 11.2 which is encountered in the culture

Processes
- Ethnographic research into the cultural views and practices concerning sickness and healing
- Ethnographic research into the cultural views and practices concerning evil spirits, deliverance, and mental illness
- Ethnographic research into the cultural views and practices concerning blessings and curses
- Ethnographic research into the cultural views and practices concerning charms, spells, and other means of manipulation using spiritual power to fulfill needs or desires
- Ethnographic research into the role, methods, and means of power of spiritual power practitioners in the culture
- Collaboration with local believers and more experienced cross-cultural church planters to develop and put into practice at least one alternative Christian practice for a non-Christian power practice

CCP12—Describe the religious system and beliefs

Unit Descriptor
This unit covers an exploration of the system and beliefs of the religion as expressed in the cross-cultural church planting context and the development of a Christian response.

Application of the Unit
To describe the religious system and beliefs of a culture involves not just an investigation of formal religious theory and practice but also folk religion and beliefs and practices of the people related to the unseen world. This unit covers ethnographic research of religious beliefs and practices, as well as research into beliefs and practices related to the unseen world. Christian responses are derived as theology, theory, and suggestions for practice. It is essential for all cross-cultural workers to have an in-depth understanding of the religion and unseen world of the people they are working among.

Element	Performance Criteria
1 Explain the relationship between formal and folk religion in the culture	• Research the religious system in the culture using ethnographic methods • Obtain a description of the formal religion of the culture through ethnographic interview of a teacher of religion • Obtain a description of religion by three lay practitioners by ethnographic interview • Describe a folk religious practice • Give an ethnographic description of the differences between formal and folk religion in the culture
2 Describe beliefs about God, the spirit world, or supernatural powers and phenomena	• Describe beliefs about divine beings or powers • Describe beliefs about spirits or other non-divine beings or powers • Explain beliefs about the relationship between the material and spiritual world and how people can or cannot manipulate spiritual powers
3 Describe and give a Christian response to the cultural view of the unseen nature of humanity	• Describe beliefs concerning the unseen nature of human beings • Identify biblical equivalents in relationship to the unseen nature of human beings • Articulate a biblical theology in relation to the unseen nature of human beings in the culture
4 Describe and give a Christian response to death in the culture	• Describe beliefs concerning death and afterlife • Research rituals and traditions associated with death using ethnographic methods • Develop a biblical theology in relation to death, the afterlife, and death practices • Identify death beliefs and practices which are consistent with biblical principles and teaching • Articulate ideas about possible contextualized Christian death practices

Evidence Guide

Overview

A person who demonstrates competency in this unit must be able to provide evidence that they can explain the difference between formal and folk religion in the culture, describe beliefs about the spiritual realm, describe and give Christian responses to the unseen nature of human beings, death, and the afterlife.

Critical Aspects of Evidence to Demonstrate Competency in This Unit
Assessment requires evidence of the following products or processes to be collected:

Products

- A description of the formal religion of the culture received from a teacher of religion
- A description of the religion derived from ethnographic interviews of a minimum of three lay practitioners
- A description of a folk religious practice
- A description of beliefs about divine beings or powers
- A description of beliefs about non-divine beings and powers
- An explanation of the relationship between the material and spiritual world and how spiritual power can be manipulated
- A description of beliefs concerning the unseen nature of human beings
- A biblical theology relating to the beliefs concerning the unseen nature of human beings in the culture
- A description of beliefs concerning death and the afterlife
- A biblical theology relating to death, the afterlife, and death practices in the culture

Processes

- Ethnographic research of the religious system
- Identification of biblical equivalents for beliefs concerning the unseen nature of human beings
- Ethnographic research exploring the rituals and traditions associated with death
- Identification of death beliefs and practices which are consistent with biblical principles and teaching
- Articulation of ideas about possible contextualized Christian death practices

CCP13—Behave and communicate appropriately cross-culturally

Unit Descriptor

In this unit trainees demonstrate their ability to function, communicate, and behave appropriately as Christians in the cross-cultural church planting context.

Application of the Unit

Behaving and communicating appropriately cross-culturally covers the essential behaviors and attitudes necessary for working as a church planter in another culture. This unit requires the trainee to demonstrate appropriate behavior in a range of different cultural situations, to communicate sensitively, respectfully, and appropriately and to understand the range of different cultures' understandings of sin. It also covers self-evaluation of attitudes which impede effective cross-cultural communication and a consideration of the way Christian practices might be expressed differently in different cultures. The context and focus of the unit is cross-cultural church planting and its aim is to develop self-awareness and discipline in relating to people from other cultures in contrast to simply pursuing a personal agenda. Effective cross-cultural church planting requires the development of relationships with people from other cultures and the sensitive interactive communication. All cross-cultural church planters need to demonstrate these competencies if they are to become effective workers in another cultural context.

Element		Performance Criteria
1	Behave appropriately within the culture and learn essential cultural skills	• Prepare three local dishes and beverages and serve them to local people
		• Wear appropriate dress in all contexts
		• Receive hospitality from members of the culture without causing offense
		• Give hospitality to members of the culture without causing offense
		• Behave appropriately towards people of different gender and status in the culture
2	Explain the relationship between sin, gospel, and culture	• Give an example of the risk of equating gospel with culture
		• Give two examples of difference between the concepts of sin in different cultures
		• Describe the nature of sin and its control and punishment in the trainee's own cross-cultural church planting context

Element	Performance Criteria
3 Address the challenges of cross-cultural communication	• Give an example of a cross-cultural encounter where no attempt was made to adjust the communication for context or hearer • Explain the consequences of poor cross-cultural communication in cross-cultural church planting • Give an illustration of a personal attempt to overcome cross-cultural communication barriers • Explain an example of a form and meaning challenge relevant to cross-cultural church planting in the trainee's own cross-cultural church planting context
4 Explore the relationship between culture, the Bible, and Christian practice	• Give an example of personal ethnocentrism • Discuss the relationship between the Bible and the transformation of culture in cross-cultural church planting • Research a practice in the culture which could be contextualized

Evidence Guide

Overview

A person who demonstrates competency in this unit must be able to provide evidence that they can behave appropriately within the culture and learn essential cultural skills. They must also be able to explain the relationship between sin, gospel, the Bible, Christian practice, and culture and address the challenge of cross-cultural communication.

Critical Aspects of Evidence to Demonstrate Competency in This Unit

Assessment requires evidence of the following products or processes to be collected:

Products

- An example of the risk of equating gospel with culture
- A minimum of two examples of sin being viewed differently in different cultures
- A description of the nature and management of sin in the trainee's own cross-cultural church planting context
- An example of a cross-cultural encounter where no attempt was made to adjust the communication for context or hearer

- An explanation of the consequences of poor cross-cultural communication in cross-cultural church planting
- An illustration of a personal attempt to overcome cross-cultural communication barriers
- An example of a form and meaning challenge relevant to cross-cultural church planting in the trainee's own cross-cultural church planting context
- An example of personal ethnocentrism
- A summary of the conclusions of the research about a practice in the culture which could be contextualized

Processes
- Prepare and serve local dishes and beverages to local people
- Wear appropriate dress in all contexts
- Receive hospitality from members of the culture without causing offense
- Give hospitality from members of the culture without causing offense
- Behave appropriately towards people of different gender and status
- Cross-cultural communication
- Discuss the relationship between the Bible and the transformation of culture
- Research a practice in the culture which could be contextualized

CCP14—Research everyday life using ethnographic methods

Unit Descriptor
In this unit trainees research the everyday life of the people in their cross-cultural church planting context using ethnographic methods.

Application of the Unit
Researching everyday life using ethnographic methods is an in-depth investigation of what people do day-by-day in the culture, the systems that support social order and the festivals, celebrations, and creative arts which bring richness to the lives of the people. This unit enables the cross-cultural church planter to develop an in-depth understanding of how society is ordered and the practical outworkings of ongoing life over the generations. It involves the use of ethnographic research methods which includes participant observation in social events and daily life. The context of the unit is another culture and the intention of the unit is the trainee's participation in the life of the people in the

culture and to become comfortable living among them. This unit is relevant for all cross-cultural workers as it leads them through an investigative process of the culture which helps them to both understand the culture and feel comfortable and safe within it.

Element	Performance Criteria
1 Research everyday life using ethnographic methods	• Research the everyday life of the people in the trainee's own cross-cultural church planting context by participant observation
	• Identify three assumptions about cultural practices in the trainee's own cross-cultural church planting context
	• Re-formulate the trainee's own assumptions about cultural practices, without judgments, into questions and ask members of the host culture these questions
	• Give a description of the everyday life of the people in the trainee's own cross-cultural church planting context
2 Describe how and why people gather	• Research three different types of gathering by participant observation
	• Research the reasons for three gatherings using ethnographic methods
	• Describe the structure, order, conduct, and leadership within three gatherings
3 Research the rites of passage	• List the rites of passage
	• Research one rite of passage using ethnographic methods.
	• Give an ethnographic description of one rite of passage
4 Research the festivals	• List the festivals
	• Research one festival using ethnographic methods.
	• Give an ethnographic description of one festival
5 Research the creative arts	• List the creative art forms
	• Experience one creative art form in the same manner that people in the culture experience it
	• Describe the means which the artist uses to communicate his/her message

Evidence Guide

Overview

A person who demonstrates competency in this unit must be able to provide evidence that they can use ethnographic methods to research the everyday life of people in the trainee's own cross-cultural church planting context, including how and why they gather, rites of passage, festivals, and their creative arts.

Critical Aspects of Evidence to Demonstrate Competency in This Unit

Assessment requires evidence of the following products or processes to be collected:

Products

- A list of a minimum of three assumptions made by the trainee about cultural practices
- A list of questions, which do not contain judgments, formulated from assumptions
- A description of everyday life in the trainee's own cross-cultural church planting context
- A list of reasons for at least three different types of gathering in the culture
- Descriptions of at least three different types of gathering with specific attention given to the structure, order, conduct, and leadership of the gatherings
- A list of rites of passage
- An ethnographic description of a rite of passage
- A list of festivals
- An ethnographic description of at least one festival
- A list of creative art forms
- A description of the means which the artist uses to communicate his/her message

Processes

- Participation in the everyday life of the people in the trainee's own cross-cultural church planting context
- Identifies and checks assumptions about things that are observed in the culture by asking people within that culture
- Participation in at least three different types of gathering
- Ethnographic research of a rite of passage
- Ethnographic research of a festival
- Experiencing a creative art form in the same manner as people in the culture experience it

CCP15—Collect data for worldview analysis using ethnographic methods

Unit Descriptor

In this unit trainees collect cultural data relating to the story of the universe, values, causality, self, truth, and wisdom using ethnographic research methods.

Application of the Unit

To collect data for worldview analysis using ethnographic methods involves in-depth research into meaning, causality, values, and ethics in the culture. The process involved in the collection of the data requires the trainee to interact extensively with local people in the culture. The aim of the unit is to discover what the people on the streets think about the world they live in and to gain a picture of their perceptions. This is an extended conversation between the cross-cultural church planter and the people of the culture. Effective development of relevant, authentic Christianity in different cultures is dependent on building bridges between the worlds of the biblical text and the worldview of different cultures. This makes the development of skills necessary for research into worldview essential for all cross-cultural church planters and for anyone who is attempting to communicate values and meaning to people from a different contextual background than their own.

Element	Performance Criteria
1 Collect cultural perspectives on the story of the universe	• Collect three foundational myths or key stories from local sources
	• Outline three of the most common themes of the creative arts through having read, seen, heard, or experienced the creative art presentations or performances
	• Derive an explanation of the cultural view of the progression of time through interviewing three people in the culture

Element	Performance Criteria
2 Collect cultural data on values	• Collect three stories of cultural heroes/anti-heroes or significant figures from local sources • Collect descriptions of a good man and a good woman from three local sources • Receive an explanation of why the men and women described above are considered good from one local person • List the most common accusations made against people in day-to-day conversation • Receive a description of what is beauty and why it is beautiful from one local person • Receive a description of what is ugly and why it is ugly from one local person
3 Collect cultural perspectives on causality	• Collect an explanation of why events in the world happen from three local people • Collect an explanation of who or what causes misfortunes to happen from three local people • Research the greatest fears in the culture by ethnographic methods • Collect an explanation from three local people of what people can do to prevent or remedy misfortune, and to have good things happen to them
4 Collect cultural data on the relationship of self to the universe	• Construct a cultural mental map of the world from data collected from three local people • Receive an explanation of the location and components of the self in relation to the body from one local person • Receive an explanation from one local person of the relationship between the groups (ethnic or other) to which the self belongs and other groups • Receive an explanation of what distinguishes humans from non-humans from one local person • Receive an explanation of the relationship of humans to nature from one local person

Element	Performance Criteria
5 Collect cultural data on the source of truth and wisdom	• Research the culture's view on the ultimate source of the knowledge of right and wrong by interviewing three local people • Research the culture's view on how it is known whether something is true or not by interviewing three local people • Research the culture's view on the nature and source of wisdom by interviewing three local people

Evidence Guide

Overview

A person who demonstrates competency in this unit must be able to provide evidence that they can collect cultural data relating to the story of the universe, values, causality, self, truth, and wisdom.

Critical Aspects of Evidence to Demonstrate Competency in This Unit

Assessment requires evidence of the following products or processes to be collected:

Products

- A minimum of three foundational myths or key stories collected from local sources
- Outlines of a minimum of three common themes of the creative arts
- An explanation of the cultural view of the progression of time in the culture
- A minimum of three stories of cultural heroes collected from local sources
- Descriptions of a good man and a good woman
- An explanation of why the man and woman described above are considered to be good
- A list of the most common accusations made against people in day-to-day conversation
- A description of beauty and why it is beautiful
- A description of ugliness and why it is ugly
- An explanation of why events in the world happen
- An explanation of who or what causes misfortunes to happen
- A list of the greatest fears in the culture

- An explanation of what people can do to prevent or remedy misfortune and to have good things happen to them
- A cultural mental map of the world
- An explanation of the location and components of the self in relation to the body
- An explanation of the relationship between the groups (ethnic or other) to which the self belongs and other groups
- An explanation of what distinguishes humans from non-humans
- An explanation of the relationship of humans to nature
- Summary of research findings regarding the ultimate source of the knowledge of right and wrong
- Summary of the research findings regarding how it is known whether something is true or not
- Summary of the research findings on the nature and source of wisdom

Processes
- Ethnographic interviewing
- Synthesis of opinions from data gathered from different people
- Research into the greatest fears in the culture
- Research into the culture's view on the ultimate source of the knowledge of right and wrong
- Research into the culture's view on how it is known whether something is true or not
- Research into the culture's view on the nature and source of wisdom

CCP16—Research and describe social systems

Unit Descriptor
This unit covers the researching and describing of social structure, including its organization, leadership, maintenance, and decision-making.

Application of the Unit
To research and describe social systems involves ethnographic research into social structures, adult learning, and leadership in another culture. The intent of the unit is to enable cross-cultural church planters to prepare a picture of societal structure and function which will allow them to make hypotheses about relevant cultural structures in the church. One of the most common mistakes cross-cultural church planters make is to reproduce the structures and functions

of their own inherited culture and tradition in cross-cultural contexts. The aim of this unit is to provide alternative blueprints for future churches which are based on authentic cultural forms rather than transplanted, foreign patterns. It is relevant for all cross-cultural church planters and for those who are teaching or doing leadership development in other cultures.

Element	Performance Criteria
1 Describe the structure of society and how its order is maintained	• Research societal structure and order using ethnographic methods
	• Draw a map of important family relationships
	• Draw a map of important relationships for individuals
	• Describe the way society is organized, including its important institutions
	• Describe the way the culture maintains order and manages those who disrupt societal order
	• Describe the way conflict is managed
	• Articulate the relationship of religion to societal order
2 Describe learning in the culture, with a particular focus on adult learning	• Research learning in the culture using ethnographic methods
	• Describe the education system
	• Describe the way in which children and young people are trained in life skills
	• Describe the way in which master craftsmen, tradesmen, and professionals train aspiring craftsmen, tradesmen, and professionals
	• Describe the way in which religious professionals are trained
	• Research the cultural values and perceptions about how adults grow in wisdom and maturity by ethnographic methods
	• Describe the role of the community in adult learning
	• Explore the dimension of youth and age in learning in the culture using ethnographic methods

Element	Performance Criteria
3 Research leadership and decision-making	• Research three different types of context where decision-making occurs by participant observation
	• Describe the process of decision-making, in small and large groups, informal and formal contexts
	• Describe the ascribing of leadership and role of leadership in decision-making
	• Interview three local people who are not leaders to research the nature and role of leadership in the culture
	• Interview one leader to research the nature and role of leadership in the culture
	• Give a summary of leadership in the culture

Evidence Guide

Overview

A person who demonstrates competency in this unit must be able to provide evidence that they can research and describe the structure of a specific culture's society, its leadership, how order is maintained, and how decisions are made.

Critical Aspects of Evidence to Demonstrate Competency in This Unit

Assessment requires evidence of the following products or processes to be collected:

Products

- A map of important family relationships
- A map of important relationships for individuals in the culture
- A description of the way society, including its institutions, is organized
- A description of the way the culture maintains its order and manages those who disrupt societal order
- A description of the way conflict is managed in the culture
- An articulation of the relationship of religion to societal order
- A description of the educational system
- A description of the way in which children and young people are trained in life skills
- A description of the way in which master craftsmen, tradesmen, and professionals train aspiring craftsmen, tradesmen, and professionals
- A description of the way in which religious professionals are trained
- A description of the role of the community in adult learning

- A description of the process of decision-making in small and large groups and informal and formal contexts
- A description of the ascription and role of leadership in decision-making
- A summary of leadership in the culture

Processes
- Ethnographic research of societal structure and order
- Ethnographic research of learning
- Ethnographic research into cultural values and perceptions concerning how adults grow in wisdom and maturity
- Ethnographic research into the dimension of youth and age in learning
- Participant observation of at least three different types of context where decision-making occurs
- Interviews of at least three local people who are not leaders
- Interview of at least one leader

CCP17—Acquire basic vocational proficiency in the language of the people where the trainee will be doing cross-cultural church planting

Unit Descriptor
In this unit trainees communicate effectively in most informal and formal situations pertinent to social and community life and everyday commerce and recreation, and in situations which are not linguistically demanding in own vocational fields.

Application of the Unit
This is a language learning unit for any second language learner. It covers basic vocational proficiency which means that the learner is able to communicate orally and using writing, and to function comfortably in group situations with native speakers. This unit is relevant for any person learning another language.

Element	Performance Criteria—Using the local language
1 Effectively understand and communicate using written media	• Where relevant and possible, use the internet in the language of the people to do basic research • Prepare three official and work-related documents • Read and understand a set range of personally relevant texts • Write three personally relevant texts
2 Communicate effectively orally	• Comfortably use the telephone to communicate • Participate easily in conversations relating to social activities relevant to normal life and leisure in the culture • Participate easily in collaborative decision-making and problem-solving • Self-correct grammatical and vocabulary errors while speaking • Provide and follow detailed oral instructions concerning everyday tasks

Evidence Guide

Overview

A person who demonstrates competency in this unit must be able to provide evidence that they can effectively understand and communicate both orally and using written media.

Critical Aspects of Evidence to Demonstrate Competency in This Unit

Assessment requires evidence of the following products or processes to be collected:

Products

- A minimum of three official or work-related documents (or equivalents for a non-literate culture)
- A minimum of three examples of any of the following: personal notes, letters, email, mobile texts, internet blogs, newspaper or magazine articles

Processes

- Using the internet in the language of the people for basic research
- Reading and understanding personal notes, letters, email, mobile texts, internet blogs, newspaper or magazine articles, popular fiction, and popular non-fiction.
- Communicating comfortably using the telephone

- Participating in conversations relating to social activities relevant to normal life and leisure in the culture
- Participating in collaborative decision-making and problem-solving
- Self-correcting grammatical and vocabulary errors while speaking
- Providing and following detailed oral instructions concerning everyday tasks

CCP18—Develop proficiency in using the language in vocationally relevant ways

Unit Descriptor
In this unit trainees develop proficiency in using the language for personal and public communication in contexts which are common in Christian ministry. They also develop in using their language skills to continue to improve their language proficiency and cultural understanding.

Application of the Unit
Developing proficiency in using the language in vocationally relevant ways involves developing competency in language use for specific ministry situations. This unit covers the use of the language for communicating personal spirituality, contextualized Bible and indigenous stories, Christian teachings, and answering questions and objections. This unit gives a guideline as to the minimum language skills necessary for Christian ministry in a second language. It is relevant for all Christian workers in a second language context.

Element	Performance Criteria—Using the local language
1 Use the language for personal communication	• Comfortably answer common personal queries
	• Conduct personal Bible study using the Bible in the local language
	• Communicate a personal life history in a culturally engaging way
	• Conduct private and public prayer in the local language and forms
	• Explain a recent personal spiritual experience in a culturally appropriate way

Element	Performance Criteria—Using the local language
2 Use the language for public communication	• Re-tell and explain three indigenous stories
	• Read the Bible aloud to a local audience in a comprehensible way using appropriate local methods related to public reading
	• Memorize and quote three Bible verses in the local language
	• Explain the trainee's conversion experience in a relevant and appropriate way
	• Tell three contextualized Bible stories
	• Tell the story of the whole Bible crafted around a relevant cultural theme
	• Explain biblical themes and principles using three contextualized Bible stories
	• Communicate a contextualized gospel presentation
	• Give answers to three common questions about Christianity
	• Give answers to three common objections to Christianity
3 Use the language to improve understanding and communication	• Elicit feedback about language usage
	• Adjust language use to incorporate feedback and improve communication
	• Consistently ask questions to better understand the audience and their response
	• Ask in-depth questions to better understand ethical and moral issues in a culturally appropriate way
	• Ask in-depth questions to better understand beliefs and meanings behind cultural practices in a culturally appropriate way

Evidence Guide

Overview

A person who demonstrates competency in this unit must be able to provide evidence that they can use the local language for personal and public communication and to improve their ability to communicate.

Critical Aspects of Evidence to Demonstrate Competency in This Unit

Assessment requires evidence of the following products or processes using the local language to be collected:

Products
- A culturally engaging personal life history
- A culturally appropriate explanation of a recent personal spiritual experience
- A minimum of three indigenous stories retold
- An explanation of at least three indigenous stories
- At least three Bible verses are memorized and quoted in the local language
- A culturally relevant and appropriate explanation of the trainee's conversion
- At least three contextualized Bible stories told
- A story of the whole Bible crafted around a relevant cultural theme
- At least three Bible stories explaining biblical themes and principles
- A contextualized gospel presentation
- Answers to at least three common questions about Christianity
- Answers to at least three common objections to Christianity

Processes
- Answering personal queries
- Using the Bible in the local language in personal devotions
- Praying in private and public
- Culturally appropriate public reading of the Bible
- Eliciting feedback about language usage
- Incorporating language feedback to improve communication
- Asking questions to better understand the audience and its response
- Asking in-depth questions to better understand ethical and moral issues
- Asking in-depth questions to better understand beliefs and meanings behind cultural questions

CCP19—Engage with a multicultural community, design a multicultural church planting strategy and begin to implement it

Unit Descriptor
In this unit the trainee participates in the secular multicultural community, researches and becomes familiar with the different cultures in the community, develops intercultural interpersonal skills, designs a multicultural church planting strategy, and begins to implement it.

Application of the Unit

To engage with a multicultural community, design a multicultural church planting strategy, and begin to implement it involves participation in that community, researching the community, developing interpersonal skills, developing a church planting strategy, and implementing it. This unit encompasses the activities that enable the trainee to do the above and leads the trainee through the process of researching, developing, and implementing a relevant, multicultural church planting strategy for a specific multicultural context. The aim of the unit is to help the trainee engage with the community and to understand its various dimensions and challenges through active participation in the community. It is recommended that this unit is covered together with CCP20 (Articulate the challenges of developing and promoting biblical multiculturalism) which helps develop an understanding of the issues and complexities inherent in multicultural work. This unit is relevant to all churches and Christian workers who are intending to develop or plant churches in multicultural contexts.

Element	Performance Criteria
1 Participate in the secular multicultural community	• Regularly participate in a secular community activity where people from the major cultures with respect to church planting in the community are also involved
	• Participate in one secular activity which serves the general multicultural community
	• Develop ease of conversing with people from any ethnic group living in the community
2 Research the community and become familiar with all the cultures represented	• Present an overview of the history of each culture in the community
	• Present an overview of the major cultural characteristics of each culture in the community, learned from a member of that ethnic group
	• Draw a map of the natural networks in the community and articulate the implications for multicultural church planting
	• Give an overview of the social demography of the community and articulate the implications for multicultural church planting
	• Describe the major secular and religious festivals celebrated by the different ethnic groups of the community and explore ways in which these could be incorporated into a multicultural church planting strategy

Element	Performance Criteria
3 Develop intercultural interpersonal skills	• Develop the interpersonal skills necessary to help people from different cultures relate to each other through practice • Develop cross-cultural mediatory skills to help with intercultural conflict management through practice • Develop strategies to cope with pressure from specific ethnic groups to force conformity to their particular cultural model
4 Develop a multicultural church planting strategy	• Present a clear representation of the model of multiculturalism being adopted in the church planting strategy • Articulate the implications of the chosen model of multiculturalism for the church planting strategy • Give a visual representation of the end vision of the multicultural church planting strategy • Articulate the approach to evangelism in relation to the mix of different ethnic groups in the community, including how follow-up will be adapted to the needs of the different ethnic groups • Define discipling strategies, including how the needs of different cultures in the community will be met • Discuss ways of finding a balance between the need for providing a model of Christian community life and the imposition of a particular cultural pattern • Articulate guiding principles for intentionally laying a foundation for inclusive multi-ethnic leadership

Element	Performance Criteria
5 Develop and implement a discipling strategy	• Consulting with cross-cultural church planters experienced with each specific ethnic group, identify the specific discipling needs and appropriate discipling methods for each of three ethnic groups in the multicultural church planting context
	• Implement an approach to discipling for a specific ethnic group recommended by an experienced cross-cultural church planter with one person from that specific ethnic group for three months.
	• Maintain the integrity of the model and strategy for multicultural church planting articulated in CCP19 Element 4 in interactions with early enquirers
	• Facilitate members of different ethnic groups who are exploring Christianity in discovering the meaning of being followers of Jesus as authentic members of their own culture

Evidence Guide

Overview

A person who demonstrates competency in this unit must be able to provide evidence that they can participate in the secular multicultural community, research and become familiar with the different cultures in the community, develop intercultural interpersonal skills, design a multicultural church planting strategy, and begin to implement it.

Critical Aspects of Evidence to Demonstrate Competency in This Unit

Assessment requires evidence of the following products or processes to be collected:

Products

- A presentation of an overview of the history of each culture in the community
- A presentation of the major cultural characteristics of each culture in the community
- A map of the natural networks in the community
- An articulation of the implications of the natural networks in the community for multicultural church planting
- An overview of the social demography of the community

- An articulation of the implications of the social demography of the community for multicultural church planting
- A description of the major secular and religious festivals celebrated by the different ethnic groups in the community
- Strategies to cope with pressure from specific ethnic groups to force conformity to their particular cultural model
- A clear representation of the model of multiculturalism being adopted in the church planting strategy
- An articulation of the implications of the chosen model of multiculturalism for the church planting strategy
- A visual representation of the end vision of the multicultural church planting strategy
- An articulation of the approach to evangelism in relation to the mix of different groups in the community and an explanation of how follow-up will be adapted to the needs of the different ethnic groups
- A presentation of the discipling strategies to be used, including how the needs of different cultures in the community will be met
- A list of guiding principles for intentionally laying a foundation for inclusive multi-ethnic leadership

Processes

- Regular participation in a multicultural secular community activity
- Participation in at least one activity which serves the general multicultural community
- Converse easily with people from any ethnic group living in the community
- Exploration of the ways in which the major secular and religious festivals celebrated by the different ethnic groups of the community could be incorporated into a multicultural church planting strategy
- Intentional development through practice of interpersonal skills which encourage people from different cultures to relate to each other
- Intentional development through practice of cross-cultural mediatory skills which aid in the management of intercultural conflict
- Discussion of ways of finding a balance between the need for providing a model of Christian community life and the imposition of a particular cultural pattern
- Consultation with experienced cross-cultural church planters

- Cross-cultural discipling of at least one person for at least three months using an approach recommended by a cross-cultural church planter who has experience working with the same ethnic group as the disciple
- Maintenance of the integrity of the model and strategy for multicultural church planting
- Facilitation of members of different ethnic groups who are exploring Christianity in discovering an authentic expression of what it means to be a follower of Jesus in their own culture

CCP20—Articulate the challenges of developing and promoting biblical multiculturalism

Unit Descriptor

This unit covers the issues involved in multicultural interactions and the development of a practical strategy for dealing with these.

Application of the Unit

Articulating the challenges of developing and promoting biblical multiculturalism involves an exploration of different models and theologies of multiculturalism, ethnicity, and the dynamics of power between different ethnic groups in different contexts. This unit also covers the different methods of decision-making, leadership, and conflict management in different cultures and the construction of a model, strategy, and evaluative tool for multicultural practice in a church planting context. The aim of the unit is to apply multicultural theory to a specific multicultural church planting context and create a practical tool which will enable the church planter to apply principles of good multicultural practice to actual practice in church planting. The intention is to develop an informed and principled approach to multiculturalism which can be reflected on and evaluated as churches develop. This unit has application to all churches which have more than one culture represented in their congregation and could be contextualized to other multicultural organizational contexts. Although specifically developed for church planting contexts, it has relevance beyond this.

Element	Performance Criteria
1 Outline a biblical theology of ethno-diversity and multiculturalism	• Explain different models of multiculturalism • Derive and outline a biblical theology of ethno-diversity and multiculturalism
2 Explain the key challenges involved in multicultural interactions	• Define the nature of ethnicity • Explain the concept of inter-ethnic boundaries and how these are maintained • Explain the nature of power and power dynamics in majority/minority situations and in multicultural situations • Analyze the concept of whiteness • Describe the concept of paternalism • Self-assess for paternalistic attitudes
3 Prepare a strategy for conflict management in a multicultural context	• Describe three different styles of conflict management as found in different cultures • Describe three different styles of decision-making as found in different cultures • Describe three different styles of leadership as found in different cultures • Prepare a strategy for managing conflict in multicultural contexts
4 Prepare a strategy for multiculturalism in a church planting situation	• Prepare a model of multiculturalism for a specific context • Write a strategy for the implementation of the above model • Derive objective measures for the assessment of the degree of true multicultural representation and freedom • Develop an evaluation tool for assessing the effectiveness of the strategy with respect to the above model

Evidence Guide

Overview

A person who demonstrates competency in this unit must be able to provide evidence that they can outline a biblical theology of ethno-diversity and multi-culturalism, explain the key challenges involved in multicultural interactions, and prepare a strategy for conflict management in a multicultural context and for multiculturalism in a team, organization, or church planting situation.

Critical Aspects of Evidence to Demonstrate Competency in This Unit
Assessment requires evidence of the following products or processes to be
collected:

Products

- An explanation of different models of multiculturalism
- A biblical theology of ethno-diversity and multiculturalism
- A definition of ethnicity
- An explanation of the concept of inter-ethnic boundaries
- An explanation of the nature of power and power dynamics in majority/
  minority and multicultural situations
- A description of paternalism
- A description of the different ways in which conflict is managed in
  different cultures
- A description of the different ways in which different cultures approach
  decision-making
- A description of different styles of leadership in different cultures
- A strategy for managing conflict in multicultural contexts
- A model of multiculturalism for a specific context
- A strategy for the implementation of a model of multiculturalism in the
  trainee's own multicultural church planting context
- A list of objective measures of the degree of true multicultural
  representation and freedom
- An evaluation tool for assessing the effectiveness of a strategy with
  respect to true multicultural representation and freedom

Processes

- Analysis of the concept of whiteness
- A self-assessment for paternalistic attitudes
- Developing a strategy based on a model of multiculturalism
- Deriving measurable indicators of true multicultural representation and
  freedom
- Designing an evaluation tool for assessing multicultural representation
  and freedom
- Testing an evaluation tool for assessing multicultural representation and
  freedom

CCP21—Maintain personal well-being

Unit Descriptor

This unit covers the preparation and implementation of plans for recognizing and managing stress, maintaining a healthy lifestyle, and maintaining spiritual health.

Application of the Unit

Maintaining personal well-being involves planning and implementing strategies for managing stress, maintaining a healthy lifestyle, and spiritual health. As this unit has been designed specifically for the cross-cultural church planter, it is particularly concerned with the stress of moving and of living in another culture. The intention of the unit is to help the cross-cultural church planter establish patterns of self-discipline and accountability that will foster longevity in a cross-cultural church planting context. While there is an overlap with the needs of anyone in Christian ministry, the particular focus of this unit is the cross-cultural church planter during the initial months in a new cultural context.

Element	Performance Criteria
1 Plan strategies for managing cross-cultural stress	• Prepare a plan for coping with the stress of moving and changing cultural contexts
	• Identify probable personal indicators of cross-cultural stress
	• Prepare a stress management plan for cross-cultural stress
	• Identify three people who could give support during cross-cultural stress
	• Develop and implement strategies for increasing personal flexibility
2 Plan and maintain a healthy lifestyle	• Maintain a balance of healthy living habits with respect to food, sleep, work, family commitments, rest, and recreation for six months.
	• Identify the probable personal indicators and precipitants of brown out
	• Prepare and implement a plan for regular and adequate rest and recreation

Element	Performance Criteria
3 Maintain spiritual health	• Prepare and implement a Bible reading and devotional plan for one year
	• Prepare and implement a plan for personal spiritual growth
	• Identify three people who will consistently pray for and encourage the trainee
	• Communicate with the people who consistently pray for the trainee regularly for six months
	• Prepare a strategy for coping with discouragement and depression

Evidence Guide

Overview

A person who demonstrates competency in this unit must be able to provide evidence that they can manage stress and maintain a healthy physical and spiritual lifestyle.

Critical Aspects of Evidence to Demonstrate Competency in This Unit

Assessment requires evidence of the following products or processes to be collected:

Products

- A plan for coping with the stress of moving and changing cultural contexts
- A list of probable personal indicators of cross-cultural stress
- A stress management plan for cross-cultural stress
- A list of a minimum of three people who could give support during cross-cultural stress
- A list of intentional strategies for increasing personal flexibility
- A list of probable personal indicators and precipitants of brown out
- A plan for regular and adequate rest and recreation
- A plan for at least a year of Bible reading and devotions
- A plan for personal spiritual growth
- A list of at least three people who will consistently pray for and encourage the trainee
- A strategy for coping with discouragement and depression

Processes
- Implementation of intentional strategies for increasing personal flexibility
- A balance of healthy living habits with respect to food, sleep, work, family commitments, rest, and recreation maintained for at least six months
- Implementation of a plan for regular and adequate rest and recreation
- Implementation of a Bible reading and devotional plan
- Implementation of a plan for personal spiritual growth
- Regular communication with prayer supporters occurring at least once a month for six months

CCP22—Investigate the formal teachings and practice of a religion

Unit Descriptor
In this unit the trainee describes another religion including its practices, obligations on its adherents, perspective of Christianity, and similarities and differences with Christianity.

Application of the Unit
This unit investigates the formal teachings and practice of a religion through direct contact with teachers and practitioners of the religion. It involves describing the religion, explaining what its adherents do, learning what its perspective of Christianity is, and comparing the religion with Christianity. The focus of the unit is on understanding the religion through the eyes of its teachers and practitioners, rather than through the perspectives of outsiders. In comparing the religion with Christianity, the intended outcomes are to understand the similarities between the two religions, including potential bridges for common understanding, and to understand any obstacles to following Jesus that a person within that religion may have. This unit is relevant for any Christian wanting to understand and interact with people who follow another religion.

Element	Performance Criteria
1 Describe the religion	• Read a book written by a teacher of the religion explaining the religion for an adherent of the religion
	• Attend a lecture or course on the religion run by a recognized teacher of the religion
	• Summarize the beliefs, teachings, and necessary practices of the religion
	• Explore the relationship of the community of the followers of the religion to individual practice with three adherents of the religion through ethnographic interview
2 Explain what adherents of the religion have to do	• Observe one practice of the religion at one of its buildings of worship
	• Research the meaning and purpose of the actions observed in association with the observed practice of religion by ethnographic interview
	• Interview three people who regularly attend a building of worship or lectures/teaching delivered by a formally recognized teacher of the religion concerning the essential rules of behavior for the religion and the consequences of breaking those rules
	• Summarize the essential rules of behavior for the adherents of the religion and the consequences for breaking them
3 Investigate the concerns the religion has about Christianity	• Study two tracts for Christians written by teachers of the religion
	• Listen to three testimonies of the conversion of Christians to the religion
	• Listen to one debate between a teacher of the religion and a Christian teacher and summarize the argument from the perspective of the non-Christian religious teacher
	• Outline the major arguments against, objections to, and problems the religion has with Christianity

Element	Performance Criteria
4 Compare the religion with Christianity	• Outline similarities between the religion and Christianity
	• Outline differences between the religion and Christianity
	• Make a comparative summary between the two religions
	• Discuss the obstacles that a person from the religion who is interested in learning more about following Jesus might have to overcome

Evidence Guide

Overview

A person who demonstrates competency in this unit must be able to provide evidence that they can describe the religion, its practices, its obligations on its adherents, its perspective of Christianity, and its similarities and differences with Christianity.

Critical Aspects of Evidence to Demonstrate Competency in This Unit

Assessment requires evidence of the following products or processes to be collected:

Products

- A summary of the beliefs, teachings, and necessary practices of the religion
- A summary of the essential rules of behavior for adherents of the religion and the consequences of breaking them
- A summary of the argument of a debate of a teacher of the religion with a Christian teacher from the perspective of the teacher of the non-Christian religion
- An outline of the major arguments against, objections to, and problems the religion has with Christianity
- An outline of the similarities between the religion and Christianity
- An outline of the differences between the religion and Christianity
- A comparative summary of the two religions

Processes

- Reading a book written by a teacher of the religion explaining the religion for an adherent of the religion
- Attending a lecture or course on the religion run by a recognized teacher of the religion

- Ethnographic interviews of at least three followers of the religion concerning the relationship of the community of the followers to individual practice
- Observation of at least one practice of the religion at one of its buildings of worship
- Researching the meaning and purpose of the actions observed in association with the observed practice of religion through ethnographic interview
- Interviews of at least three people who regularly attend a building of worship or teaching in the religion concerning the essential rules of behavior and consequences of breaking those rules
- Study of at least two tracts written by teachers of the religion for the purpose of converting Christians
- Listening to at least three conversion testimonies of Christians to the religion
- Listening to and analyzing the argument of a teacher of the religion who debates with a Christian teacher
- A discussion of the obstacles that a person from the religion who is interested in learning more about following Jesus might have to overcome

CCP23—Communicate complex concepts in another language

Unit Descriptor

In this unit the trainee uses a language other than their mother tongue to sensitively communicate about complex and difficult concepts.

Application of the Unit

Communicating complex concepts in another language involves advanced language ability and the ability to sensitively elicit information about meaning and values in another cultural context. This unit covers appropriate behavior and attitudes towards people from other cultures as well as the ability to use a second language to discuss concepts. In keeping with the context of the Diploma, of particular concern is the ability to discuss spiritual concepts in a second language and culture. This unit is applicable to any person learning a second language to an advanced level.

Element	Performance Criteria
1 Communicate appropriately in another language cross-cultural context	• Use a language other than the mother tongue • Address people with the honor and respect due them in their own culture • Listen to people of the hosting culture • Question and carry out discussions with appropriate people, in appropriate contexts at appropriate times
2 Discuss concepts	• Elicit information about beliefs • Elicit information about worldview concepts • Discuss moral and ethical issues
3 Communicate spiritual concepts	• Use questions and other communication styles appropriate to the hosting culture to stimulate thinking about spiritual issues • Use stories to communicate Christian principles and spiritual challenges • Use non-Christian religious language and forms to communicate Christian principles and spiritual challenges

Evidence Guide

Overview

A person who demonstrates competency in this unit must be able to provide evidence that they can communicate and discuss concepts appropriately in another language and in a different culture than the trainee's home culture.

Critical Aspects of Evidence to Demonstrate Competency in This Unit

Assessment requires evidence of the following processes to be collected:

Processes

- Use of a language other than the mother tongue of the trainee
- Demonstrating appropriate respect and honor towards people
- Listening to people
- Asking questions and having discussions with appropriate people, in appropriate contexts at appropriate times, according to the codes of conduct of the hosting culture
- Eliciting information about beliefs
- Eliciting information about worldview concepts
- Discussing moral and ethical issues

- Stimulating thinking about spiritual issues by using questions and other communication styles appropriate to the hosting culture
- Using stories to communicate Christian principles and spiritual challenges
- Using non-Christian religious language and forms to communicate Christian principles and spiritual challenges

ADVANCED DIPLOMA

Assessor Competencies

Cross-cultural church planting competency needs to be assessed by experienced cross-cultural church planters. Appropriate and relevant industrial experience for assessing Advanced Diploma competencies requires the trainer to have had at least six years of continuous cross-cultural church planting experience in another language context and to have been involved in the planting of at least one church in that same context.

To have been involved in the planting of a church means to have been involved in the processes of evangelism, discipling, gathering, and leadership development and that at the time of leaving the context (or time of training if the assessor is still in the context) there exists at least one group of believers in a specific locality who meet together regularly and are committed to knowing and obeying God as he is revealed in the Bible; help each other obey the commands of Jesus Christ, including being salt and light in their community; have a biblically and culturally appropriate structure for leadership and discipline; actively share their faith with others and make disciples.

Units of Competency

CCP29—Describe cultural themes and prepare a biblical response

Unit Descriptor
This unit covers practical steps to understanding deeper levels of culture and relating these to biblical themes which are communicated through storytelling.

Application of the Unit

Describing cultural themes and preparing a biblical response involves collecting themes found in a range of cultural data, analyzing the cultural data, and comparing it with biblical data to articulate a biblical response to those themes. It covers the analysis of the worldview of a culture and preparing a relevant Christian counterpoint. The unit does not focus on the gathering of the data but assumes the necessary research has already been done (as is required by achieving the competencies outlined for the Diploma in Cross-Cultural Church Planting which is an entry requirement for the Advanced Diploma in Cross-Cultural Church Planting). The intention of the unit is the development of a simple theological primer based on the questions and concerns of the culture and a correspondent catechism and list of essentials for discipleship. The conclusions of the analysis are checked with local and expatriate experts and a set of related stories are crafted and told to local people. The unit emphasizes the importance of cultural understanding for effective cross-cultural communication of Christian teachings, as well as the importance of practical outcomes which can be used in real ministry situations. It is a specialized unit relevant for anyone committed to communicating Christianity to people from other cultures but is dependent on prior extensive ethnographic research into worldview.

Element	Performance Criteria
1 Identify cultural themes	• Analyze gossip and common topics of conversation for cultural themes
	• Analyze behavioral patterns for cultural themes
	• Analyze stated beliefs for cultural themes
	• Identify the reasons why people seek spiritual help
	• Analyze indigenous interpretations of creative media for cultural themes
	• Explain sources of comfort, peace, and life-meaning in the culture
	• Analyze three life stories and myths of cultural heroes for cultural themes
	• Articulate the intersection of cultural themes with given biblical themes

Element		Performance Criteria
2	Analyze the interaction between formal and folk religion in a specific ethnic group	• Describe the formal religion of a specific ethnic group • Describe the folk religion of a specific ethnic group • Explain the interaction between formal and folk religion and daily life in a specific ethnic group
3	Construct a worldview outline	• With reference to collected cultural data, prepare a worldview outline concentrating on the construction of meaning in a specific culture • Identify the most significant themes in the worldview • Check the prepared worldview outline and its significant themes with local people
4	Articulate a biblical response to the worldview	• For each section of the worldview outline, prepare a biblical response • Based on the worldview outline and biblical response, construct a simple theological primer • Based on the theological primer, construct a catechism • Based on the theological primer and catechism, identify essential areas for training new believers • Check the conclusions and construction of the theological primer, catechism, and list of essential areas for discipleship with local Christian leaders and expatriate experts
5	Communicate a biblical worldview using storytelling	• Craft three stories communicating a biblical worldview in relation to the constructed worldview outline • Tell the crafted stories to local people and receive feedback

Evidence Guide

Overview

A person who demonstrates competency in this unit must be able to provide evidence that they can identify cultural themes, analyze the interaction between formal and folk religion, construct a worldview outline, articulate a biblical response to the worldview, and tell stories which communicate a biblical worldview in relation to the worldview of the culture in the trainee's own cross-cultural church planting context.

Critical Aspects of Evidence to Demonstrate Competency in This Unit

Assessment requires evidence of the following products or processes to be collected:

Products
- A list of cultural themes derived from:
  - gossip
  - conversation
  - behavioral patterns
  - stated beliefs
  - reasons for people seeking spiritual help
  - indigenous interpretations of creative media
  - sources of comfort, peace, and life-meaning
  - life stories and myths of cultural heroes
- An outline of intersection points between biblical themes and cultural themes
- A description of formal religion
- A description of folk religion
- An explanation of the interaction between formal and folk religion and daily life
- A worldview outline
- A list of significant worldview themes
- A biblical response to each section of the worldview outline
- A simple theological primer
- A catechism
- A list of essential areas for training new believers
- A minimum of three stories communicating a biblical worldview

Processes
- Analysis of cultural data and derivation of cultural themes
- Analysis of cultural data and construction of a worldview outline particularly focused on meaning construction
- Analysis of cultural data and assessment of the significance of different cultural themes
- Checking of conclusions regarding worldview and cultural themes with local people
- Checking of the theological primer, catechism, and list of essential areas for discipleship with local leaders and expatriate experts
- Telling the crafted biblical worldview stories to local people and receiving feedback

CCP30—*Communicate a contextualized gospel*

Unit Descriptor

This unit develops an understanding of different cultural concepts of sin and enables the trainee to articulate and communicate concepts of sin and salvation in culturally relevant ways.

Application of the Unit

To communicate a contextualized gospel involves an exploration of the nature of sin in different cultures and the developing of the skills of crafting stories which relate salvation to these different dimensions of sin. This unit covers the identification of the nature of experienced sin in the culture, felt needs, and the crafting of relevant salvation stories. This is a practical unit in which the crafted stories are told to local Christians and non-Christians, feedback and objections are received, and responses prepared. This is a relevant unit for any Christian worker involved in evangelism among people from other cultures.

Element	Performance Criteria
1 Describe the concept of sin as guilt, shame and uncleanness and its expression in different cultures	• Explain the concept of sin as guilt • Identify cultures where sin as guilt is more prominent, and describe the way this is expressed in the culture • Explain the concept of sin as shame • Identify cultures where sin as shame is more prominent, and describe the way this is expressed in the culture • Explain the concept of sin as uncleanness • Identify cultures where sin as uncleanness is more prominent, and describe the way this is expressed in the culture • Articulate a comprehensive exploration of sin and salvation in all its dimensions as presented in the Bible • Articulate the consequences of miscommunication in relation to the concept of sin in cross-cultural church planting • Develop a biblical theology of shame from given resources • Develop a biblical theology of uncleanness from given resources • Develop a biblical theology of guilt from given resources
2 Prepare contextualized gospel stories	• Communicate the gospel in relation to shame and uncleanness using three stories • Identify Bible stories which illustrate biblical answers to felt needs • Craft three Bible stories which illustrate answers to identified felt needs and which suit the intended audience • Prepare locally reproducible and contextually appropriate tools or props for communicating the stories
3 Tell the contextualized stories and collect feedback	• Tell three stories to local non-Christians and receive feedback • Enable local believers to tell the stories to others

Element	Performance Criteria
4 Prepare a biblical response to objections to the contextualized gospel	• Collect objections to the contextualized gospel message • Prepare a biblical response for three objections using stories • Check the prepared biblical responses with local Christian leaders and expatriate experts • Communicate the prepared stories to local people and receive feedback • Create an evangelism tool using the developed apologetic

Evidence Guide

Overview

A person who demonstrates competency in this unit must be able to provide evidence that they can describe the concepts of sin as guilt, shame, and uncleanness and their various expressions in different cultures. They must also provide evidence of their being able to prepare and tell contextualized gospel stories, gather feedback, and prepare a biblical response to objections made to the contextualized gospel stories.

Critical Aspects of Evidence to Demonstrate Competency in This Unit

Assessment requires evidence of the following products or processes to be collected:

Products
- Explanations of the concepts of sin as guilt, shame, and uncleanness
- Descriptions of how the above concepts of sin are expressed in different cultures
- An articulation of the comprehensiveness of sin and salvation as presented in the Bible
- An articulation of the consequences of miscommunication in relation to the concept of sin in cross-cultural church planting
- Biblical theologies of shame, uncleanness, and guilt
- A minimum of three stories communicating the gospel in relation to shame and uncleanness
- A list of Bible stories which illustrate biblical answers to felt needs
- A minimum of three contextualized Bible stories which illustrate answers to felt needs

- Tools or props to aid storytelling which are locally reproducible and contextually appropriate
- Feedback from people to whom stories are told
- List of objections to the contextualized gospel stories collected from local non-Christians
- For each of at least three of the objections to the contextualized gospel stories: a story which embodies a biblical response
- An apologetic evangelism tool

Processes
- At least three of the prepared stories are told to local non-Christians and feedback is received
- Local believers are enabled to tell the stories to others
- Collecting objections to the gospel and preparation of a biblical response
- Checking the apologetics with local believers and expatriate experts
- Telling the apologetic stories to local people and receiving feedback

CCP31—Articulate the challenges of facilitating reproducibility and preventing dependency in cross-cultural church planting

Unit Descriptor
This unit covers the issue of dependency in cross-cultural church planting and helps the trainee prepare some practical strategies for avoiding dependency and facilitating reproducibility.

Application of the Unit
Articulating the challenges of facilitating reproducibility and preventing dependency in cross-cultural church planting involves the derivation of principles which promote reproducibility and avoid dependency in cross-cultural church planting ministry. This unit covers the articulation of biblical and missiological principles as well as the analysis of case studies of cross-cultural church planting. The aim of the unit is for the trainee to develop a personal set of guiding principles and a strategy for putting those principles into practice in his/her own cross-cultural church planting context. This unit has relevance for any worker who is engaged in Christian work in other cultures. It is particularly relevant for those workers who come from contexts of higher socioeconomic status than the people they work among.

Element	Performance Criteria
1 Derive principles of approach which facilitate reproducibility in cross-cultural church planting	• Articulate biblical principles which inform a cross-cultural church planting strategy that encourages reproducibility and self-sustainability • Describe common characteristics of indigenous church planting movements • Define the expected outcomes of reproducible cross-cultural church planting • Explain key principles for empowering local leadership • Explain key principles for ensuring local ownership of Christian activities • Describe the role of cross-cultural church planter in reproducible cross-cultural church planting
2 Derive principles for avoiding dependency in cross-cultural church planting	• Define dependency • Articulate the reasons why dependency in cross-cultural church planting is negative • Articulate biblical principles concerning the use of money and material resources in cross-cultural church planting • Analyze the nature and causes of dependency, especially the specific role of foreign resources and personnel, in three contexts • Analyze three case studies of cross-cultural church planting where dependency has not been a problem • Analyze the nature of the power dynamics between the cross-cultural church planter, other ethnic groups in the context, and the ethnic group among whom new churches are being planted
3 Outline key strategy steps for empowering indigenous leaders and facilitating local ownership of Christian activities in a specific cultural context	• Derive a set of principles for preventing dependency and promoting reproducibility • Prepare a strategy for putting the above principles into practice

Evidence Guide

Overview

A person who demonstrates competency in this unit must be able to provide evidence that they can derive principles of approach to cross-cultural church planting that facilitate reproducibility and prevent dependency. They must then demonstrate that they can design a cross-cultural church planting strategy which puts their derived principles into practice.

Critical Aspects of Evidence to Demonstrate Competency in This Unit
Assessment requires evidence of the following products or processes to be collected:

Products

- A list of biblical principles which encourage reproducibility and self-sustainability in a cross-cultural church planting context
- A list of characteristics that are common to indigenous church planting movements
- A list of expected outcomes for reproducible cross-cultural church planting
- An explanation of the key principles for empowering local leadership
- An explanation of the key principles for ensuring local ownership of Christian activities
- A description of the role of the cross-cultural church planter in reproducible cross-cultural church planting
- A definition of dependency
- A list of reasons as to why dependency is negative in cross-cultural church planting
- A list of biblical principles concerning the use of money and material resources in cross-cultural church planting
- Outlines of the nature and causes of dependency in a minimum of three cross-cultural church planting contexts
- A set of principles for preventing dependency and promoting reproducibility in the trainee's own cross-cultural church planting context
- A strategy for putting the above principles into practice in the trainee's own cross-cultural church planting context

Processes

- Derivation of principles of reproducibility and self-sustainability from the biblical text
- Derivation of principles concerning the use of money and material resources in cross-cultural church planting from the biblical text
- Analysis of the nature and causes of dependency in a minimum of three cross-cultural church planting contexts
- Analysis of a minimum of three cross-cultural church planting contexts where dependency has not been a problem
- Analysis of the nature of the power dynamics between the cross-cultural church planter, other ethnic groups in the context, and the ethnic group among whom new churches are being planted

CCP32—Develop a cross-cultural church planting strategy

Unit Descriptor

This unit leads the trainee through a process which results in a practical, detailed church planting strategy for a specific cross-cultural context.

Application of the Unit

The development of a cross-cultural church planting strategy involves the analysis of indigenous religious practices, articulation of biblical principles, evaluation of existing church planting models, and the writing and implementation of a strategy for cross-cultural church planting for a specific cross-cultural context. The focus of the unit is the trainee's own cross-cultural church planting context and the intention is that a relevant, appropriate strategy is developed and put into practice. This unit is applicable to more experienced cross-cultural church planters who want to evaluate their work and also for new cross-cultural church planters.

Element	Performance Criteria
1 Describe and apply the essential elements of a local church according to the Bible	• Derive a biblical description highlighting the essential elements of a local church
	• Describe and compare three contemporary models of church according to the biblical essential elements of a local church
	• With reference to ethnographic research concerning gathering in the culture, hypothesize a contextualized model of church
	• With reference to ethnographic research concerning social networks in the culture, articulate the implications of societal organization to the contextualized model of church
	• Create an experimental model of biblical church

Element	Performance Criteria
2 Analyze indigenous religious practices with respect to biblical and missiological principles	• Identify important religious practices for a specific ethnic group • Evaluate the compatibility of those religious practices with biblical principles • Articulate possible church planting strategies incorporating pre-Christian religious practices • Identify risks associated with incorporating pre-Christian religious practices into Christian practice • Describe ways in which these risks could be minimized
3 Outline biblical principles of cross-cultural church planting	• Articulate a biblical theology of cross-cultural church planting • Articulate biblical principles which inform cross-cultural church planting practice
4 Research different models of church planting	• Research church planting movements in closely equivalent people groups and derive principles for church planting practice • Evaluate three models of church planting with respect to facilitating multiplication and indigeneity • Describe the process of institutionalization in church planting movements, evaluate risks of institutionalization, and describe methods of ensuring ongoing life
5 Write policies which inform the church planting strategy	• Prepare policies concerning use of foreign (or other outside) money, material resources, and personnel • Articulate the relationship between the cross-cultural church planter and locals with respect to the conduct of evangelism, discipling, the establishing of churches, and church leadership

Element	Performance Criteria
6 Plan the church planting strategy and begin to implement it	• Develop an integrative set of principles which will inform the trainee's own cross-cultural church planting practice • Clearly define the end vision of the church planting strategy • Define goals for the strategy • Indicate methods of research to inform the strategy • State methods and plans for stimulating prayer backing • Articulate three strategies for evangelism • Identify three appropriate evangelistic tools, state the means of their production and distribution, and define feedback loops • State intended methods of discipleship, including tools, and evaluate them with respect to reproducibility and empowerment of local Christians • Outline a reproducible and locally-empowering method for leadership training • Define the process and end point for the withdrawal of the cross-cultural church planter • Put the strategy with respect to research, prayer, and evangelism into practice

Evidence Guide

Overview

A person who demonstrates competency in this unit must be able to provide evidence that they can describe and apply the essential elements of a local church according to the Bible; analyze indigenous religious practices with respect to biblical and missiological principles; outline biblical principles of cross-cultural church planting; research different models of church planting; write policies which inform a church planting strategy; and plan and start to implement a cross-cultural church planting strategy.

Critical Aspects of Evidence to Demonstrate Competency in This Unit

Assessment requires evidence of the following products or processes to be collected:

Products
- A biblical description of a local church highlighting the essential elements
- A comparison of a minimum of three contemporary models of church with the biblical essentials of a local church
- A hypothesized model of a contextualized local church
- A simulated or real experimental model of contextualized church
- A list of important religious practices for a specific ethnic group
- A list of possible church planting strategies incorporating pre-Christian religious practices
- A list of the risks associated with incorporating pre-Christian religious practices into Christian practice
- Descriptions of ways in which the risks of incorporating pre-Christian religious practices into Christian practice could be minimized
- A biblical theology of cross-cultural church planting
- A list of biblical principles for cross-cultural church planting practice
- A list of principles for church planting practice derived from research into church planting movements in closely equivalent people groups
- A description of the process of institutionalization
- A description of methods of ensuring ongoing life in institutionalization
- A written policy concerning the use of foreign (or other outside) money, material resources, and personnel
- A written policy defining the relationship between the cross-cultural church planter and locals with respect to the conduct of evangelism, discipling, the establishing of churches and church leadership
- An integrative list of principles for cross-cultural church planting practice
- A cross-cultural church planting strategy for a specific ethnic group including:
  - Clearly defined end vision
  - Clearly defined goals
  - Methods of research
  - Methods and plans for stimulating prayer backing
  - A minimum of three strategies for evangelism

- A minimum of three appropriate evangelistic tools, including statements about their means of production, distribution, and feedback loops
- Intended methods of discipleship, including tools
- A method for leadership training
- A process and stated end point for the withdrawal of the cross-cultural church planter
- A reflective log of the initial three months of the implementation of the cross-cultural church planting strategy with specific attention to the aspects of research, prayer, and evangelism
- A Field Supervisor's report of observing the implementation of the strategy

Processes

- Ethnographic research into gathering in the culture where the cross-cultural church planting is taking place
- Ethnographic research concerning social networks in the culture
- Articulation of the implications of societal organization in the culture in relation to the contextualized model of church
- The creation of a contextualized model of local church
- Evaluation of the compatibility of the important religious practices with biblical principles
- Researches church planting movements in closely equivalent people groups
- Evaluation of the risks of institutionalization
- The cross-cultural church planting strategy's initial stages of research, prayer, and evangelism are put into practice

CCP33—Develop a reproducible strategy for discipling all believers

Unit Descriptor

This unit covers the evaluation of different models of discipling and the development of a reproducible strategy for discipling in a specific cross-cultural context.

Application of the Unit

Developing a reproducible strategy for discipling all believers involves identifying key principles from the biblical text and human experience, preparing a strategy, and putting it into practice. This unit covers the theory relevant to good discipling practice and requires that theory to be tested in a real discipling context. Disciples of the trainee are facilitated in telling Christian stories to others and in learning to understand the Bible. This unit is relevant to those who are already in cross-cultural church planting contexts and have people they are discipling.

Element	Performance Criteria
1 Identify key biblical principles for discipling	• Give a definition of discipling
	• Describe Jesus' method of discipling his followers
	• Describe other New Testament methods of discipling
	• Describe Old Testament approaches to the development of faith, understanding, and right living among the people of God
	• Describe biblical commands and guidelines relevant to the process of developing faith, understanding, and right living among the people of God
	• Prepare an integrated list of key biblical principles for discipling
2 Identify key principles for discipling from human experience	• Explain the specific challenges of discipling in a cross-cultural discipling relationship
	• Describe how adults learn and are trained in the trainee's own cross-cultural church planting context
	• Give a summary of adult education principles and explain their relevance to discipleship
	• Analyze three historical models of discipleship
	• Analyze three contemporary models of discipleship
	• Prepare an integrated list of key principles for discipling derived from human experience
3 Prepare a strategy for reproducible discipling	• Prepare an outline of a competency profile for a disciple from the Bible
	• Develop a strategy for reproducible discipling based on the above profile
	• For those parts of the profile and strategy where it is relevant, develop a story-based knowledge curriculum

Element	Performance Criteria
4 Implement the discipling strategy	• Gather illustrations of the outworking of the discipleship competency elements in the life of local believers from three local believers • Discuss the strategy with three local believers and incorporate their feedback into the strategy • Implement the strategy • A local trainee tells Bible stories to people who have never heard them before • A local trainee does simple, inductive Bible exegesis

Evidence Guide

Overview

A person who demonstrates competency in this unit must be able to provide evidence that they can identify key principles for discipling, prepare a discipling strategy, and implement it in a cross-cultural church planting context.

Critical Aspects of Evidence to Demonstrate Competency in This Unit

Assessment requires evidence of the following products or processes to be collected:

Products

- A definition of discipleship
- A description of Jesus' method of discipling his followers
- Descriptions of other New Testament methods of discipling
- Descriptions of ways in which faith, understanding, and right living is developed among the people of God in the Old Testament
- A list of biblical commands and guidelines relevant to the process of developing faith, understanding, and right living among the people of God
- A list of key biblical principles for discipling
- An explanation of the specific challenges of discipling in a cross-cultural context
- A description of how adults learn and are trained in the trainee's own cross-cultural church planting context.
- A summary of adult education principles
- An explanation of the relevance of adult education principles to discipleship
- An analysis of at least three historical models of discipleship
- An analysis of at least three contemporary models of discipleship
- A list of key principles for discipling derived from human experience

- A competency profile for a disciple derived from the Bible
- A strategy for discipleship
- A story-based knowledge curriculum for discipleship
- A cultural profile of a disciple

Processes

- Analysis of at least three historical models of discipleship
- Analysis of at least three contemporary models of discipleship
- Designing a strategy
- Gathering data for the cultural profile of a disciple from at least three local believers
- Discussion of the strategy, with the gathering and incorporation of feedback from at least three local believers
- Implementation of the strategy
- A local trainee has been empowered to tell Bible stories to others
- A local trainee has been enabled to exegete the Bible using a simple, inductive method

CCP34—Develop a culturally appropriate strategy for leadership development

Unit Descriptor

This unit covers the analysis of leadership development in a specific culture and the development of a culturally appropriate leadership development strategy.

Application of the Unit

Developing a reproducible strategy for leadership development involves identifying key principles from the biblical text and human experience, analyzing different models of leadership development, and preparing a strategy. This unit covers the development of a set of key principles for leadership development and the application of those principles to a specific cross-cultural church planting context. Its aim is to match biblical principles with cultural patterns rather than imposing a foreign approach on the local church. It is concerned that leaders are selected and developed in ways that are congruent with cultural values and that local leaders are empowered to develop their own theologies, patterns of approach, and methods for managing resources. The focus of the unit is working with the culture, not against it, and the necessary pre-requisite is respect for the culture and the leadership and leadership structures already existing in the culture. It is recommended that this unit is covered together with the elective unit CCP39 (Explore leadership in different cultures and the impact of intercultural interaction on leadership of new churches) as it promotes an understanding of the different ways different cultures approach leadership and the complexity of intercultural interaction in cross-cultural church planting situations. The unit assumes an in-depth knowledge of the culture and particularly its social and leadership structures (as is required by achieving the competencies outlined for the Diploma in Cross-Cultural Church Planting which is an entry requirement for the Advanced Diploma in Cross-Cultural Church Planting). This unit would be of benefit to any cross-cultural church planter and to any person involved in a teaching or support role in relation to established churches in other cultures.

Element	Performance Criteria
1 Identify key principles for leadership development cross-culturally	• Articulate a biblical theology of leadership
	• Prepare a biblical job description for church leaders
	• Explain biblical models of leadership and their relevance to the church
	• Describe biblical patterns of leadership development
	• Give a summary of adult education principles, and explain their relevance to leadership development
	• Analyze three historical and contemporary methods of leadership development
	• Identify cultural patterns of adult learning and leadership development from within the trainee's own cross-cultural church planting context
	• Define the relationship between the cross-cultural church planter and the local leadership
	• Define the relationship between the local leadership and the leadership of churches in neighboring and more distant ethnic groups or communities
	• Evaluate a model of leadership development (including tools) used in a specific cross-cultural context with respect to cross-cultural communication theory and reproducibility, as well as the principles derived above

Element	Performance Criteria
2 Prepare a reproducible strategy for leadership development	• Formulate a reproducible strategy for effective leadership development
	• Identify key issues and questions specific to the local context
	• Outline an appropriate method for enabling potential leaders to define and answer their own questions
	• Outline methods for facilitating the development of indigenous Christian stories, theologies, and apologetics
	• Define selection criteria for trainees
	• Define material and financial support policies with reference to reproducibility principles
	• Define selection criteria for trainers
	• Clearly define the relationship of the leadership development to the indigenous church

Evidence Guide

Overview

A person who demonstrates competency in this unit must be able to provide evidence that they can identify key principles for leadership development in a cross-cultural context and prepare a reproducible strategy for leadership development appropriate to the cross-cultural context it is designed for.

Critical Aspects of Evidence to Demonstrate Competency in This Unit

Assessment requires evidence of the following products or processes to be collected:

Products
- A biblical theology of leadership
- A biblical job description for church leaders
- Descriptions of different biblical models of leadership
- Explanations of the relevance of different biblical models of leadership to leadership in the church
- Descriptions of different biblical patterns of leadership development
- A summary of adult education principles
- An explanation of the relevance of adult education principles to leadership development
- Analyses of at least three different historical and contemporary methods of leadership development

- A description of the cultural patterns of adult learning and leadership development from the culture in which the church planter is working
- A definition of the relationship between the cross-cultural church planter and local leadership
- A definition of the relationship between the local leadership and the leadership of churches in neighboring and more distant ethnic groups or communities.
- An evaluation of a model of leadership development used in a specific cross-cultural context
- A strategy for reproducible and effective leadership development in which:
  - Key issues and questions specific to the local context are identified
  - An appropriate method for enabling potential leaders to define and answer their own questions is outlined
  - Methods for facilitating the development of indigenous Christian stories, theologies, and apologetics are outlined
  - Selection criteria for trainees are defined
  - Material and financial support policies are defined with reference to reproducibility principles
  - Selection criteria for trainers are defined
  - The relationship of the leadership development to the indigenous church is clearly defined

Processes
- Analysis of different models of leadership—biblical, historical, and contemporary
- Evaluation of a model of leadership development used in a specific cross-cultural context
- Strategy design, writing, and evaluation

CCP35—Acquire vocational proficiency in the language of the people where the trainee will be doing cross-cultural church planting

Unit Descriptor

Through this unit the trainees demonstrate that they can perform very effectively in almost all situations pertinent to social and community life and everyday commerce and recreation, and generally in almost all situations pertinent to their own "vocational" fields.

Application of the Unit

To acquire vocational proficiency in the language of the people where the trainee will be doing cross-cultural church planting involves the development of advanced fluency and competence in a second language, particularly in areas essential for good cross-cultural church planting practice. This unit develops the trainee's competence in discussion and debate, understanding and communicating concepts and themes, including implicit or para-messages, written language to an advanced level in areas related to Christian ministry, confidence in small and large group contexts, and the ongoing development of language ability. The aim of the unit is to develop a high level of confidence and fluency in language use in all areas usually encountered in cross-cultural church planting practice. This unit is relevant to all Christian workers working in a second language in another culture, particularly those involved in church planting, teaching, or leadership development.

Element	Performance Criteria
1 Comfortably use and understand the language	• Actively participates in debates and general discussions
	• Discusses themes communicated in the creative arts
	• Understands and uses local humor forms
	• Perceives and explains hidden messages and subtexts in advertising and other media
2 Use and understand written language	• Writes a formal letter to the authorities in the culture
	• Explains a written non-Christian religious text
	• Writes a contextualized Bible story in the local language
	• Writes an explanation of Christian teaching or theology
	• Communicates Christian teaching through written creative language (creative writing, poetry, drama, song)

Element	Performance Criteria
3 Use language to communicate Christian teachings	• Leads a discussion about beliefs towards a Christian perspective • Discusses ethical issues communicating a Christian perspective • Debates Christian teachings with non-Christian religious teachers • Tells three stories in the local cultural style • Leads small groups of local people in discussions of Christian teaching • Addresses large groups of local people formally in the style of the local culture
4 Plan for ongoing language development	• Identifies areas of weakness in own language ability • Prepares a plan for continuing language development • Implements the plan for continuing language development

Evidence Guide

Overview

A person who demonstrates competency in this unit must be able to provide evidence that they can comfortably use and understand the language in general and vocational contexts and plan for ongoing language development.

Critical Aspects of Evidence to Demonstrate Competency in This Unit

Assessment requires evidence of the following products or processes to be collected:

Products

- Discussion of themes in the creative arts
- Explanation of local humor
- Explanation of hidden messages and subtexts in advertising and other media
- Formal letter to authorities in the culture
- Evidence of the acceptability of the above letter through an official response
- An explanation of a written non-Christian religious text
- A written contextualized Bible story

- Evidence of understanding of the written contextualized Bible story by its intended recipients
- A written explanation of Christian teaching or theology
- Evidence of understanding of the written explanation of Christian teaching or theology by its intended recipients
- A piece of creative writing communicating Christian teaching
- Evidence of use or understanding of the creative writing communicating Christian teaching by its intended recipients
- A minimum of three stories told in the local cultural style
- A formal address to a large group of people in an appropriate local cultural style
- List of areas of weakness in the trainee's own language ability
- A plan for continuing language development

Processes

- Participation in general discussions
- Participation in general debates
- Understanding local humor
- Use of local humor
- Perceiving hidden messages and subtexts in advertising and other media
- Leading a discussion about beliefs towards a Christian perspective
- Discussion of ethical issues from a Christian perspective
- Debates of Christian teaching with non-Christian religious teachers
- Leading small group discussion of Christian teaching
- Implementation of the plan for continuing language development

CCP36—Explore indigenous theologies, and apply principles of indigenous theologizing to a specific cross-cultural context

Unit Descriptor

In this unit different indigenous theologies are analyzed, their relationship to inherited theologies are explained, and the relevance of indigenous theology to cross-cultural church planting is articulated.

Application of the Unit

To explore indigenous theologies and apply principles of indigenous theologizing to a specific cross-cultural context involves an understanding of the relationship between indigenous and inherited theologies, the way indigenous theologies are developed and communicated, and the development of the ability to appreciate indigenous theologies and their implications in a cross-cultural church planting context. The aim of the unit is to enable the cross-cultural church planter to perceive, listen to, and appreciate the importance of indigenous theologies in contrast to the more common foreign missionary approach, which has been to judge and suppress. The intention of the unit is the development of an attitude of learning with respect to theology and the way a new Christian culture develops in its understanding of and relationship with God, and to enable the cross-cultural church planter to work with the people in their discovery of God, rather than having an agenda of transplanting his/her own culture's experience of God. This unit has applicability to all cross-cultural workers, with particular relevance to cross-cultural church planters, teachers, and those working with leaders from other cultures.

Element		Performance Criteria
1	Explain the nature of indigenous theology and its relationship to inherited theologies	• Define the essential elements of an indigenous theology
		• Discuss the relationship between indigenous theologies and systematic and other inherited theologies
		• Articulate the common reasons for expatriate rejection of indigenous theologies
2	Analyze three indigenous theologies	• Outline the teachings of three indigenous theologies
		• Outline the development of three indigenous theologies in relation to the history, context, and felt needs of the respective cultures
		• Analyze and evaluate the teachings of three indigenous theologies according to the Bible
3	Explore the origin, sources, and means of communication of indigenous theologies in church planting movements	• Examine three case studies of church planting movements and the origins, sources, and means of communication of the indigenous theologies in those movements
		• Discuss the concept of oral theologies
		• Describe the role of creative media in the dissemination of indigenous theologies in church planting movements

Element	Performance Criteria
4 Explore the use of indigenous theology in the trainee's own or closely equivalent cross-cultural church planting context	• Research and analyze three examples of creative media and other means of communication for indigenous theologies
	• Research and analyze three testimonies of believers, teaching in churches, and other forms of oral communication for indigenous theologies
	• Outline the themes and content of the indigenous theologies
	• Analyze and evaluate the indigenous theologies according to the Bible
	• Integrate the content of the indigenous theologies appropriately into the theological primer, catechism, gospel presentations, and outline of essential areas for discipleship

Evidence Guide

Overview

A person who demonstrates competency in this unit must be able to provide evidence that they can explain the nature of indigenous theology and its relationship to inherited theologies, analyze indigenous theologies, describe how indigenous theologies are communicated, and research and apply indigenous theological principles in their own cross-cultural church planting context.

Critical Aspects of Evidence to Demonstrate Competency in This Unit

Assessment requires evidence of the following products or processes to be collected:

Products
- List of essential elements of an indigenous theology
- List of common reasons for expatriate rejection of indigenous theologies
- Outline of teachings of at least three indigenous theologies
- Outline of the development process for at least three indigenous theologies
- Biblical evaluation of an analysis of at least three indigenous theologies
- Descriptions of the origins, sources, and means of communication of at least three indigenous theologies associated with church planting movements
- Description of the role of creative media in the dissemination of indigenous theologies in church planting movements

- Analysis of at least three examples of creative media and other means of communication in the trainee's own or closely equivalent cross-cultural church planting context for indigenous theologies
- Analysis of at least three examples of testimonies of believers or summaries of teaching delivered in the trainee's own or closely equivalent cross-cultural church planting context for indigenous theologies
- Outline of the themes and content of the indigenous theologies from the trainee's own or closely equivalent cross-cultural church planting context
- Analysis of the indigenous theologies from the trainee's own or closely equivalent cross-cultural church planting context
- Biblical evaluation of the indigenous theologies from the trainee's own or closely equivalent cross-cultural church planting context
- Evidence of appropriate integration of indigenous theological content into the trainee's theological primer, catechism, gospel presentations, and outline of essential areas for discipleship.

Processes
- Discussion of the relationship between indigenous and inherited theologies
- Discussion of the concept of oral theologies
- Research into indigenous theologies in trainee's cross-cultural church planting context (evidenced by the collection of items for analysis)
- Integration of elements of indigenous theology with derived theology done in a manner appropriate to the theological concepts and manner of communication

CCP37—Examine history to derive principles for cross-cultural church planting practice today

Unit Descriptor
In this unit the trainees identify why mass religious movements occur, how the cross-cultural church planter can help or hinder this process, and explain how their view on truth can affect a developing church planting movement.

Application of the Unit
Examining history to derive principles for cross-cultural church practice today involves historical analysis of mass religious movements in the past and the role of the cross-cultural church planter in facilitating or hindering these movements. It also explores the historical development of truth and doctrine and

cultural hegemonies in relation to the propagation of truth in other cultures. The aim of the unit is to enable the cross-cultural church planter to learn from the past, understand the common dynamics in cross-cultural church planting situations, reflect on his/her own attitudes, and develop a set of principles which can be applied to his/her own church planting practice. This unit has specific relevance for cross-cultural church planters and for those wanting to understand the role of the cross-cultural church planter in church planting movements.

Element	Performance Criteria
1 Identify causative agents in mass religious movements	• Examine three case studies of mass religious movements from different perspectives
	• Identify the reasons why each mass religious movement occurred from three contrasting perspectives
	• Identify contextual factors encouraging the movements that cannot be changed by a cross-cultural church planter
	• Identify contextual factors in the movements that may be able to be affected or influenced by a cross-cultural church planter
	• Give a brief overview of the anthropology of conversion
2 Give an overview of the historical development of the concept of truth in Christianity and its impact on cross-cultural church planting	• Explain the way in which the Bible was compiled and validated as the authentic revelation of God
	• Outline the historical development of approach to interpreting and applying the Bible
	• Discuss the historical development of doctrine and its relationship to truth and right living
	• Discuss the historical and contemporary reasons for the hegemony of Anglo-European cultural approaches to biblical interpretation
	• Give an explanation of interpretive approach to the Bible from three Christian texts from non-Anglo-European cultures
	• Explain three case studies in which imposed culturally-determined biblical interpretations either impeded a church planting movement or caused it to develop a syncretistic parallel practice with respect to what happened and why they happened.

Element	Performance Criteria
3 Explain, with reference to history, how cross-cultural church planters can help or hinder the development of church planting movements	• Analyze three case studies of different historical examples of models of unsuccessful cross-cultural church planting with respect to the attitudes and methodology of the church planter(s) • Analyze three case studies of different historical examples of models of successful cross-cultural church planting with respect to the attitudes and methodology of the church planter(s) • Derive a set of principles for cross-cultural church planting practice from the experience of cross-cultural church planters in the past

Evidence Guide

Overview

A person who demonstrates competency in this unit must be able to provide evidence that they can identify causative agents in mass religious movements, give an overview of the development of the concept of truth in Christianity, and explain, with reference to history, how cross-cultural church planters can help or hinder the development of church planting movements.

Critical Aspects of Evidence to Demonstrate Competency in This Unit

Assessment requires evidence of the following products or processes to be collected:

Products

- List of reasons for occurrence for each of a minimum of three mass religious movements
- A list of contextual factors which encouraged the mass religious movements but which are outside the control of a cross-cultural church planter
- A list of contextual factors which encouraged the mass religious movements which may be affected or influenced by a cross-cultural church planter
- An overview of the anthropology of conversion
- An explanation of the way in which the Bible was compiled and validated as the authentic revelation of God
- An outline of the historical development of approach to interpreting and applying the Bible
- Explanations of interpretative approaches to the Bible from a minimum of three Christian texts from non-Anglo-European cultures.

- An explanation of what happened and why to cause the impeding of a church planting movement or its development of a syncretistic parallel practice through the imposition of culturally-determined biblical interpretations
- Lists of attitudes in cross-cultural church planters that help or hinder the development of church planting movements
- Lists of methods used by cross-cultural church planters that help or hinder the development of church planting movements
- A list of principles for cross-cultural church planting practice derived from the experience of cross-cultural church planters in history

Processes
- Examination of a minimum of three case studies of mass religious movements from at least three different perspectives for each
- Discussion of the historical development of doctrine and its relationship to truth and right living
- Discussion of the historical and contemporary reasons for the hegemony of Anglo-European cultural approaches to biblical interpretation
- Analysis of the attitudes and methodology of the church planter in a minimum of three historical models of unsuccessful cross-cultural church planting
- Analysis of the attitudes and methodology of the church planter in a minimum of three historical models of successful cross-cultural church planting

CCP38—Explain, analyze, and put into practice the process of contextualization

Unit Descriptor
In this unit the process of contextualization is explained, analyzed, and put into practice in the trainee's own cross-cultural church planting context.

Application of the Unit
In this unit trainees explain the process of contextualization, examine its application in different cultural contexts, and apply it in their own context. This is a practical unit in which the cross-cultural church planter enables local believers to contextualize a range of cultural practices. The aim of the unit is to facilitate the development of an authentic cultural expression of Christianity and to clarify and facilitate the cross-cultural church planter's role in this through a combination

of theory and practice. This unit is relevant to cross-cultural church planters and others who are involved in cross-cultural discipleship and leadership development.

Element	Performance Criteria
1 Explain the process of contextualization	• Explain the importance of contextualization to the future of Christianity • Define syncretism • Articulate the relationship between contextualization, syncretism, and imposition of foreign forms (without contextualization) • Discuss common objections to contextualization • Define the role of the cross-cultural church planter in contrast to the role of local believers in contextualization • Outline the process of contextualization in relation to specific issues or practices
2 Analyze case studies of contextualization	• Analyze a case study of contextualization relating to a biblically neutral practice • Analyze a case study of a biblically ambiguous practice • Analyze a case study of a practice that other expatriates have condemned but for which there is no consistent indigenous formal opinion • Analyze a case study of the replacing or contextualizing of a major indigenous festival
3 Work through the process of contextualization with local believers	• Apply the process of contextualization to a biblically neutral practice • Apply the process of contextualization to a biblically ambiguous practice • Apply the process of contextualization to an aspect of a major indigenous ritual, ceremony, or festival

Evidence Guide

Overview

A person who demonstrates competency in this unit must be able to provide evidence that they can explain the process of contextualization, analyze its application with respect to a number of different practices, and put the process into practice in their own cross-cultural church planting context.

Critical Aspects of Evidence to Demonstrate Competency in This Unit

Assessment requires evidence of the following products or processes to be collected:

Products

- An explanation of the importance of contextualization to the future of Christianity
- A definition of syncretism
- An articulation of the relationship between contextualization, syncretism, and the imposition of foreign forms
- A definition of the role of the cross-cultural church planter in contrast to the role of local believers in contextualization
- A list of the steps involved in contextualization
- Analysis of a case study involving contextualization of a biblically neutral practice
- Analysis of a case study involving contextualization of a biblically ambiguous practice
- Analysis of a case study involving contextualization of a practice condemned by expatriates
- Analysis of a case study involving contextualization of a major indigenous festival

Processes

- Discussion of the common objections to contextualization
- Analysis of contextualization of a biblically neutral practice
- Analysis of contextualization of a biblically ambiguous practice
- Analysis of contextualization of a practice condemned by expatriates
- Analysis of contextualization of a major indigenous festival
- Contextualization of a biblically neutral practice in the trainee's own cross-cultural church planting context
- Contextualization of a biblically ambiguous practice in the trainee's own cross-cultural church planting context
- Contextualization of an aspect of a major indigenous ritual, ceremony, or festival in the trainee's own cross-cultural church planting context

CCP39—Explore leadership in different cultures and the impact of intercultural interaction on leadership of new churches

Unit Descriptor
In this unit the range of expression of different dimensions of leadership in different cultures is explored alongside the effects of intercultural interaction on the leadership of new churches in cross-cultural church planting contexts.

Application of the Unit
Exploring leadership in different cultures and the impact of intercultural interaction on leadership of new cultures involves a survey of different approaches to leadership in different cultures and biblical equivalents of similar practice, research into leadership in a specific culture, and an exploration of the power dynamics and other issues involved in intercultural interaction between foreigners and local leadership in cross-cultural contexts. The aim of the unit is to develop an understanding of the challenges and issues involved in cross-cultural interactions relating to leadership of churches and to develop a set of guiding principles for the cross-cultural church planter's own practice. This unit is relevant to all cross-cultural church planters, teachers, and persons interacting with leaders of churches in other cultures.

Element	Performance Criteria
1 Outline the different styles of leadership found among the cultures of the world, and articulate a biblical response to each	• Describe the way in which different cultures select and appoint leaders, and articulate a biblical response • Describe the way in which different cultures ascribe status to leaders, and articulate a biblical response • Describe the degree and nature of power in relation to leaders in different cultures, and articulate a biblical response • Describe the way in which leaders make decisions in different cultures, and articulate a biblical response • Describe the way in which leaders in different cultures manage and resolve conflict, and articulate a biblical response • Describe the expectations which followers have of leaders in different cultures, and articulate a biblical response • Describe the way in which leaders are developed in different cultures, and articulate a biblical response
2 Perform in-depth research of leadership in the trainee's own cross-cultural church planting context	• Give a description of each dimension of leadership • Give an integrated summary of leadership in the culture • Based on the above in-depth research of leadership in the local culture, derive implications for leadership practice and development in the church
3 Explore the effects of intercultural interactions on leadership in churches in cross-cultural church planting contexts	• Give an explanation of the concept of paternalism and its impact in cross-cultural church planting • Give an explanation of the concept of orientalism and its impact in cross-cultural church planting • Explore the nature, extent, and impact of power dynamics in the trainee's own cross-cultural church planting context • Discuss the reasons for the dominance of Western cultural forms in churches around the world • Discuss ways of preventing cross-cultural church planters from imposing their own inherited Christian cultural forms on new churches in different cultures • List the risks of a cross-cultural church planter leading new churches in another culture • Define the role of the cross-cultural church planter in relationship to the leadership of new churches in another culture

Evidence Guide

Overview

A person who demonstrates competency in this unit must be able to provide evidence that they can outline the different styles of leadership from around the world and articulate a biblical response to each. They must demonstrate that they have performed in-depth research into leadership in their own cross-cultural church planting context. That they have also explored the effects of intercultural interaction on the leadership of churches in cross-cultural church planting contexts must also be shown.

Critical Aspects of Evidence to Demonstrate Competency in This Unit

Assessment requires evidence of the following products or processes to be collected:

Products

- A comprehensive description of the ways in which different cultures do the following leadership functions must be provided:
  - Selection and appointment of leaders
  - Ascription of status
  - Ascription of power
  - Nature of power
  - Decision-making
  - Conflict management and resolution
  - Expectations of followers
  - Leadership development
- A biblical response to each of the above areas
- A description of leadership covering each of the above areas for the culture of the people in the trainee's own cross-cultural church planting context
- A summary description of leadership in the trainee's own cross-cultural church planting context
- A statement outlining the implications of the above for leadership practice and development in the trainee's own cross-cultural church planting context
- An explanation of the concept of paternalism and its impact on cross-cultural church planting
- An explanation of the concept of orientalism and its impact on cross-cultural church planting
- A list of the risks relating to a cross-cultural church planter leading new churches

- A definition of the role of the cross-cultural church planter in relationship to the leadership of new churches

Processes

- Research into leadership in the trainee's own cross-cultural church planting context
- Discussion on power dynamics in cross-cultural church planting contexts
- Discussion on the issue of Western dominance in cross-cultural church planting contexts
- Discussion on methods of preventing the imposition of foreign forms in cross-cultural church planting

Creative Arts Elective Units

CCP40—Perform and write drama in a different culture's drama style

Unit Descriptor

This unit covers the skill of understanding, writing, and performing drama in a cultural style different from the trainee's home culture.

Application of the Unit

Performing and writing drama in a different culture's drama style involves explaining a range of different drama styles that are used in different cultures around the world, creating drama in a specific culture's style, and using the drama style of another culture to appropriately communicate Christian concepts. This unit covers the understanding and performance of drama in a different cultural style and the missiological implications of doing so. The aim of the unit is to enable the cross-cultural church planter to appreciate and use the creative arts of another culture rather than to impose the creative art forms of his/her own culture on the churches that are planted. This unit is of particular relevance to those who already have experience with drama in their own culture and want to use the medium of drama to communicate Christian concepts in another culture. It would also be of relevance to those who have an interest in the creative arts of other cultures and want to understand and experiment with the expression of creative arts in other cultures.

Element	Performance Criteria
1 Explain different cultural drama styles and the implications of using these styles with respect to cross-cultural communication	• Demonstrate and explain three different cultural drama systems • Articulate the meanings communicated by and associated with different drama styles in a specific culture • Articulate principles of communication through drama in relation to a specific culture • Articulate missiological issues related to using indigenous drama styles in evangelism, worship, and teaching
2 Appropriately use drama created in a specific culture's style to communicate Christian concepts	• Create a drama in a specific culture's style • Use indigenous drama or a drama created in a specific culture's style to appropriately communicate a Christian concept

Evidence Guide

Overview

A person who demonstrates competency in this unit must be able to provide evidence that they can explain different cultural drama styles and the implications of using these styles with respect to cross-cultural communication, as well as appropriately use a specific cultural drama style to communicate a Christian concept.

Critical Aspects of Evidence to Demonstrate Competency in This Unit

Assessment requires evidence of the following products or processes to be collected:

Products

- Explanations of at least three different cultural drama systems
- Demonstrations of at least three different cultural forms of drama
- An articulation of the meanings communicated by and associated with different drama styles in a specific culture
- A list of principles of communication through drama in relation to a specific culture
- An articulation of the missiological issues related to using indigenous drama styles in evangelism, worship, and teaching
- A drama created in a specific culture's style

Processes

- Appropriate use of drama in a specific cultural style to communicate a Christian concept

CCP41—Perform and choreograph dance in a different culture's dance style

Unit Descriptor

This unit covers the skill of understanding, choreographing, and performing dance in a cultural style different from the trainee's home culture.

Application of the Unit

Performing and choreographing dance in a different culture's dance style involves explaining a range of different dance styles that are used in different cultures around the world, creating dance in a specific culture's style, and using the dance style of another culture to appropriately communicate Christian concepts. This unit covers the understanding and performance of dance in a different cultural style and the missiological implications of doing so. The aim of the unit is to enable the cross-cultural church planter to appreciate and use the creative arts of another culture rather than to impose the creative art forms of his/her own culture on the churches that are planted. This unit is of particular relevance to those who already have experience with dance in their own culture and want to use the medium of dance to communicate Christian concepts in another culture. It would also be of relevance to those who have an interest in the creative arts of other cultures and want to understand and experiment with the expression of creative arts in other cultures.

Element	Performance Criteria
1 Explain different cultural dance styles and the implications of using these styles with respect to cross-cultural communication	• Demonstrate and explain three different cultural dance systems • Articulate the meanings communicated by and associated with different dance styles in a specific culture • Articulate principles of communication through dance in relation to a specific culture • Articulate missiological issues related to using indigenous dance styles in evangelism, worship, and teaching
2 Appropriately use dance choreographed in a specific culture's style to communicate Christian concepts	• Choreograph a dance in a specific culture's style • Use indigenous dance or a dance choreographed in a specific culture's style by the trainee to appropriately communicate a Christian concept

Evidence Guide

Overview

A person who demonstrates competency in this unit must be able to provide evidence that they can explain different cultural dance styles and the implications of using these styles with respect to cross-cultural communication, as well as appropriately use a specific cultural dance style to communicate a Christian concept.

Critical Aspects of Evidence to Demonstrate Competency in This Unit

Assessment requires evidence of the following products or processes to be collected:

Products

- Explanations of at least three different cultural dance systems
- Demonstrations of at least three different cultural forms of dance
- An articulation of the meanings communicated by and associated with different dance styles in a specific culture
- A list of principles of communication through dance in relation to a specific culture
- An articulation of the missiological issues related to using indigenous dance styles in evangelism, worship, and teaching
- A dance created in a specific culture's style

Processes

- Appropriate use of dance in a specific cultural style to communicate a Christian concept

CCP42—Perform and compose music in a different culture's musical style

Unit Descriptor

This unit covers the understanding, performance, composition, and teaching of music in a cultural style different to that of the trainee's home culture.

Application of the Unit

Performing and composing music in a different culture's music style involves explaining a range of different music styles that are used in different cultures around the world, creating music in a specific culture's style, and using the music style of another culture to appropriately communicate Christian concepts. This unit covers the understanding and performance of music in a different cultural style and the missiological implications of doing so. The aim of the unit is to enable the cross-cultural church planter to appreciate and use the creative arts of another culture rather than to impose the creative art forms of his/her own culture on the churches that are planted. This unit is of particular relevance to those who already have experience with music in their own culture and want to use the medium of music to communicate Christian concepts in another culture. It would also be of relevance to those who have an interest in the creative arts of other cultures and want to understand and experiment with the expression of creative arts in other cultures.

Element	Performance Criteria
1 Explain different cultural musical styles and the implications of using these different styles with respect to cross-cultural communication	• Demonstrate and explain three different cultural musical systems • Articulate the meanings communicated by or associated with different musical styles within a specific culture • Articulate principles of communication through music as they relate to a specific culture • Articulate missiological issues related to using indigenous music styles in evangelism, worship, and teaching
2 Perform, compose, and use music in a different culture's musical style to communicate a Christian concept	• Perform a piece of music in a different cultural style • Write and perform a new composition in a different cultural musical style • Use indigenous music or music composed in a specific culture's style to appropriately communicate a Christian concept

Evidence Guide

Overview

A person who demonstrates competency in this unit must be able to provide evidence that they can explain different cultural music styles and the implications of using these styles with respect to cross-cultural communication, as well as appropriately use a specific cultural music style to communicate a Christian concept.

Critical Aspects of Evidence to Demonstrate Competency in This Unit

Assessment requires evidence of the following products or processes to be collected:

Products

- Explanations of at least three different cultural music systems
- Demonstrations of at least three different cultural forms of music
- An articulation of the meanings communicated by and associated with different music styles in a specific culture

- A list of principles of communication through music in relation to a specific culture
- An articulation of the missiological issues related to using indigenous music styles in evangelism, worship, and teaching
- A performance of a piece of music from a specific culture
- A performance of a piece of music composed by the trainee in a specific cultural style

Processes

- Appropriate use of music in a specific cultural style to communicate a Christian concept

CCP43—Create visual art in a different culture's artistic style

Unit Descriptor
This unit covers the understanding, creation, and use of art in a culture different than the trainee's home culture.

Application of the Unit
Creating visual art in a different culture's artistic style involves explaining a range of different artistic styles that are used in different cultures around the world, creating visual art in a specific culture's style, and using the artistic style of another culture to appropriately communicate Christian concepts. This unit covers the understanding and creating of visual art in a different cultural style and the missiological implications of doing so. The aim of the unit is to enable the cross-cultural church planter to appreciate and use the creative arts of another culture rather than to impose the creative art forms of his/her own culture on the churches that are planted. This unit is of particular relevance to those who already have experience with visual art in their own culture and want to use the medium of visual art to communicate Christian concepts in another culture. It would also be of relevance to those who have an interest in the creative arts of other cultures and want to understand and experiment with the expression of creative arts in other cultures.

Element	Performance Criteria
1 Explain different cultural artistic styles and the implications of using these styles with respect to cross-cultural communication	• Demonstrate and explain three different cultural visual art systems • Articulate the meanings communicated by and associated with different art styles in a specific culture • Articulate principles of communication through visual art in relation to a specific culture • Articulate missiological issues related to using indigenous art styles in evangelism, worship, and teaching
2 Appropriately use art created in a specific culture's style to communicate Christian concepts	• Create a piece of visual art in a specific culture's style • Use indigenous art or a piece of art created in a specific culture's style to appropriately communicate a Christian concept

Evidence Guide

Overview

A person who demonstrates competency in this unit must be able to provide evidence that they can explain different cultural visual art styles and the implications of using these styles with respect to cross-cultural communication, as well as appropriately use a specific cultural visual art style to communicate a Christian concept.

Critical Aspects of Evidence to Demonstrate Competency in This Unit

Assessment requires evidence of the following products or processes to be collected:

Products
- Explanations of at least three different cultural visual art systems
- Demonstrations of at least three different cultural forms of visual art
- An articulation of the meanings communicated by and associated with different visual art styles in a specific culture
- A list of principles of communication through visual art in relation to a specific culture
- An articulation of the missiological issues related to using indigenous visual art styles in evangelism, worship, and teaching
- A piece of visual art created in the style of a specific culture

Processes

- Appropriate use of visual art in a specific cultural style to communicate a Christian concept

	Monday	Tuesday	Wednesday	Thursday	Friday	Saturday	Sunday
Early morning		Discussion of church planter biography & reflection on/ debriefing ministry (including team work) over past week	Informal sessions based around theory and skill development, e.g. teambuilding and planning, storytelling, intercultural communication. *Lunch is eaten communally.*			Church planting activities	Visiting different ethnic churches
Early afternoon	DAY OFF	Ministry planning & further research				Community involvement	Church planting activity with team
Mid-late afternoon and evening	Reading, church planting activities, and community involvement						House church

APPENDIX 3
Ethnographic Questions

This list of questions was compiled and adapted from "Missionaries and Anthropologist Cooperate in Research" by Jacob A. Loewen in *Readings in Missionary Anthropology II*, enlarged 1978 edition, pages 860–76.

These questions should be used as a stimulus for discussion and not considered to be exhaustive. The questions should be answered considering what happens in the culture each person comes from, rather than giving the "correct" Christian answer. Westerners should also be careful in answering the questions and be ready to evaluate their own answers in terms of cultural values, rather than what is "scientifically right." Please refer to the source book for a more extensive list of questions.

Adults

- What are the most significant relationships in a person's life? Who is in that network of relationships? Who influences whom?
- Who made people? How were they made?
- How important are family relationships? What are the outer boundaries of the extended family group?
- How many different ranks of status are recognized?
- How does a person mark the transition from one rank of status to the next?
- Are any age groups recognized?
- Are there any voluntary associations? Are they graded in status?
- What is the status of widows? Widowers? Who looks after them?
- What are their topics of conversation?
- What different professions are recognized?
- Is there any kind of election or choosing for leadership?
- How does one become a warrior?
- What kind of class distinctions are there?
- How does one become a worker?

- How does one become a hunter?
- Are there judges who will classify people?
- How does one become a counselor?
- How does one become a wise man?
- How does one become leader?
- How does one become a medicine man?
- Does a person need a sponsor from above to move up in status? Does he need supernatural sponsorship?
- Must one have power in order to become a man of worth?
- Is there any struggle for status?
- Can one lose one's status?
- Can one rise in status?
- Can women become leaders? In what areas?
- Does the wife of a leader have any more authority than an ordinary woman?
- Can a foreigner be accepted into the social group? Can he/she initiate this?
- Can rank be inherited? Through what lineage?
- For what purposes is the family important? Marriage? Festivity? Soul power? Status?
- How does one earn rank?
- What is the division of labor between leaders and followers?

Advertising

- Describe what is advertised.
- What is considered the most effective method of advertising in the culture?
- Describe the major themes of advertising.
- Analyze how different media are used by advertisers to communicate their messages.

Birth

- Who may be present at the delivery?
- Why are some children born dead?
- How does one get twins? Are both permitted to live?
- Why is delivery occasionally so difficult?
- Why are some children born in different positions? What do each of these mean?

- Why are some children born prematurely?
- Why is the top of the child's head soft at birth?
- How must the navel be cared for?
- With what does one cut the umbilical cord?
- What is done with the afterbirth?
- May evil spirits find entrance into the newly born body? How? How is this prevented? When is the danger of evil spirits greatest for the child?
- If children are killed at birth, who does the killing? Is this considered good? Is it punished? Who does the punishing? How? Does the relevant deity care? Is he/she involved in the punishing?
- How do people come into existence? What were they before they were born?

Children

- How do they treat their children?
- How are children disciplined?
- At what age is a child responsible for him/herself?
- Does one pay attention to the birthday?
- What is viewed as children's work?
- Is there any special training for children before puberty?
- Is there any type of child adoption?
- Do grandparents have responsibility for grandchildren?
- How important are other adults in socializing the child?
- How does the child get his/her name? When?
- How many children does one want?
- Which sex of the child makes the parents happier? Why?
- How is a child weaned? At what age?
- Can a woman become pregnant while she is nursing?
- Can a mother's milk be destroyed or damaged? How? What effect does this have?
- How does the child receive toilet training? At what age does one begin?
- What are the methods of toilet training?
- By what age is the child expected to be toilet trained? If they are not, what happens?
- Who wants more children, the husband or the wife?
- With whom does a child have the most intimate relationship?
- Who trains the children after weaning?

- How are children protected from illness?
- Who does the child love most? How does he/she show it?
- Who loves the child most? How does this person show their love?

Clothing and Ornamentation

- Describe the clothing of daily life, festive life, dancing, and for special ceremonies.
- Does the cut of the hair distinguish rank? Age?
- May hair be cut?
- How do children wear their hair?
- How do women wear their hair?
- How do men wear their hair?
- Describe the ornaments that are worn daily, for special festivals, for weddings, war, leaders.
- Is there filing of teeth? Capping of teeth with gold? Does this have any meaning?
- Is there any meaning in any of the ornamentation worn?
- What types of tattooing are practiced? Why?

Conflict Management

- How does the family settle quarrels? Describe some quarrels you have seen or have been told about.
- Are gifts used in conflict management?
- How does the community settle quarrels?

Cultural Adaptation

- What daily life issues have surprised you as you have settled in?
- Describe the issues you struggle with as you adapt to your new surroundings.
- Do the differences between your preferences with those of your host culture make you uncomfortable in any way? Give some examples of the kinds of things that will challenge you for long-term cultural adjustment.

Death and Burial

- What external signs of mourning does a man, woman, child, or other relative have?
- Is mercy killing of the old practiced? Of crippled children? How is this explained?
- What is done with the bodies of leaders?
- What must the widow or widower do?
- What are the results if these rules (of widowhood) are not obeyed?
- How long does the mourning period last?
- How long must one wait before one can remarry after the death of the marriage partner?
- Will relationship in life be carried on by souls after death?
- What happens to a person when he/she dies?
- At what point does the soul leave the body in connection with death? Where does it go?
- Can spirits of the dead do damage? How? How can one protect himself against them?
- How are people buried? Describe what happens and why each thing is done.
- Is there a special burial place?
- What must the widow or widower do?
- Are there different kinds of burials for different kinds of death?
- What happens to the possessions of the dead person if they are not destroyed?
- How long can the body be left before they must be buried?
- Is natural death recognized?
- Can/is the body burned? Why/why not?
- Are the possessions of the dead person buried/burned with them? Why?
- Why do people die?
- Do souls leave the body willingly?
- Must the soul do certain things?
- Where does the soul go after death?
- What is the relationship of the souls of the dead to living people?
- What remains after the death of a person?
- How long does the soul remain in the vicinity after death?
- To which different areas can a soul go after death?

- May souls of the dead do damage? How? How can one protect himself against them?
- What are the results if these rules concerning mourning and remarriage are not obeyed?
- Was reburial ever practiced? For what reasons?
- How is the remaining part of a dead man related to the living person?
- How does the soul travel to wherever it goes after death?

Decision-making

- Are old people considered wise?
- Do old people have authority?
- Where does one seek advice?
- How does the family make decisions? Who takes the lead? Is there discussion?
- What is the community decision-making unit? What is the process?
- How much can each member participate in the gathering? On what basis is this determined?
- Is there any ranking in the right to speak?

Economic System

- What do economists think are the country's chief economic problems? Its assets? Its economic opportunities?
- What is the national, regional, or local policy regarding economic practice?
- How are large political and economic organizations likely to affect these people over the next ten years? Give an example.
- What are some of the most powerful political and economic organizations in the environment of these people? How do they feel about these?
- What percent own their own land and/or business?
- Is there a Marxist movement among university students? What are their specific complaints?
- What trade routes or economic ties exist between this people and neighboring people or urban centers or neighboring countries?
- To what extent does geography dictate economics for this people?

- How does this people's economic situation compare with that of the rest of the nation and with the rest of the world?
- What is the distribution of wealth among this people like?
- What is the economic status of this people?
- Is there economic tension between ethnic groups?
- What economic trends do you see among this people?
- What do your host people think the country's chief economic problems are? How do these impact them personally?

Festivities

- Who are the principal participants? What do they do? Or what is done to them?
- Where do festivities take place?
- When do festivities take place?
- What are the principal characteristics of the festivals?
- Are certain rules of the society relaxed during the festival period? How long does the lax period last? For whom are the rules relaxed? What is the purpose of this liberty?
- Is there any instruction bound up with the festival? Who gives the instruction?
- What is the origin of the celebration of each festivity?
- What kind of festivities are celebrated? (e.g. fertility festivals, birth or name, puberty, engagement, wedding, ceremonies relating to war, hunt, religion, officials, rank, mourning, burial, victory, dedication of property)
- What is the purpose of the festivals?
- Who initiates festivities?
- Who takes care of the drunks?

Food

- What are the food staples?
- Are there any polite gestures for eating?
- How does one show that one likes the taste of food?
- Does all the family eat together?
- Who cooks?
- Who does the planting? The gathering?

- What is the average daily diet?
- Which foods, meats, plants must be avoided by sick people? Pregnant women? Children? By the aged?
- If food is given as a gift, does it have to be reciprocated? How is this done?
- Can one eat all types of meat?
- What determines the rhythm of life and festivities?
- If there is a shortage of food, who eats first, who eats last?
- Are there any special ceremonies connected with planting or harvesting?
- What is the worst thing you can think of having to eat?

Gathering

- What are the patterns of social gathering for everyone: men, women, and children?
- Why do people gather?
- Who gathers them?
- What do they do when they gather?
- How often do they gather?
- Who leads them once they are gathered?
- How is the gathered group led?
- How much can each member participate in the gathering? On what basis is this determined?

Gender Roles

- Who cooks?
- What is the role of each member of the family?
- What are the responsibilities of the old people in the household? In child training? At festivities?
- What must the widow or widower do?
- What is the responsibility of the mother? Father? Grandfather? Grandmother? Paternal uncle? Maternal uncle? Paternal aunt? Maternal aunt?
- What is considered men's work?
- What is considered women's work?
- What happens if a man does woman's work?

- How much does the father play with the child? How long do the parents control the child's choices? Is there a generation gap? How do people try to bridge it?
- What is the division of labor between men and women?
- If girls don't marry, why don't they marry and who looks after them?
- Can women ever be inherited?
- Are women ever stolen to become wives? Will such a woman ever run away? What is her status then?
- What is expected from children? Males? Females?
- Who is considered smarter?—boys or girls?
- Who instructs a girl in the art of housekeeping?
- Who instructs boys? In what?
- What characteristics do women look for in a man?
- Do all girls get married?
- How much freedom does the woman have? How much authority? Give examples. How much education has she had? What is her economic role?

Geography

- What percentage of these people currently live in cities, and what percentage in villages?
- What natural contacts exist between this people and other ethnolinguistic groups living outside this region?
- What are the major towns, cities, and villages where they live?
- How much movement is there from villages to cities and vice versa? How much interaction between city and villages is there?
- In what major urban centers do these people live?
- How does the terrain affect the people's lifestyle (health, livelihood, isolation etc.)?
- What are the terrain and climate like?
- In what geographic region are they dispersed?
- What is the total population of this people?
- What are the local natural resources?
- To what extent does geography dictate economics for this people?
- How many have access to television and radio?
- What technological trends do you see among this people?
- How many have electricity?

- Briefly describe the people's physical and political environment.
- What boundaries exist between people in this city or people group? What is their significance for church planting?
- Where are they traveling?

Gifts and Reciprocity

- If food is given as a gift, does it have to be reciprocated? How is this done?
- Are gifts used in conflict management?
- What kind of gifts can one make to God?

God

- What do they turn to in a time of crisis?
- Who does a person first go to for help? Why do they go to them?
- Who or what sustains life?
- How does God relate to people?
- When is God kind?
- Where is God, and what is he made of?
- For what reason would God punish men during life?
- What are their ideas of Jesus?
- What are their ideas of God?
- Is God kindly disposed towards man?
- What are their ideas of the supernatural?
- How does God show his good concern for man?
- How often does God show his good concern for man?
- Does God punish? How often? How? (sickness, death, loss of property or honor/respect)
- Is God like a policeman who watches behavior?
- When is God kind?
- What kind of gifts can one make to God?
- By what standards does God judge? Violation of taboo? Violation of laws? Neglect of worship?
- How can one placate God's anger?
- May God's name be freely used/not be used? Why?
- In what ways is God like men?

- Do they think there is any transcendent power in the universe? Do they think they can relate to it? How?
- What are their ideas of man?

Heart Issues

- What are the most significant relationships in a person's life? Who is in that network of relationships? Who influences whom?
- What are their achievements (from their point of view)?
- What are their joys (from their point of view)?
- Who does a person first go to for help? Why do they go to them?
- Where do people go when they or a family member is sick? What power do they rely on? Can people find out what will happen to them in the future? How?
- What are they reading?
- What are the important stories for your people?
- What stories are expressed through the rituals of your people?
- What stories are told again and again among your people?
- What are their failures (from their point of view)?
- Who are their heroes?
- How do people feel about romantic love, being alone, pleasure, family pride, friendliness, achievement, communal solidarity?
- What are they listening to?
- What questions are they asking?
- What do these people consider to be the significant events of the last thirty years? Of the last five hundred years? How have they reacted to these events?
- What are their topics of conversation?
- What is expressed in the dances of the people?
- Analyze how different media are used by advertisers to communicate their messages.
- Explain the relationship of different styles of music to when each style might be used and what it is used to communicate.
- Do your people expect to receive justice from any system? How? What are they looking for?
- What are the themes which underlie the most important stories?

- What are the major rituals of the people, and what themes are expressed in them?
- What are the major themes expressed in the poetry and other literature of the people?
- What are the themes of the stories, legends, and myths of the people?
- Identify why people seek spiritual help.
- What are the main themes of editorials in national newspapers and magazines?
- What do they think is man's destiny? Man's origin?
- What do they think will provide a full and meaningful life?
- From what you have experienced so far, what would you suggest as the order of importance for fear, guilt, and shame in the worldview of the people around you? What makes you think this?
- Describe the major themes of myths and stories.
- How do they feel about their identity and ethnicity?
- Is their ethnic identity maintained more because of a sense of satisfaction in their primordial roots, or because their ethnic identity gives them economic/political advantage?
- If a meeting exists among this people, in what ways has Christianity enhanced their sense of their heritage?
- What is most important—the past, the present, or the future?
- Is time linear, cyclical, or like an oscillating pendulum?
- What is beautiful/ugly, and what are the dominant emotional themes (mystery/awe, peace, ecstasy, joy/sorrow, pessimism/optimism, etc.).
- What are the major themes which come through the music/singing of the people?
- What major themes are expressed in the drama of the people?
- Describe the major themes of advertising

Humor

- What do they consider funny?
- What makes them laugh?
- Are there professional comedians? If so, what sort of humor do they use and what is their message? What gender are the comedians usually and why?
- Give an example of something they consider funny.
- Are there different types of humor and what are their roles?

Leadership

- Who are the most influential people in the community? (These may include media and national as well as local figures.)
- How are leaders developed?

Learning

- What is the literacy rate?
- What is the status of education among this people?
- What kinds of media do they prefer: books, magazines, newspapers, leaflets, comics, radio, TV, tapes, drama, music, demonstrations, posters?
- Is this a literate or an oral language only?
- What problems are there regarding education?
- Who is defined as "wise" and what defines this?
- What are the recognized professions in the culture, and how are these people trained?
- How are people trained in skills?
- How are people trained in the creative arts?
- How are cultural forms and rituals passed on?
- Is there any special training for children before puberty?
- If an adult needs to know something, where does he/she go?
- If an adult needs to master a particular skill, where does he/she go?
- How are leaders developed?
- Who is defined as "educated" and what defines this?
- What were the indigenous forms of learning before schools were introduced?
- Describe all informal learning processes in the culture (that is, not institution-based).
- Is there any instruction bound up with the festival? Who gives the instruction?
- How are the children taught?
- How do people learn about their religion?
- How do adults learn?
- How are excellent teachers identified?
- How are young people mentored?
- Describe any indigenous education systems.
- How are excellent teachers developed?
- Do they have any distinct kinds of humor?

Legal/Justice System

- Where do people gather?
- By what mechanism can prisoners be freed?
- Describe all the national and social legal systems and administration of justice to which your people are subject.
- What moral system do they actually try to live by?
- Which is worst—guilt (of breaking a moral code), shame (and the breaking of relationship), or defilement (ritual uncleanness)?
- Do your people expect to receive justice from any system? How? What are they looking for?

Life Cycle

- How does a person mark the transition from one rank of status to the next?
- Is there a special burial place?
- What determines the rhythm of life and festivities?
- Are there different types of time?
- Does a person need a sponsor from above to move up in status? Does he need supernatural sponsorship?
- What are the major rituals of the people, and what themes are expressed in them?

Money

- How is the white/Western/Asian person seen in the culture of your host country? (In relation to money or other forms of material support)
- What expectations do the people have towards foreigners? (In relation to money or other forms of material support)
- How is money viewed?
- Do people ask, beg for money?
- Do people borrow money? From whom?
- Who lends money? To whom?
- What happens if a loan is not paid back?
- Can people refuse to give? Yes/No—in which cases?
- Can money be given as a gift? At what occasions?
- How do people save money?
- Why do they not save money?
- Who holds the money in the family?

- Who decides how money is spent?
- Do husband and wife have separate financial means?
- Who is financially responsible—for what?
- What are the financial obligations in the extended family system?

Music

- Are songs private property? Can everyone sing certain songs?
- What are the major themes which come through the music/singing of the people?
- Explain the musical system of your people group.
- Explain the relationship of different styles of music to when each style might be used and what it is used to communicate.

Marriage

- How do they treat their children?
- What kind of festivities take place?
- Who initiates the marriage festivities?
- Who serves as master of ceremonies?
- Who should be punished in adultery? Who performs the punishment?
- Were wives ever killed when the husband died?
- Is virginity expected before marriage?
- How does courtship take place? Who takes the initiative?
- What type of contacts between sexes are permitted before marriage?
- Do parents seek to protect the girl?
- Is virginity a cultural ideal? If it is not realized, how is this rationalized?
- How long must one wait before one can remarry after the death of the marriage partner?
- How many children does one want?
- Is divorce possible?
- Is there any education for marriage? Who gives it?
- Is marriage an agreement between the two young people or between the families?
- Who makes the approach for marriage, the young man, the young woman, the parents, the uncle, or some other individual?
- How is the marriage arrangement made?
- Which acts are termed adultery?

- Is there any type of engagement?
- What is one's relationship with one's in-laws?
- Which kind of marriages would be preferred?
- What are the ideals of engagement?
- How companionable is the husband-wife relationship? How much trust, respect, and understanding is there? How much disrespect, deception, or tension?
- What is the goal of marriage?
- What is considered beautiful?
- What is the relationship between the respective sets of parents?
- What is the status relationship between husband and wife?
- Who experiences shame in the case of adultery?
- What is the ideal of marriage? What is the practice?
- Is there trial marriage? For how long a period? Under what conditions? Is it considered good or bad?
- Do wives or husbands ever bewitch their spouses? For what reasons? How? What must then be done?
- Why does a man become unfaithful to his wife? (Bewitchment? Too strong sex drive? Stolen by another woman?)
- Why does a woman become unfaithful to her husband?
- Who punishes the wife if she makes a mistake?
- What is called handsome in a man?

Old People

- Are old people honored?
- Are old people killed?
- Are old people hidden away?
- Where do old people live?
- What is the attitude towards old age?
- Why do women stop menstruating?
- Are old people dangerous to children?
- What are the responsibilities of the old people in the household? In child training? At festivities?
- Do grandparents have responsibility for grandchildren?
- Where does one seek advice?
- Do old people have authority?

- Are old people considered wise?
- Do old people have any special organization?
- Are the souls of old people considered stronger, wiser, better than those of young people?
- Why do people get old?
- Does the soul also get old?

Names

- Can the child change his/her name?
- Does a person have several names?
- Are names private?
- Can names be inherited? Along which lines of inheritance?
- Must names be kept secret? If so, who may know the intimate name of a person?
- Can power be inherited with a name? May one speak the name of a dead person? If not, for how long is it taboo?

Performing Arts

- Which of the following forms of communication do the people group use most: non-fiction, narrative, poetry, myth, proverbs, comics, debates, direct, or indirect?
- What stories underlie the dramas and dances of your people?
- How are people trained in the creative arts?
- What major themes are expressed in the drama of the people?
- What is expressed in the dances of the people?
- Do they have any distinct kinds of humor?
- Describe the major themes of the creative arts.

Politics

- To what extent does geography dictate economics for this people?
- What is the national, regional, or local policy regarding economic practice?
- What is the regional political structure?
- What is the national political structure?
- What is the current political status of this people?
- How are large political and economic organizations likely to affect these people over the next ten years? Give an example.

- What are some of the most powerful political and economic organizations in the environment of these people? How do they feel about these?
- To what extent is this people engaged in the local, regional, or national political structure?
- What, if any, political events relate this people to the broader political context?
- Briefly describe the people's physical and political environment.

Pregnancy

- Who performs abortion?
- For what reasons is abortion justified?
- How is abortion practiced?
- What is the attitude towards abortion?
- What may a pregnant woman do or not do?
- What is conceived—the soul or the body?
- Can a woman prevent pregnancy? What types of contraceptives (medical, traditional and spiritual) does she use?
- What type of "spiritual" receptivity does a woman need to become pregnant?
- What are the beliefs concerning how a woman becomes pregnant?

Property

- What percent own their own land and/or business?
- Beyond basic necessities, what do they prefer to spend their money on? Clothes, parties, insurance policies, investments, labor-saving gadgets?
- Who pays for property or goods used for religious or spiritual purposes?
- May ceremonial objects be sold?
- How is private property sold? How is the exchange effected? Who is responsible for setting the price—the buyer or the seller? Is such an exchange termed "giving"?
- Can borrowing become permanent?
- What kinds of expenditure do they consider extravagant?
- What is the relationship between people and nature—the earth, plants, and animals?
- Will the magical charm of one person work for another?
- Do people have their own private magical charms?

- Are certain areas privately owned?
- How did the current owners (in terms of nation or tribe) get possession of their land?
- What type of property can one own?
- Can one own land?
- Can one own fruit trees?
- Are clothes private property?

Punishment

- How are children disciplined?
- How important are other adults in socializing the child?
- What wrongs does the group punish?
- How does the group punish?
- What crimes or wrongs does a family punish?
- For what offenses is a child punished?
- What crimes or wrongs does a family punish?
- What is punished by the clan/village/larger social grouping? How do they punish?
- Who should be punished in adultery? Who performs the punishment?
- If the child is delayed in their toilet training who punishes the child and how?
- Does God punish? How often? How? (Sickness, death, loss of property or honor/respect?)
- For what reason would God punish men during life?
- How does the individual punish or avenge wrongs?
- For what reason would the spirits punish man?
- Can one become punishable through ignorance?
- What are the results if these rules concerning mourning and remarriage are not obeyed?
- Is God like a policeman who watches behavior?
- By what standards does God judge? Violation of taboo? Violation of laws? Neglect of worship?
- How can one placate God's anger?
- Will good and bad deeds bring natural results in reward or judgment?
- Does punishment have any kind of religious sanction?
- Is there any grading of punishment?

Relatives

- To which clan do the offspring belong?
- Who are the most loyal family members? Who are the least loyal? Are there some marginal members?
- Are adopted children considered blood relatives?
- What rights do adopted children have?
- Who must a man avoid?
- Who must a woman avoid?
- How is the family related to other structures in society? To the neighborhood? To kin? To community organizations?
- Are the relatives on the mother's side considered blood relatives?
- What kind of relatives are recognized? From mother's side? From father's side?
- Which individuals are excluded from marriage because of blood relationship?
- How many generations are distinguished in kinship?
- Are orphans recognized?
- Who is responsible for orphans?
- What would be the results of incest?
- How is incest defined?
- Who punishes incest?
- Is the relevant deity concerned about incest?

Religion

- What religious trends are underway among this people?
- What is the percentage of this people adhering to each of the main religions?
- What is the predominant religion?
- What minority religions or sects exist?
- What peculiar characteristics or deviations from the mainstream of these religions exist among this people?
- Do they participate in more than one religion? If so, when, where, and concerning what do they express each faith?
- Who does a person first go to for help? Why do they go to them?
- What do they turn to in a time of crisis?
- Identify why people seek spiritual help.

- Determine what priority people give to obtaining spiritual help.
- Is there any struggle for spiritual power?
- Are there sacred places? Where? Why are they sacred?
- Are there polluted or defiled places? Where? Why are they polluted/defiled?
- How is the control of spirits exercised? (e.g. magic, special words, ceremonies, rituals, sacrifices)
- Who can become a shaman or person who can control or manipulate spirits?
- How is the shaman (or spirit-manipulator) chosen?
- Can the shaman (or spirit-manipulator) foretell events? How?
- Is the shaman (or spirit-manipulator) paid? When?
- Is there circumcision? Clitoridectomy (female circumcision)? Piercing of ear lobes or nasal septum? At what age? Who does it? Why is it done?
- May ceremonial objects be sold?
- What determines the rhythm of life and festivities?
- How is the earth made fertile?
- Is there any relationship between human fertility and the fertility of the earth?
- Are there any special ceremonies connected with planting or harvesting?
- What is most important—the past, the present, or the future?
- What are their ideas of sin?
- What are their ideas of man?
- How are the results of sexual relations dealt with? (e.g. ritual washing to be made clean) Do both men and women have to do it?
- What are the major rituals of the people, and what themes are expressed in them?
- What moral system do they actually try to live by?
- Does punishment have any kind of religious sanction?
- If a Christian meeting exists among this people, in what ways has Christianity enhanced their sense of their heritage?
- What is the status of Scripture translation into this language?
- What are their ideas of Christians?

Religious System/Organizations

- How is the religious system organized?
- How much power do religious/spiritual leaders have over adherents of that religion?

- Who pays for property or goods used for religious or spiritual purposes?
- What religious institutions exist?
- How do people learn about their religion?
- How are decisions made in the religious community?
- What is the system of accountability for spiritual leaders?
- What is the relationship between religious leaders and political or social leaders?
- Who can broker spiritual power?
- How much power do religious/spiritual leaders have in the wider community?
- How are spiritual leaders chosen and organized?

Sexual Relations

- Who taught man the art of sex relations?
- May a pregnant woman continue to have sex relations? What about a nursing woman or a menstruating woman?
- Who takes the initiative in sexual relations?
- Where may sex relations be practiced? When? How often?
- Which would be considered worse, for a girl to sleep with a married man, or with an unmarried youth?
- What is done with the premarital child? The extra-marital child?
- How are the results of sexual relations dealt with? (e.g. ritual washing to be made clean) Do both men and women have to do it?
- How are sexual relations perceived? (Do they make you unclean? Leave "fire" in the body?)

Sin

- Will good deeds be rewarded?
- What are the results if rules are not obeyed?
- What is punished by the clan/village/larger social grouping?
- Which deeds get social recognition?
- What do people feel if they do something wrong?
- With what do they feel that they've done something wrong?
- Are there any wrongs that are against the whole society?
- What wrongs does the group punish?
- What is the attitude towards drunken behavior?

- Is mercy killing of the old practiced? Of crippled children? How is this explained?
- Which deeds get social recognition?
- Can harm be done through curses?
- What is the greatest good and what are the greatest evil actions?
- What are their ideas of sin?
- What is worst—guilt (of breaking a moral code), shame (and the breaking of relationship), or defilement (ritual uncleanness)?
- Which sins are worse than others?
- What are the most important characteristics of a good person?
- Are there certain wrongs that cannot be forgiven? (By men?) Why are they unpardonable?
- Are there polluted or defiled places? Where? Why are they polluted/defiled?
- Are certain body parts good? Are others considered bad?
- Are certain body parts clean? Are others considered unclean?
- What is beautiful/ugly, and what are the dominant emotional themes (mystery/awe, peace, ecstasy, joy/sorrow, pessimism/optimism, etc.)
- From what you have experienced so far, what would you suggest as the order of importance for fear, guilt and shame in the worldview of the people around you? What makes you think this?
- What is clean and what is unclean?
- What is good and what is bad?
- What causes God to be angry?
- By what standards does God judge? Violation of taboo? Violation of laws? Neglect of worship?
- What are the results if these rules concerning mourning and remarriage are not obeyed?
- What is good and what is shameful?
- What is honorable and what is shameful?
- Is there badness apart from morality?
- How does the individual punish or avenge wrongs?
- How does one determine guilt? (E.g. the witness of others? Confession of the individual? A vision or declaration by a prophet?)
- Is a moral transgression more serious than a taboo?
- Is there any distinction between holiness and goodness?
- Is there any kind of holy—evil distinction?
- Is there any distinction between the holy and the profane?

- Can one become punishable through ignorance?
- How does one know which sins are worse than others?
- Does punishment have any kind of religious sanction?
- Will good and bad deeds bring natural results in reward or judgment?
- Is there ceremonial cleanness apart from morality?
- Is there shame apart from morality?

Social Control

- Describe all the national and social legal systems and administration of justice to which your people are subject
- To what degree does the group restrict interaction with members of other groups?
- How important is the child's peer group in socializing the child?
- How important are other adults in socializing the child?
- Are members of the family/clan/village/larger social grouping ever avoided because of what they have done? How strong is the avoidance? What had they done? What deeds would cause such treatment? How strong is the avoidance? Must the culprits go away?
- Which deeds get social recognition?
- How is bravery rewarded?
- What moral system do they actually try to live by?

Social Demography

- What is the relationship between this language and the national language?
- What other ethnolinguistic groups live in the vicinity of this people?
- What is the relationship between this people and the larger national/regional population?
- What is the status of literacy in this language and in the national language?
- In what geographic region are they dispersed?
- What bilingual dictionaries are available for this language?
- Where do diaspora communities exist from which to learn this language?
- To what linguistic family does this language belong, and what are some related languages?
- With what other people groups does this people share cultural affinities?

- What is the history of this people, including ethnolinguistic origins and recent history?
- What percent are rich, comfortable, subsistence level, or destitute? Do these economic class lines coincide with other classifications (i.e., kin, caste, etc.) or do they cut across these divisions, tying people together?
- What religious trends are underway among this people?
- What is the percentage of this people adhering to each of the main religions?
- In the main, what social class in the national system do these people occupy? What are the functions or potential functions of this class in the total system?
- What is the current political status of this people?
- What natural contacts exist between this people and other ethnolinguistic groups living outside this region?
- What is the total population of this people?
- How does this people's economic situation compare with that of the rest of the nation, and with the rest of the world?
- What is the economic status of this people?
- Are significant parts of these people required to function customarily in terms of two (or more) cultural systems?
- What other cultural systems have influence on your people group: near neighboring peoples; early foreign colonizers/immigrants who helped form the nation; recent foreign colonizers/traders?
- What boundaries exist between people in this city or people group? What is their significance for church planting?
- What subgroups exist within your people group?
- To what extent are the people bilingual?
- Where are they traveling?
- Do the people consider themselves poor, or not?

Social Organization

Beyond the family

- To what degree does the group(s) you have identified see itself as distinct within society?
- To what degree does the group restrict interaction with members of other groups?

- What is the most important group(s) a person belongs to?
- How does a person relate to the members of their ingroup(s)?
- To what degree do group members see themselves as being connected together through influential relationships?
- How does a person relate to members of their people group who are not in their ingroup?
- How is the world of relationships organized?
- What kind of boundaries are there between groups? How rigid or fuzzy are these boundaries?
- How do the people identify themselves? With what specific traits would they identify someone who is a _____ (member of their group)? How do their near neighbors identify them (i.e. with what specific traits)?
- How important are family relationships? What are the outer boundaries of the extended family group?
- What various networks tie members of this people to other people outside the group? What are the strongest of these ties?
- How many different ranks of status are recognized?
- How does a person mark the transition from one rank of status to the next?
- Are there any voluntary associations? Are they graded in status?
- Does a person need a sponsor from above to move up in status? Does he need supernatural sponsorship?

Soul

- Will relationship in life be carried on by souls after death?
- What is the seat of emotions? (e.g. heart, liver, spleen)
- Are thinking and desiring related?
- With what does one feel love? Hate? Desire?
- Can soul and spirit be distinguished?
- How are soul, spirit, feelings and thinking related to the brain? To the personality?
- Does a tribe have a common spirit or soul?
- What are people made of? What are the parts of a person? Which part of a person is most important? Why?
- Does man have several natures? (e.g. higher, better nature and lower, worse nature)
- Does a people group have a common spirit or soul?

- With what does one think?
- Do animals have a nonphysical aspect about them, similar to human beings?
- Where does the soul originate from? (Mother? Father? A receptacle of souls in the environment? The beyond?)
- How many souls does a person get? How are these distinguished from each other?
- When does the soul take possession of the body of the newly conceived child? (At conception? At the first movement of the child? At birth? At some special ceremony?)
- Can the soul of the deceased be born another time?
- Do souls leave the body willingly at death?
- Is the soul or spirit related to man's breath? His blood?
- What is human personality?
- What are the basic parts of man?

Spirit World

- Can spirits be misled?
- Can spirits be caught?
- Does the shaman (or spirit-manipulator) have power over the spirits?
- What kind of power does the shaman have over the spirits?
- Does a shaman (or spirit-manipulator) become possessed by spirits?
- What is the relationship of Christian angels to the spirit world?
- Can sorcery be practiced without any kind of contact?
- Is there an upper world? Who lives there?
- Is there an underworld? How did it get there? Is it populated? By whom?
- Have people from the underworld ever visited the present world?
- Where do the spirits live?
- Is there a special spirit world? Where is it located?
- Can one carry some type of spirit protection with him? How does one acquire this?
- Can spirits be deceived by humans?
- If a spirit is resident in a man, which is the seat of its residence? (e.g. liver, heart, belly)
- What types of witchcraft are there?
- Can anyone practice sorcery or witchcraft?
- Can one do harm with body hair, fingernails, names, body fluids, clothes, or any kind of personal property?

- Is supernatural power available to both sexes?
- Can harm be done through curses?
- Can good be done through blessings?
- Are certain places recognized as the habitation of spirits?
- Can people control the spirits? How?
- How should people relate to the spirits?
- Can a spirit enter a person's body? How? Why? What happens to the person?
- Can one feel the presence of spirits? How does one feel it?
- Can a spirit be made to leave the body? How?
- What kind of power does the shaman have over the spirits?
- Where do dreams come from? (Can the soul or spirit leave the body during dreams?)
- What kinds of spirits are there? Which ones are good and which ones are bad?
- Why does a spirit do kind things to a man?
- Why does a spirit do harm to a man?
- How does one know of the presence of a spirit in the body?
- How does the spirit leave the body?
- How does a spirit gain entrance to a human body? Which is the port of entry?
- Can spirits be controlled by people? Who?
- How is the control of spirits exercised? (e.g. magic, special words, ceremonies, rituals, sacrifices)
- Are there ranks of spirits?
- May evil spirits find entrance into the newly born body? How? How is this prevented? When is the danger of evil spirits greatest for the child?
- What happens when a person dreams? (Can the soul or spirit leave the body during dreams?)
- Can one lose his/her soul or spirit?
- For what reason would the spirits punish man?
- Do different spirits favor different sexes?

Stories

- Collect some common stories and myths.
- Which of the following forms of communication does the people group use most: non-fiction, narrative, poetry, myth, proverbs, comics, debates, direct, or indirect?

- What stories are told again and again among your people?
- What stories underlie the dramas and dances of your people?
- What stories are expressed through the rituals of your people?
- What are the important stories (or story) for your people?
- What is an example of a brave act?
- Who tells the stories?
- With whom can one joke?
- What are the themes of the stories, legends, and myths of the people?
- Describe the major themes of myths and stories.
- What are the themes which underlie the most important stories?

Taboo

Taboo is distinguished from sin in that taboo is negative magic.
If one disobeys a taboo, it will avenge itself.

- Are there any deeds considered taboo?
- Who enforces the taboo?
- What is the result of the violation of a taboo?
- How does the taboo manifest itself? (Must it not be touched, looked at, mentioned, eaten?)
- Are there taboo people?
- Are there any taboo objects?
- Can one taboo object pass the taboo on to others? How?
- Are there any taboo words or names (e.g. the names of the dead)?
- How was the taboo created?
- Who or what empowers the taboo?
- Is there any difference between holy things and unclean things?
- Is there any relationship between taboo and morality?

Universe

- How many seasons are there, and how are they distinguished?
- What are the stars, and what do they mean?
- Where did the rainbow come from, and what does it mean?
- Is there only one world in existence? Is there another world? If so, how did it get there, and what is in it?
- Have people from the other world ever visited the present world?

- Have people from the present world ever been able to visit the other world? How?
- Why are some animals enemies of man?
- When was the world made?
- Who made the world?
- Who made people?
- What is the relationship between people and animals?
- Where does the world come from? When was it made? Who made it?
- What is the relationship between man and the earth?

Visual Arts

- Who can become an artist?
- What is the status of the artist in the culture?
- Who pays artists?
- How are artists trained?
- Are different styles of visual art associated with different purposes of use or communication?
- Who defines acceptable or exceptional art?
- Describe the distinctives of the visual arts of your people group.
- What is the association between art and religion?
- What defines good art?
- Describe the major themes of the visual arts.

War

- Who is permitted to go to war?
- Is there a special war cry?
- Is there any special clothing for war?
- Do people paint for going into war?
- Are there any deities or spirits of war?
- Are there specialists in making weapons?
- Do weapons have to be dedicated?
- What kind of weapons are used for war?
- Do prisoners ever try to escape?
- By what mechanism can prisoners of war be freed?
- What is an example of a brave act in war?
- How is bravery in battle rewarded?

- How are prisoners of war disposed of?
- Are prisoners taken in war? Who?
- With whom do they fight? Why?
- Is it necessary to abstain from sexual relations before war? Why?
- What preparations does the warrior make?
- Is there a proper time for fighting, and how is that time determined?
- What role do women and children have in war?

Working

- Within your people group, what are the main occupations?
- What are the common local products made for home use or for sale?
- Does one have to work in exchange, or can one give gifts or pay wages?
- Can one hire other people to do one's work?
- For which work must one begin as an apprentice?
- Are there special times when certain jobs cannot be done?

Youth

- How does a boy become a youth? At what age?
- What are the qualities that one looks for in a young woman?
- Does anyone pay attention to her first menstruation? How? Who initiates this celebration? What is the intent of this celebration?
- Is virginity expected before marriage?
- How does a girl become a young woman and ready for marriage?
- What are the responsibilities of the youth?
- When does a boy become ready for marriage?
- How does a boy become recognized as a young man?
- Is there any young men's society? What function does it fill?

APPENDIX 4
Learning Language and Culture:
Performance Criteria and Evidence of Competency

Suggested Order	Competency	Performance Criteria		Product Or Process
1	21	3	A Bible reading and devotional plan for at least one year is prepared and implemented	Regular reports on devotional time
2	21	3	A set number of people who will consistently pray for and encourage the trainee are identified	List of people
3	21	3	Communication with the people who consistently pray for the trainee occurs regularly for at least six months	Prayer letters
4	21	1	A plan for coping with the stress of moving and changing cultural contexts is prepared	Plan
5	14	1	The everyday life of the people in the trainee's own cross-cultural church planting context is researched by participant observation	Research by participant observation
6	14	1	A description of the everyday life of the people in the trainee's own cross-cultural church planting context is given	Ethnographic description
7	13	3	An example of a cross-cultural encounter where no attempt was made to adjust the communication for context or hearer is given	Observation and reflection on missionary practice or other cross-cultural communication around them
8	13	3	Consequences of poor cross-cultural communication in cross-cultural church planting are explained	Reflection on theory
9	14	4	The festivals are listed	List of festivals
10	14	1	A set number of own assumptions about cultural practices in the trainee's own cross-cultural church planting context are identified	Personal reflection on ethnographic research

Suggested Order	Competency	Performance Criteria		Product Or Process
11	14	4	At least one festival is researched using ethnographic methods	Ethnographic research
12	14	4	An ethnographic description of at least one festival is given	Ethnographic description of a festival
13	21	2	A plan for regular and adequate rest and recreation is prepared and implemented	Plan for rest & recreation *and* its implementation
14	21	1	Probable personal indicators of cross-cultural stress are identified	List of personal indicators of cross-cultural stress *plus discussion with Field Supervisor*
15	21	1	A stress management plan for cross-cultural stress is prepared	Stress management plan
16	21	1	A set number of people who could give support during cross-cultural stress are identified	Identifying at least three people who could give support during cross-cultural stress
17	13	2	An example of the risk of equating gospel with culture is given	Reflection on theory re: equating gospel with culture
18	16	1	The way society is organized, including its important institutions, is described	Ethnographic research
19	14	3	The rites of passage are listed	Ethnographic research
20	16	2	The education system is described	Ethnographic research
Basic language, uses language to improve language, observes, & asks basic questions				
21	16	1	A map of important family relationships is drawn	Ethnographic research
22	14	1	The trainee's own assumptions about cultural practices are re-formulated, without judgments, into questions which are asked of members of the host culture	Ethnographic research
23	13	3	An illustration of a personal attempt to overcome cross-cultural communication barriers is given	Reflection on own experience with respect to overcoming cross-cultural communication barriers
24	12	1	A folk religious practice is described	A description of a folk religious practice
25	14	3	At least one rite of passage is researched using ethnographic methods	Ethnographic research

Suggested Order	Competency	Performance Criteria		Product Or Process
26	14	3	An ethnographic description of at least one rite of passage is given	Ethnographic description of a rite of passage
27	14	5	The creative art forms are listed	Ethnographic research into creative art forms in the culture
28	15	2	The most common accusations made against people in day-to-day conversation are listed	Participant observation of common conversation topics
29	13	4	An example of personal ethnocentrism is given	Personal reflection on behavior and attitudes
Starting to conduct basic interviews				
30	12	1	The religious system in the culture is researched using ethnographic methods	Ethnographic research of religious system
31	16	1	A map of important relationships for individuals in the culture is drawn	Ethnographic research of social networks
32	14	5	At least one creative art form is experienced in the same manner that people in the culture experience it	Ethnographic research, especially participant observation of a creative art form
33	16	2	The way in which children and young people are trained in life skills is described	Ethnographic research of learning in the culture
34	16	2	The way in which religious professionals are trained is described	
35	16	2	The way in which master craftsmen, tradesmen, and professionals train aspiring craftsmen, tradesmen, and professionals is described	
36	16	2	Learning in the culture is researched using ethnographic methods	
37	21	1	Intentional strategies for increasing personal flexibility are developed and implemented	Personal reflection on behavior with respect to flexibility and the ability to change and grow in the area of personal flexibility

Suggested Order	Competency	Performance Criteria		Product Or Process
Comfortable in more detailed conversations				
38	16	1	Societal structure and order is researched using ethnographic methods	Ethnographic research concerning societal structure and order
39	16	1	The way in which the culture maintains order and manages those who disrupt societal order is described	Ethnographic research concerning the maintenance of societal order
40	16	3	A set number of different types of context where decision-making occurs are researched by participant observation	Participant observation of different types of context where decision-making occurs
41	13	4	The relationship between the Bible and the transformation of culture in cross-cultural church planting is discussed	Reflection on theory in the light of experience
Starts communicating personal spirituality and can follow group conversations/interactions				
42	13	3	An example of a form and meaning challenge relevant to cross-cultural church planting in the trainee's own cross-cultural church planting context is explained	Reflection on theory in the light of experience
43	13	2	At least two examples of difference between the concepts of sin in different cultures are given	Understanding anthropological theory concerning the concept of sin
44	14	2	A set number of different types of gathering is researched by participant observation	Participant observation of different types of gathering in the culture
45	14	2	The structure, order, conduct, and leadership within a set number of gatherings are described	Ethnographic research concerning different types of gathering in the culture
46	14	2	The reasons for a set number of gatherings are researched using ethnographic methods	Ethnographic research into the reasons for different gatherings
47	16	3	The process of decision-making, in small and large groups, informal and formal contexts is described	Ethnographic research concerning decision-making in the culture
48	16	3	The ascribing of leadership and role of leadership in decision-making is described	Ethnographic research concerning the role of leadership in decision-making

Suggested Order	Competency		Performance Criteria	Product Or Process
49	12	1	A description of religion by a set number of lay practitioners is obtained by ethnographic interview	At least three ethnographic interviews regarding the practice of religion
50	16	1	The relationship of religion to societal order is articulated	Ethnographic research into relationship of religion to societal order
51	12	1	A description of the formal religion of the culture is obtained through ethnographic interview of a teacher of religion	Ethnographic interview of a teacher of religion concerning formal religion
52	12	1	An ethnographic description of the differences between formal and folk religion in the culture is given	Reflection, analysis, and synthesis of ethnographic research
More in-depth interviewing, collects stories and re-tells them (with practice)				
53	16	2	The dimension of youth and age in learning in the culture is explored using ethnographic methods	Ethnographic research into youth and age, especially with respect to learning
54	15	1	A set number of foundational myths or key stories are collected from local sources	Research to collect stories from local sources
55	15	2	A set number of stories of cultural heroes are collected from local sources	Research to collect stories from local sources
56	21	3	A strategy for coping with discouragement and depression is prepared	Relating theory to experience or potential experience
Interview for beliefs behind major cultural practices				
57	15	2	A description of what is beauty and why it is beautiful is received from at least one local person	Ethnographic interview about beauty
58	15	2	A description of what is ugly and why it is ugly is received from at least one local person	Ethnographic interview about ugliness
59	11	2	Cultural views and practices concerning sickness and healing are researched using ethnographic methods	Ethnographic research into sickness and healing
60	11	1	The concept of the excluded middle is explained	Reflection on theory in the light of experience
61	11	2	Cultural views and practices concerning charms, spells, and other means of manipulation using spiritual power to fulfill needs or desires are researched using ethnographic methods	Ethnographic research concerning charms, spells, and other means of manipulation using spiritual power to fulfill needs or desires

Suggested Order	Competency	Performance Criteria	Product Or Process
62	15	3	An explanation of who or what causes misfortunes to happen is collected from a set number of local people	Ethnographic research including interviewing at least three people into who or what causes bad things in life and what people can do to prevent or remedy them or to make good things happen
63	15	3	An explanation of what people can do to prevent or remedy misfortune and to have good things happen to them is collected from a set number of local people	
64	11	2	The role, methods, and means of power of spiritual power practitioners in the culture are researched using ethnographic methods	Ethnographic research into the role, methods, and means of power of spiritual power practitioners in the culture
65	11	1	A biblical survey of the spiritual world and its interaction with the material world is conducted	Biblical survey related to the spiritual world and its interaction with the material world
66	11	3	For each belief and practice outlined in 11.2 which is encountered in the culture, a biblical response is prepared	Reflection on experience and research findings in the light of the Bible
67	11	1	A practical theology of the supernatural is developed	
68	15	3	An explanation of why events in the world happen is collected from a set number of local people	Ethnographic research including interviews of at least three different people of why things happen in the world
69	12	4	Rituals and traditions associated with death are researched using ethnographic methods	Ethnographic research into the rituals and traditions associated with death
70	13	2	The nature of sin and its control and punishment in the trainee's own cross-cultural church planting context are described	Ethnographic research into the nature of sin and its control and punishment
71	13	4	A practice in the culture which could be contextualized is researched	Reflection on theory in the light of experience
72	15	2	Descriptions of a good man and a good woman are collected from a set number of local sources	Ethnographic interview of at least three local people to elicit descriptions of a good man and a good woman

Suggested Order	Competency	Performance Criteria		Product Or Process
73	15	1	A set number of the most common themes of the creative arts are outlined through having read, seen, heard, or experienced the creative art presentations or performances	Reflection on experience of the creative arts
74	16	3	At least one leader is interviewed to research the nature and role of leadership in the culture	Ethnographic interview of at least one local leader re: nature and role of leadership
75	16	3	A set number of local people who are not leaders are interviewed to research the nature and role of leadership in the culture	Ethnographic interview of at least three local people who are not leaders regarding the nature and role of leadership in the culture
76	16	3	A summary of leadership in the culture is given	Analysis and synthesis of cultural data
In-depth interviewing about beliefs				
77	11	2	Cultural views and practices concerning evil spirits, deliverance, and mental illness are researched using ethnographic methods	Ethnographic research concerning evil spirits, deliverance, and mental illness
78	11	2	Cultural views and practices concerning blessings and curses are researched using ethnographic methods	Ethnographic research concerning blessings and curses
79	12	2	Beliefs about the relationship between the material and spiritual world and how people can or cannot manipulate spiritual powers is explained	Ethnographic research concerning the relationship between the material and spiritual world and how people can or cannot manipulate spiritual powers
First language supervisor report				
80	15	4	An explanation of the relationship between the groups (ethnic or other) to which the self belongs and other groups is received from at least one local person	Ethnographic interview of at least one person to explore the relationship of the groups to which that person belongs to other groups
81	16	2	The role of the community in adult learning is described	Ethnographic research concerning the role of the community in adult learning

Suggested Order	Competency		Performance Criteria	Product Or Process
82	15	4	A cultural mental map of the world is constructed from data collected from a set number of local people	Synthesis of cultural data obtained by ethnographic interview of at least three people regarding a mental map of the world
83	12	2	Beliefs about divine beings or powers are described	Ethnographic research concerning beliefs about divine beings or powers
84	12	2	Beliefs about spirits or other non-divine beings or powers are described	Ethnographic research concerning beliefs about spirits and other non-divine beings or powers
85	21	2	The probable personal indicators and precipitants of brown out are identified	Reflection on theory in the light of experience
86	11	3	In collaboration with local believers and more experienced cross-cultural church planters, a Christian practical alternative to at least one non-Christian power practice is developed and put into practice	Experimenting with putting theory into practice—synthesis of a practical theology of the supernatural with spiritual beliefs and practices encountered in the culture
Interviewing for complex concepts which locals may even find difficult to articulate & collaborative discussion about Christian practices				
87	15	4	An explanation of the relationship of humans to nature is received from at least one local person	Ethnographic interview of at least one person about the relationship of humans to nature
88	15	2	An explanation of the bases on which men and women are considered good is received from at least one local person	Ethnographic interview of at least one person about how and why "good" is defined in the culture
89	14	5	The means which the artist uses to communicate his/her message is described	Ethnographic research into artistic communication methods
90	15	1	An explanation of the cultural view of the progression of time is derived through interviewing a set number of people in the culture	Ethnographic interview of at least three people concerning the cultural view of the progression of time
91	12	3	Beliefs concerning the unseen nature of human beings are described	Ethnographic research concerning the unseen nature of human beings

Suggested Order	Competency	Performance Criteria		Product Or Process
92	15	4	An explanation of the location and components of the self in relation to the body is received from at least one local person	Ethnographic interview of at least one person concerning the components of self in relation to the body
93	15	4	An explanation of what distinguishes humans from non-humans is received from at least one local person	Ethnographic interview of at least one person concerning what distinguishes humans from non-humans
94	12	3	Biblical equivalents in relationship to the unseen nature of human beings are identified	Biblical survey concerning the concepts of the unseen nature in the culture
95	12	3	A biblical theology in relation to the unseen nature of human beings in the culture is articulated	Construction of a biblical theology concerning the unseen nature of the human beings in the culture
96	15	3	The greatest fears in the culture are researched by ethnographic methods	Ethnographic research into the greatest fears in the culture
97	12	4	Beliefs concerning death and afterlife are described	Ethnographic research concerning death and the afterlife
Second language supervisor report				
98	12	4	A biblical theology in relation to death, the afterlife, and death practices is developed	Biblical survey relating to death, the afterlife, and death practices
99	12	4	Death beliefs and practices which are consistent with biblical principles and teaching are identified	Comparative analysis of cultural data with biblical data
100	12	4	Ideas about possible contextualized Christian death practices are articulated	Reflection on experience in the light of theory
101	15	5	The culture's view on the nature and source of wisdom is researched by interviewing a set number of local people	Ethnographic interview of at least three people concerning the nature and source of wisdom
102	15	5	The culture's view on how it is known whether something is true or not is researched by interviewing a set number of local people	Ethnographic interview of at least three people concerning how it is known whether something is "true"

Field Supervisor Report (End of First Year)
Regarding General Adjustment and Basic Cultural Skills

Competency		Performance Criteria	What Product or Process are They Assessing?
Maintaining a healthy lifestyle (~ 1 month NB need regular checks over next 6 months)			
21	2	A balance of healthy living habits with respect to food, sleep, work, family commitments, rest, and recreation is maintained for at least six months	Behavior
Behaving appropriately in the culture			
13	1	Appropriate dress is worn in all contexts	Behavior
13	1	Behaves appropriately towards people of different gender and status in the culture	Behavior
13	1	Receives hospitality from members of the culture without causing offense	Receives hospitality from members of the culture without causing offense
13	1	A set number of local dishes and beverages are prepared and served to local people	Prepares and serves at least three local dishes and/or drinks to local people
13	1	Gives hospitality to members of the culture without causing offense	Gives hospitality without causing offense

Language Supervisor (LS)/Field Supervisor (FS) Reports

Note: The time frame will differ according to the difficulty of the language and the language ability of the new missionary.

Approx. Time	Comp		Performance Criteria	What Product or Process is Being Assessed?	Evidence to Be Collected
Basic language, uses language to improve language, observes & asks basic questions					
~ 6 months	18	1	Common personal queries are comfortably answered	Using the language comfortably in basic conversation	FS/LS report of observing trainee answering common personal queries comfortably
~ 12 months	18	3	Feedback about language usage is elicited	Eliciting feedback about language usage	FS/LS report of observing trainee eliciting feedback about language usage

Approx. Time	Comp		Performance Criteria	What Product or Process is Being Assessed?	Evidence to Be Collected
~ 12 months	18	3	Language use is adjusted to incorporate feedback and improve communication	Improving language usage by adjusting language according to feedback	FS/LS report of trainee improving language usage by adjusting language according to feedback
~ 12 months	18	3	Questions are consistently asked to better understand the audience and their response	Using language to better understand the audience	FS/LS report of trainee's consistent asking of questions to better understand the audience and their response
~ 12 months	18	1	A personal life history is communicated in a culturally engaging way	Giving a personal history or a testimony	FS/LS report of trainee communicating a personal life history in a culturally engaging way
~ 12 months	18	2	The trainee's conversion experience is explained in a relevant and appropriate way	Giving a personal conversion testimony	FS/LS report of trainee communicating a personal conversion testimony in a relevant and appropriate way
~ 12 months	18	2	The Bible is read aloud to a local audience in a comprehensible way using appropriate local methods related to public reading	Reading the Bible aloud to a local audience	FS/LS report of trainee reading the Bible aloud to a local audience in a comprehensible way and using appropriate local methods related to public reading
~ 12 months	18	2	A set number of Bible verses in the local language are memorized and quoted	Quoting the Bible verses	FS/LS report of Bible verses being quoted
~ 18 months	17	2	Participates easily in conversations relating to social activities relevant to normal life and leisure in the culture	Improving language usage by adjusting language according to feedback	FS/LS report of trainee's easy participation in conversations relating to social activities relevant to normal life and leisure in the culture

Approx. Time	Comp		Performance Criteria	What Product or Process is Being Assessed?	Evidence to Be Collected
~ 18 months	17	1	Reads and understands a set range of personally relevant texts	Reading and understanding personal emails, notes, mobile texts, novels	FS/LS report of trainee's reading and understanding a set range of personally relevant texts
~ 18 months	17	2	Provides and follows detailed oral instructions concerning everyday tasks	Providing and following detailed oral instructions concerning everyday tasks	FS/LS report of trainee's providing and following detailed oral instructions concerning everyday tasks
~ 18 months	17	2	Self-corrects grammatical and vocabulary errors while speaking	Self-correcting grammatical and vocabulary errors while speaking	FS/LS report of trainee's self-correcting grammatical and vocabulary errors while speaking
~ 18 months	18	2	A set number of indigenous stories are retold and explained	The ability to tell the stories and the trainee's understanding of them	FS observes trainee retelling at least three indigenous stories to locals OR the trainee tells the indigenous stories to the FS PLUS explanations of the context and meaning of each of them to the FS (or FS observes trainee giving the explanations back to locals)
~ 18 months	17	1	Writes a set number of personally relevant texts	Writes personally relevant texts	At least three personally relevant texts sighted by the FS
Interacts with people on a spiritual level, including contextualizing spiritual truth and experience					
	18	1	Personal devotions are conducted using the Bible in the local language	Uses the Bible in the local language in personal devotions	Self-report to FS
	18	1	Private and public prayer is conducted in the local language and forms	Prays using local language and forms in private and public	Self-report of private prayer to FS Observation of FS of public prayer

Approx. Time	Comp	Performance Criteria	What Product or Process is Being Assessed?	Evidence to Be Collected
	18	2	A set number of contextualized Bible stories are told	Telling contextualized Bible stories	FS observation of at least three contextualized Bible stories being told to local people
	18	2	A contextualized gospel presentation is communicated	Communicating a contextualized gospel	FS observes a contextualized gospel presentation being communicated to local people
	18	2	Answers are given to a set number of common questions about Christianity	Answering common questions about Christianity	FS observes trainee answering at least three common questions from locals about Christianity
	18	2	Answers are given to a set number of common objections to Christianity	Answering common objections to Christianity	FS observes trainee answering at least three common objections from locals about Christianity
	18	1	A recent personal spiritual experience is explained a culturally appropriate way	Communicating a testimony of recent spiritual experience	FS observes trainee giving a testimony about recent spiritual experience to local people
Comfortable in all aspects of general language usage					
~ 2 years	17	1	Where relevant and possible, uses the internet in the language of the people to do basic research	Uses the internet in the language of the people to do basic research	FS observes trainee using the internet
~ 2 years	17	2	Communicates comfortably using the telephone	Comfortably communicates using the telephone	FS observes trainee using the telephone
Extensive general research, official language usage, easily adjusts and contextualizes spiritual communication					
~ 2 years	18	2	The story of the whole Bible crafted around a relevant cultural theme is told	Crafts and tells a story of the whole Bible around a relevant cultural theme	FS observes trainee telling a story of the whole Bible crafted around a relevant cultural theme to local people

Approx. Time	Comp	Performance Criteria		What Product or Process is Being Assessed?	Evidence to Be Collected
~ 2 years	17	1	Prepares a set number of official and work-related documents	Writing official documents	FS sights the documents
~ 2 years	18	2	A set number of contextualized Bible stories are used to explain biblical themes and principles	Crafts and tells at least three contextualized Bible stories explaining biblical themes and principles	FS observes trainee telling at least three contextualized Bible stories explaining biblical themes and principles to local people
~ 2 years	17	2	Participates easily in collaborative decision-making and problem-solving	Collaborates easily with locals	FS observes trainee participating in collaborative decision-making and problem-solving

Field/Language Supervisor Report (End of ~ 2 Years)— Advanced Cross-cultural Communication Skills

Competency		Performance Criteria
18	3	Where appropriate, in-depth questions are asked to better understand ethical and moral issues
23	2	Moral and ethical issues are discussed
18	3	Where appropriate, in-depth questions are asked to better understand beliefs and meanings behind cultural practices
23	2	Information about beliefs is *elicited*
23	2	Information about *worldview concepts* is *elicited*
23	1	*People are addressed with the honor and respect due them in their own culture*
23	1	The people of *the hosting culture* are listened to
23	1	Questions and discussions are carried out with *appropriate people* in *appropriate contexts* at *appropriate times*
23	3	Questions and other communication styles appropriate to *the hosting culture* are used to stimulate thinking about spiritual issues
23	3	Christian principles and *spiritual challenges* are communicated using stories
23	3	Christian principles and *spiritual challenges* are communicated *using non-Christian religious language and forms*

APPENDIX 5
Seminar Outlines

Worldview—Week 1

Time	Day 1	Day 2	Day 3	Day 4	Day 5	Day 6
Theme for the Day	*Culture & Conversion; Worldview Categories; Logic, Self, Time, Space*	*Affective & Evaluative Themes & Counterthemes*	*Sin & Causality*	*Story of the Universe & Visual Map of Worldview*	*Indigenous Theologies*	*Rest*
8:30–9:30	Introduction	Reflection on Reading	Reflection on Reading	Reflection on Reading	Reflection on Reading	
9:30–11	Worldview	Affective Themes & Counter-themes	Sin	Story of the Universe	Indigenous Theology Case Studies	
11:30–1	Religion Describing Cultural Themes	Evaluative themes Emotional Expression vs Control Group vs Individual		Visual Map of Worldview Themes		
1–2	Lunch					
2–5	Worldview Categories: Logic Self Time Space	Hierarchy vs Equality Ascription vs Achievement Holistic vs Dichotomistic Control vs Freedom	Gospel for Shame & Uncleanness Stories Causality	Visual Map with Intersection Points with Biblical Worldview	*Rest*	

Worldview—Week 2

Time	Day 7	Day 8	Day 9	Day 10
Theme for the Day	*Indigenous Theology & Preparing a Theological Primer*	*Crafting & Practicing Contextualized Gospel Stories*	*Catechism & Discipleship Essentials* *Biblical Worldview Stories*	*Preparing Evangelism Tools* *Apologetics*
8:30–9:30	Reflection on Reading	Reflection on Reading	Reflection on Reading	Reflection on Reading
9:30–11 11:30–1	Indigenous Theology in Own Church Planting Context	Gospel Stories	Discipleship Essentials	Create Contextualized Abundant Gospel Sowing Tools using the Contextualized Gospel Stories Review Each Other's Tools
1–2	Lunch			
2–5	Prepare the Theological Primer	Catechism—including thinking about how to use it	Worldview Stories	Hypothesize on Some Objections to your Stories and Practice the Process of Creating an Apologetic Biblical Response then Crafting a Story for It

Developing a Relevant Discipleship Strategy

Time	Day 1	Day 2	Day 3	Day 4	Day 5
Theme for the Day	*Discipling in the Bible*	*Principles for Discipling AND Contextualization*	*Models of Discipling AND the Role of the Discipler AND Critical Issues for Discipling in the Culture*	*Designing a Discipling Strategy*	*Storying and Discipling*
8:30–9:30	Reflection on Reading	Reflection on Reading	Reflection on Reading	Reflection on Reading	Reflection on Reading
9:30–11	Dreams Relevance of Discipleship as a Route to Those Dreams Can You Disciple Pre-conversion? Definition of Discipleship	NT & OT Guidelines for Developing Faith/Teaching New (& Old) Believers Integrated List of Biblical Principles	Adult Education Theory & Relevance to Discipleship Historical Models Contemporary Models	Biblical Competency Profile for a Disciple of Jesus	Storying Developing a Story-based, Event-oriented Curriculum
11:30–1	Jesus' Way of Discipling	Contextualization Discussion of Issues Outline of Process	Integrated List of Principles from Human Experience	Design a Strategy	
1–2	Lunch				
2–4	Other New Testament Methods Old Testament Methods	Contextualization Case Studies	Sin & the Role of the Holy Spirit vs the Foreign Discipler Worldview/ Theological Primer/Catechism	Strategy Design Continued Evaluate Each Other's Strategies	

Developing a Contextualized Leadership Development Strategy

Time	Day 1	Day 2	Day 3	Day 4	Day 5	Day 6
Theme for the Day	*Leadership in the Bible*	*Leadership & Culture*	*Leadership & Culture*	*Models of & Principles Related to Leadership Development*	*Attitudes, Issues, Principles, & Strategy Development*	*Evaluation & Where to from Here*
8:30–9:30	Reflection on Reading	Reflection on Reading	Reflection on Reading	Reflection on Reading	Reflection on Reading	Reflection on Reading
9:30–11	Biblical Theology of Leadership	Selection & Appointment	Conflict Resolution	Biblical Models Historical Models Contemporary Models	Orientalism, Paternalism, Power Dynamics, Western Dominance, etc.	Evaluate Each Other's Strategies
11:30–1	Biblical Job Description of a Leader	Status	Expectations of Followers		Principles & Guidelines Evaluate Any Existing Models in the Cross-cultural CP Context Already	Where to from Here . . . How & When to Identify Leaders and Start Training Them
1–2	Lunch					
2–4		Power Decision-making	Leadership Development Integrated Summary of Leadership in the Culture List of Implications for Leadership Development Strategy Design	Adult Learning in the Culture Adult Education Principles Adult Education Principles & Leadership Development Cross-cultural Communication Principles Reproducibility Principles	Design a Strategy	Preparing for Work back On-field • What Needs to be Checked—How & When? • What Needs to be Done to Implement? • How to Do It • Accountability for Doing It

BIBLIOGRAPHY

Africa Inland Mission. "Timo (Training in Ministry Outreach)." http://www
.aimint.org/usa/serve/timo.

Allen, Roland. *The Spontaneous Expansion of the Church and the Causes Which
Hinder It.* 2nd ed. London: The World Dominion Press, 1949.

Baker, Dwight P. "Missiology as an Interested Discipline—and Where Is It
Happening?" *International Bulletin of Missionary Research* 38, no. 1
(2014): 17–20.

Ball, Les. *Transforming Theology: Student Experience and Transformative
Learning in Undergraduate Theological Education.* Preston, Victoria:
Mosaic Press, 2012.

Banks, Robert J. *Reenvisioning Theological Education: Exploring a Missional
Alternative to Current Models.* Grand Rapids, MI: W.B. Eerdmans,
1999.

Bartel-Radic, Anne. "Intercultural Learning in Global Teams." *Management
International Review* 46, no. 6 (2006): 647–78.

Blöcher, Detlef. "Training Builds up Missionaries: Lessons from ReMAP II."
*Connections: The Journal of the World Evangelical Alliance Missions
Commission* 4 (2005).

———. "What ReMAP I Said, Did, and Achieved." In *Worth Keeping: Global
Perspectives on Best Practice in Missionary Retention,* edited by Rob
Hay, Valerie Lim, Detlef Blöcher, Jaap Ketelaar, and Sarah Hay, 9–22.
Pasadena, CA: William Carey Library, 2007.

Blöcher, Detlef, and Jonathan Lewis. "Further Findings in the Research Data."
In *Too Valuable to Lose: Exploring the Causes and Cures of Missionary
Attrition,* edited by William David Taylor, xviii, 380. Pasadena, CA:
William Carey Library, 1997.

Boa, Kenneth. *Conformed to His Image: Biblical and Practical Approaches to
Spiritual Formation.* Grand Rapids, MI: Zondervan, 2001.

Box, Harry. *Don't Throw the Book at Them: Communicating the Christian Message to People Who Don't Read.* Pasadena, CA: William Carey Library, 2014.

Brasher, Herbert. *Important Factors in Pre-Field and Field-Based Preparation of Missionaries Serving with Cross and Crescent International.* Evangelical Missiological Society Dissertation Series. Pasadena, CA: WCIU Press, 2007.

Brierley, Peter. "Missionary Attrition: The ReMAP Research Report." In *Too Valuable to Lose: Exploring the Causes and Cures of Missionary Attrition,* edited by William David Taylor, 85–103. Pasadena, CA: William Carey Library, 1997.

Brown, Ron. "Resilience in Ministry Despite Trauma." In *Worth Keeping: Global Perspectives on Best Practice in Missionary Retention,* edited by Rob Hay, 315–18. Pasadena, CA: William Carey Library, 2007.

Brueggemann, Walter. *Theology of the Old Testament: Testimony, Dispute, Advocacy.* Minneapolis: Fortress Press, 1997.

Brynjolfson, Robert. "Mission Training Review: Piecing Together the Puzzle; Executive Summary Report." In *Integral Ministry Training: Design and Evaluation,* edited by Robert Brynjolfson and Jonathan Lewis, 202–206. Pasadena, CA: William Carey Library, 2006.

———. "Student Assessment in an Outcomes-Based Program." In *Integral Ministry Training: Design and Evaluation,* edited by Robert Brynjolfson and Jonathan Lewis, 212–17. Pasadena, CA: William Carey Library, 2006.

Brynjolfson, Robert, and Jonathan Lewis, eds. *Integral Ministry Training: Design and Evaluation.* Pasadena: William Carey Library, 2006.

Bulley, Colin. "Non-Formal and Community-Based Learning." In *Integral Ministry Training: Design and Evaluation,* edited by Robert Brynjolfson and Jonathan Lewis, 186–87. Pasadena: William Carey Library, 2006.

Carter, Greg. *Skills, Knowledge, Character: A Church-Based Approach to Missionary Candidate Preparation.* Valparaiso, IN: Snowfall Press, 2010.

Cheesman, David. "Do Leaders Grow Colleges? Leadership, Prosperity, and Decline in Theological Education." *The Theological Educator* 6 (2013).

Chen, Guo-Ming. "Intercultural Effectiveness." In *Intercultural Communication: A Reader,* edited by Larry A. Samovar, Richard E. Porter, and Edwin R. McDaniel, 393–400. Boston, MA: Wadsworth Cengage Learning, 2009.

Chiu, Chi-Yue, Walter J. Lonner, David Matsumoto, and Colleen Ward. "Cross-Cultural Competence: Theory, Research, and Application." *Journal of Cross-Cultural Psychology* 44, no. 6 (2013): 843–48.

Coleman, Robert Emerson. *The Master Plan of Discipleship.* The Personal Evangelism Library. Old Tappan, NJ: F.H. Revell Co., 1987.

Conde-Frazier, Elizabeth, S. Steve Kang, and Gary A. Parrett. *A Many Colored Kingdom: Multicultural Dynamics for Spiritual Formation.* Grand Rapids, MI: Baker Academic, 2004.

Covell, Ralph R. *Confucius, the Buddha, and Christ: A History of the Gospel in Chinese.* American Society of Missiology Series. Maryknoll, NY: Orbis Books, 1986.

Daloz, Laurent A. "Mentorship." In *Adult Learning Methods: A Guide for Effective Instruction,* edited by Michael W. Galbraith. Malabar, FL: Krieger, 2004.

Dirkx, John M. "The Meaning and Role of Emotions in Adult Learning." Chap. 23 in *The Jossey-Bass Reader on Contemporary Issues in Adult Education,* edited by Sharan B. Merriam and Andrâe P. Grace, 349–62. San Francisco, CA: Jossey-Bass, 2011.

Donovan, Vincent J. *Christianity Rediscovered.* 25th anniversary ed. Maryknoll, NY: Orbis Books, 2003.

Downs, Perry G. *Teaching for Spiritual Growth: An Introduction to Christian Education.* Grand Rapids, MI: Zondervan, 1994.

Elliston, Edgar J., and J. Timothy Kauffman. *Developing Leaders for Urban Ministries.* American University Studies Series vii, Theology and Religion. New York: P. Lang, 1993.

Elmer, Duane. *Cross-Cultural Connections: Stepping Out and Fitting In around the World.* Downers Grove, IL: InterVarsity, 2002.

———. *Cross-Cultural Conflict: Building Relationships for Effective Ministry.* Downers Grove, IL: InterVarsity, 1993.

Espinoza, Benjamin D. "Practicing the Welcoming Gospel: Hospitality in Cross-Cultural Ministries." *Evangelical Missions Quarterly* 50, no. 4 (2014): 464–71.

Esterline, David, Dietrich Werner, Todd Johnson, and Peter Crossing. "Global Survey on Theological Education 2011–2013: Summary of Main Findings." Busan: Global Digital Library on Theology and Ecumensim, 2013.

Farley, Edward. *Theologia: The Fragmentation and Unity of Theological Education.* Philadelphia, PA: Fortress Press, 1983.

Ferris, Robert, ed. *Establishing Ministry Training: A Manual for Program Developers.* Pasadena, CA: William Carey Library, 1995.

———. "Standards of Excellence in Missionary Training Centers." *Training for Cross-Cultural Ministries* 1 (2000): 1–4.

Flemming, Dean E. *Contextualization in the New Testament: Patterns for Theology and Mission.* Downers Grove, IL: InterVarsity, 2005.

———. *Recovering the Full Mission of God: A Biblical Perspective on Being, Doing, and Telling.* Downers Grove, IL: IVP Academic, 2013.

Foster, Richard. *Celebration of Discipline.* London: Hachette UK, 2012.

Fox, Michael V. "The Pedagogy of Proverbs 2." *Journal of Biblical Studies* 113, no. 2 (1994): 233–43.

Freire, Paulo. *Pedagogy of the Oppressed.* New rev. 20th anniversary ed. New York: Continuum, 1993.

Frost, M., and A. Hirsch. *The Shaping of Things to Come.* Peabody, MA: Hendrickson Publishing, 2003.

Gardner, Howard. *Frames of Mind: The Theory of Multiple Intelligences.* New York: Basic Books, 1993.

Gava, Omar. "Comibam Training Coordinator's Report: Towards Excellence in Missionary Training." *Connections* 4, no. 2 (2005): 18–21.

Gnanakan, Ken. "The Training of Missiologists for Asian Contexts." In *Missiological Education for the Twenty-First Century: The Book, the Circle, and the Sandals: Essays in Honor of Paul E. Pierson,* edited by Paul Everett Pierson, John Dudley Woodberry, Charles Edward van Engen, and Edgar J. Elliston, xxv, 310. Maryknoll, NY: Orbis Books, 1996.

Gudykunst, William B. "Managing Anxiety and Uncertainty." In *Bridging Differences: Effective Intergroup Communication,* 18–35. London: Sage Publications, 2004.

Gupta, Paul R., and Sherwood G. Lingenfelter. *Breaking Tradition to Accomplish Vision: Training Leaders for a Church-Planting Movement: A Case from India.* Winona Lake, IN: BMH Books, 2006.

Hale, Thomas, and Gene Daniels. *On Being a Missionary.* Rev. ed. Pasadena, CA: William Carey Library, 2012.

Hall, E. *Beyond Culture.* New York: Anchor Press, 1976.

Hambrick, D.C., S.C. Davison, S.A. Snell, and C.C. Snow. "When Groups Consist of Multiple Nationalities: Towards a New Understanding of the Implications." *Organization Studies* 19, no. 2 (1998): 181–205.

Harley, C. David. "Missionary Training: The History of All Nations Christian College and Its Predecessors (1911–1981)." Doctoral diss., Rijksuniversiteit Utrecht, 2000.

———. *Preparing to Serve: Training for Cross-Cultural Mission.* Pasadena, CA: William Carey Library, 1995.

Hay, Rob. *Worth Keeping: Global Perspectives on Best Practice in Missionary Retention.* Globalization of Mission Series. Pasadena, CA: William Carey Library, 2007.

Heath, Shirley Brice. *Ways with Words: Language, Life, and Work in Communities and Classrooms.* New York: Cambridge University Press, 1983.

Herppich, Birgit. "Cultural Bias in Missionary Education: The Unintentional Dynamic of Trained Incapacity." Association of Professors of Mission. University of Northwestern, St Paul, MN: First Fruits Press, 2014.

Hibbert, Evelyn Catherine. "Designing Training for Adults." In *Integral Ministry Training: Design and Evaluation,* edited by Robert Brynjolfson and Jonathan Lewis, 51–64. Pasadena, CA: William Carey Library, 2006.

Hibbert, Evelyn, and Richard Hibbert. *Leading Multicultural Teams.* Pasadena, CA: William Carey Library, 2014.

Hibbert, Richard, and Evelyn Hibbert. "Report on Hindrances to and Needs in Reaching the Unreached and Church Planting in WEC Fields." Rehe, Germany: WEC Intercon, 2002.

Hibbert, Richard Yates. "Negotiating Identity: Extending and Applying Alan Tippett's Model of Conversion." *Missiology: An International Review* 43, no.1 (2015): 59–72.

Hibbert, Richard Yates, and Evelyn Catherine Hibbert. "Assessing the Need for Better Integration in Theological Education: Proposals, Progress, and Possibilities from the Medical Education Model." In *Learning and Teaching Theology: Some Ways Ahead,* edited by Les Ball and James R. Harrison. Sydney: Morning Star Publishing, 2014.

———. "Contextualising Sin for Cross-Cultural Evangelism." *Missiology: An International Review* 42, no. 3 (2014): 309–21.

———. "Nurturing Missionary Learning Communities." Association of Professors of Mission. University of Northwestern, Saint Paul, MN: First Fruits Press, 2014.

Hibbert, Richard Yates, Evelyn Catherine Hibbert, and Tim Silberman. "The Journey Towards Long-Term Missionary Service: How Australian Missionaries Are Being Called and Choose Mission Agencies." *Missiology: An International Review* 43, no. 4 (2015):469–482.

Hiebert, Paul G. "The Flaw of the Excluded Middle." *Missiology: An International Review* 10 (1982): 35–47.

———. *The Gospel in Human Contexts: Anthropological Explorations for Contemporary Missions.* Grand Rapids, MI: Baker Academic, 2009.

Hiebert, Paul G., R. Daniel Shaw, and Tite Tienou. *Understanding Folk Religion: A Christian Response to Popular Beliefs and Practices.* Grand Rapids, MI: Baker Books, 1999.

Hill, Harriet. *The Bible at Cultural Crossroads: From Translation to Communication.* Kinderhook, NY: St Jerome Publishing, 2006.

Hughes, Selwyn, Trevor J. Partridge, and Robert Backhouse. *Cover to Cover Complete.* Farnham, Surrey, UK: CWR, 2012.

Indian Missions Association. "Qualifications for Indian Missionaries." In *Establishing Ministry Training: A Manual for Program Developers,* edited by Robert Ferris, 153–59. Pasadena, CA: William Carey Library, 1995.

International Council for Evangelical Theological Education. "ICETE Manifesto on the Renewal of Evangelical Theological Education." http://www.icete-edu.org/manifesto/index.htm.

Knowles, Malcolm S. *The Adult Learner: A Neglected Species.* Houston, TX: Gulf Publishing, 1990.

Kolb, David A. *Experiential Learning: Experience as the Source of Learning and Development.* Englewood Cliffs, NJ: Prentice-Hall, 1984.

Kraft, Charles H. *Worldview for Christian Witness.* Pasadena, CA: William Carey Library, 2008.

Krallmann, Günter. *Mentoring for Mission: A Handbook on Leadership Principles Exemplified by Jesus Christ.* 2nd ed. Waynesburo, GA: Gabriel Publishing, 2002.

Lanier, Sarah A. *Foreign to Familiar: A Guide to Understanding Hot- and Cold-Climate Cultures.* Hagerstown, MD: McDougal Publishing, 2000.

LeBar, Mary. "The Wilderness School." In *Education That Is Christian,* edited by Lois E. LeBar and Jim Plueddemann, 107–25. Colorado Springs, CO: ChariotVictor, 1995.

Leung, Angela K.-Y., Sau-Lai Lee, and Chi-Yue Chiu. "Meta-Knowledge of Culture Promotes Cultural Competence." *Journal of Cross-Cultural Psychology* 44, no. 6 (2013): 992–1006.

Lewis, Jonathan. "The Outcomes Profiling Process." Chap. 7 In *Integral Ministry Training: Design and Evaluation,* edited by Robert Brynjolfson and Jonathan Lewis, 79–92. Pasadena: William Carey Library, 2006.

———. "Philosophy of Integral Ministry Training." In *Integral Ministry Training: Design and Evaluation,* edited by Robert Brynjolfson and Jonathan Lewis, 15–26. Pasadena: William Carey Library, 2006.

———. "Stakeholder Assumptions and Consensus Building." Chap. 6 in *Integral Ministry Training: Design and Evaluation,* edited by Robert Brynjolfson and Jonathan Lewis, 67–78. Pasadena, CA: William Carey Library, 2006.

Loong, Titus, and Steve Hoke. "Working Consultation for Asian Missionary Trainers." *Training for Cross-Cultural Ministries,* no. 2 (1993): 4–6.

Magesa, Laurenti. *What Is Not Sacred? : African Spirituality.* Maryknoll, NY: Orbis Books, 2013.

Mahmood, Saba. *Politics of Piety: The Islamic Revival and the Feminist Subject.* Princeton, NJ: Princeton University Press, 2005.

Mezirow, Jack. "Learning to Think Like an Adult: Core Concepts of Transformation Theory." Chap. 1 in *Learning as Transformation : Critical Perspectives on a Theory in Progress,* edited by Jack Mezirow, 3–34. San Francisco, CA: Jossey-Bass, 2000.

———. "Transformative Learning: Theory to Practice." *New Directions for Adult and Continuing Education* 74 (1997): 5–12.

Mulholland, Kenneth. "Missiological Education in the Bible College Tradition." In *Missiological Education for the Twenty-First Century: The Book, the Circle, and the Sandals: Essays in Honor of Paul E. Pierson,* edited by Paul Everett Pierson, John Dudley Woodberry, Charles Edward van Engen and Edgar J. Elliston, xxv, 310. Maryknoll, NY: Orbis Books, 1996.

———. "Teaching Them All Things: Three Dots and a Pilgrimage." In *Teaching Them Obedience in All Things: Equipping for the 21st Century,* edited by Edgar J. Elliston, vii, 286. Pasadena, CA: William Carey Library, 1999.

Newbigin, Lesslie. *The Gospel in a Pluralist Society.* Grand Rapids, MI: W.B. Eerdmans, 1989.

O'Malley, John W. *The First Jesuits*. Cambridge, MA: Harvard University Press, 1993.

Offstein, Evan H., and Ronald L. Dufresne. "Building Strong Ethics and Promoting Positive Character Development: The Influence of HRM at the United States Military Academy at West Point." *Human Resource Management* 46, no. 1 (2007): 95–114.

Ott, Bernhard. *Beyond Fragmentation: Integrating Mission and Theological Education: A Critical Assessment of Some Recent Developments in Evangelical Theological Education*. Irvine, CA: Regnum Books International, 2001.

———. "Mission Oriented Theological Education: Moving Beyond Traditional Models of Theological Education." In *Christianity and Education: Shaping Christian Thinking in Context,* edited by David Emmanuel Singh and Bernard C. Farr, 49–65. Eugene, Oregon: Wipf & Stock, 2011.

Palmer, Parker J. *The Courage to Teach: Exploring the Inner Landscape of a Teacher's Life*. 1st ed. San Francisco, CA: Jossey-Bass, 1998.

Parshall, Phil. "How Spiritual Are Missionaries?" Chap. 9 in *Helping Missionaries Grow: Readings in Mental Health and Missions,* edited by Michele Lewis O'Donnell and Kelly S. O'Donnell, 75–82. Pasadena, CA: William Carey Library, 1988.

Patrick. "Tentmaking Unveiled— 'the Survey Says.'" *Evangelical Missions Quarterly* April (2007): 168–75.

Patterson, George, and Richard Scoggins. *Church Multiplication Guide: The Miracle of Church Reproduction*. Rev. ed. Pasadena, CA: William Carey Library, 2002.

Pazmiño, Robert W. *Foundational Issues in Christian Education: An Introduction in Evangelical Perspective*. 3rd ed. Grand Rapids, MI: Baker Academic, 2008.

Pedersen, Paula J. "Assessing Intercultural Effectiveness Outcomes in a Year-Long Study Abroad Program." *International Journal of Intercultural Relations* 34, no. 1 (2010): 70–80.

Piper, John. "Training the Next Generation of Evangelical Pastors and Missionaries." In *Teaching Them Obedience in All Things: Equipping for the 21st Century,* edited by Edgar J. Elliston, vii, 286. Pasadena, CA: William Carey Library, 1999.

Plueddemann, James E. "Culture, Learning, and Missionary Training." In *Internationalizing Missionary Training: A Global Perspective,* edited by William David Taylor, xiv, 286. Grand Rapids, MI: Baker Book House, 1991.

Poston, Larry. "The Role of Higher Education in the Christian World Mission: Past, Present, and Future." In *Teaching Them Obedience in All Things: Equipping for the 21st Century,* edited by Edgar J. Elliston, 144–184. Evangelical Missiological Society. Pasadena, CA: William Carey Library, 1999.

"Report of Commission V." Edinburgh & London: World Missionary Conference, 1910.

Roffey, Sue. *Positive Relationships: Evidence Based Practice across the World.* London: Springer, 2012.

Sanders, J. Oswald. *Spiritual Leadership: Principles of Excellence for Every Believer.* Chicago, IL: Moody Publishers, 2007.

Sanneh, Lamin O. *Translating the Message: The Missionary Impact on Culture.* American Society of Missiology Series. Maryknoll, NY: Orbis Books, 1989.

Schön, Donald A. *Reflective Practitioner: How Professionals Think in Action.* New ed. Aldershot, England: Arena, 1995.

———. *The Reflective Practitioner: How Professionals Think in Action.* Aldershot, England: Arena, 1991.

Shaw, Perry. *Transforming Theological Education: A Practical Handbook for Integrative Learning.* Carlisle, UK: Langham Partnership, 2014.

Sheldon, Charles M. *In His Steps.* New York: Grosset & Dunlap, 1935.

Sieck, Winston R., Jennifer L. Smith, and Louise J. Rasmussen. "Metacognitive Strategies for Making Sense of Cross-Cultural Encounters." *Journal of Cross-Cultural Psychology* 44, no. 6 (2013): 1007–23.

Sills, Michael David. *The Missionary Call: Find Your Place in God's Plan for the World.* Chicago, IL: Moody Publishers, 2008.

Sinclair, Amanda. *Leadership for the Disillusioned: Moving Beyond Myths and Heroes to Leading That Liberates.* Crows Nest, NSW: Allen & Unwin, 2007.

Smith, Claire Seymour. *Pauline Communities as 'Scholastic Communities': A Study of the Vocabulary of "Teaching" in 1 Corinthians, 1 and 2 Timothy and Titus.* Tubingen, Germany: Mohr Siebeck, 2012.

Steffen, Tom A, and Lois McKinney Douglas. *Encountering Missionary Life and Work: Preparing for Intercultural Ministry.* Grand Rapids, MI: Baker Academic, 2008.

Stetzer, Ed. "Missions Vs. Missional? We Really Need Both." *Christianity Today,* 9 September 2013.

Tan, Kang San. "What Is So Theological About Contextual Mission Training?" In *Contextualisation and Mission Training: Engaging Asia's Religious Worlds,* edited by Jonathan Ingleby, Kang San Tan and Loun Ling Tan, 1–16. Oxford: Regnum, 2013.

Taylor, William. "Foreword." In *Integral Ministry Training: Design and Evaluation,* edited by Robert Brynjolfson and Jonathan Lewis, vii–xiv. Pasadena, CA: William Carey Library, 2006.

Taylor, William David. "Setting the Stage." In *Internationalizing Missionary Training: A Global Perspective,* edited by William David Taylor, 2–12. Grand Rapids, MI: Baker Book House, 1991.

———, ed. *Too Valuable to Lose: Exploring the Causes and Cures of Missionary Attrition.* Globalization of Mission Series. Pasadena, CA: William Carey Library, 1997.

Thomas, Gary. *Sacred Pathways: Discover Your Soul's Path to God.* Grand Rapids, MI: Zondervan, 2000.

Thompson, J. Allen. "Training Church Planters: A Competency-Based Learning Model." In *With an Eye on the Future: Development and Mission in the 21st Century: Essays in Honor of Ted W. Ward,* edited by Ted Warren Ward, Duane Elmer, Lois McKinney, and Muriel I. Elmer, 141–52. Monrovia, CA: MARC, 1996.

Tienou, Tite. "The Training of Missiologists for an African Context." In *Missiological Education for the Twenty-First Century: The Book, the Circle, and the Sandals: Essays in Honor of Paul E. Pierson,* edited by Paul Everett Pierson, John Dudley Woodberry, Charles Edward van Engen and Edgar J. Elliston, 93–100. Maryknoll, NY: Orbis Books, 1996.

Tippett, Alan. "The Cultural Anthropology of Conversion." In *Handbook of Religious Conversion,* edited by Newton Maloney and Samuel Southard, 192–258. Birmingham, AL: Religious Education Press, 1992.

Turkle, Sherry. *Alone Together: Why We Expect More from Technology and Less from Each Other.* New York: Basic Books, 2011.

Walls, Andrew F. *The Missionary Movement in Christian History: Studies in the Transmission of Faith.* Maryknoll, NY: Orbis Books, 1996.

Ward, Ted W. "Evaluating Metaphors of Education." Chap. 3 In *With an Eye on the Future: Development and Mission in the 21st Century,* edited by Duane H. Elmer and Lois McKinney, 43–54. Monrovia, CA: MARC, 1996.

Ward, Ted Warren, and Samuel F. Rowen. "The Significance of the Extension Seminary." *Evangelical Missions Quarterly* 9, no. 1 (1972): 17–27.

Watkins, Megan, and Greg Noble. *Disposed to Learn: Schooling, Ethnicity and the Scholarly Habitus.* New York: Bloomsbury Academic, 2013.

Wenger-Trayner, Etienne, and Beverly Wenger-Trayner. "Communities of Practice: A Brief Introduction." http://wenger-trayner.com/theory/.

Wenger, Etienne. *Communities of Practice: Learning, Meaning, and Identity.* Learning in Doing. New York: Cambridge University Press, 1998.

Whiteman, Darrell. "Contextualization: The Theory, the Gap, the Challenge." *International Bulletin of Missionary Research* 21 (1997).

Willard, Dallas. *Renovation of the Heart.* Hovel Audio, 2005.

———. *The Spirit of the Disciplines.* Hodder & Stoughton, 1996.

Wingate, Andrew. "Training for Ministry in a Multifaith Context: A Case Study from Britain." In *Handbook of Theological Education in World Christianity: Theological Perspectives, Regional Surveys, Ecumenical Trends,* edited by Dietrich Werner, David Esterline, Namsoon Kang, and Joshva Raja, 223–29. Oxford: Regnum Books International, 2010.

Wright, Christopher J. H. *Deuteronomy.* New International Biblical Commentary Old Testament Series. Peabody, MA: Hendrickson Publishers, 1996.

Zahniser, Matthias. "The Trinity: Paradigm for Mission in the Spirit." *Missiology: An International Review* 17 (1989).

Zwick, Joel, Rita Wilson, Tom Hanks, Gary Goetzman, Nia Vardalos, John Corbett, Lainie Kazan, et al. 2003. *My Big Fat Greek Wedding.* New York: HBO Home Video.